A NARRATIVE OF THE CAMPAIGN INDIA, WHICH TERMINATED THE WAR WITH TIPPOO SULTAN, IN 1792.

WITH MAPS AND PLANS ILLUSTRATIVE OF THE SUBJECT, AND A VIEW OF SERINGAPATAM

BY MAJOR DIROM,
DEPUTT ADJUTANT GENERAL OF HIS MAJESTY'S FORCES IN INDIA

GYAN

Published by

GYAN

Gyan Publishing House
5, Ansari Road
Daryaganj, New Delhi-110002
Phone: 011-47034999, 9811692060
E-mail: books@gyanbooks.com

Distribution Network
gyanbooks.com
India, USA, Canada, UK, Australia, France

ISBN : 978-81-212-4538-8 (HB)
First Published, 1793

2nd Impression 2020

Printed at: Gyan Press, Delhi.

The book at your disposal is the edition of an old book originally published long back. The Text quality of this book may not be at par as compared to our other books but many readers approached us to reprint this important book so that it could satiate their hunger. We request all the readers of this book to help us to improve its quality by providing the necessary text of those pages which are not properly visible. Your valuable support in this case will be highly appreciated and acknowledged and our future readers will be benefitted immensely.

A NARRATIVE OF THE CAMPAIGN INDIA, WHICH TERMINATED THE WAR WITH TIPPOO SULTAN, IN 1792.

A

NARRATIVE

OF

THE CAMPAIGN IN INDIA,

WHICH TERMINATED THE WAR

WITH

TIPPOO SULTAN,

IN 1792.

WITH MAPS AND PLANS ILLUSTRATIVE OF THE SUBJECT,

AND A VIEW OF SERINGAPATAM.

BY MAJOR DIROM,

DEPUTY ADJUTANT GENERAL OF HIS MAJESTY'S FORCES IN INDIA.

LONDON:

PRINTED BY W. BULMER AND CO.

AND SOLD BY W. FADEN, CHARING-CROSS; G. NICOL, PALL-MALL; AND

J. SEWELL, CORNHILL.

1793.

No. 1

NORTH EAST VIEW of SERINGAPATAM.

Drawn by L. Smith from a View taken on the Spot

Engraved by W. Byrne

TO

THE RIGHT HONOURABLE

HENRY DUNDAS,

ONE OF HIS MAJESTY'S PRINCIPAL SECRETARIES OF STATE,

AND ONE OF THE COMMISSIONERS

FOR THE

AFFAIRS OF INDIA,

&c. &c. &c.

THIS WORK IS RESPECTFULLY INSCRIBED,

By

His most obedient and

Most humble servant,

THE AUTHOR.

London, 1st Feb.
1793.

PREFACE.

THE prospect of leisure for several months, during the voyage from India, suggested to the writer of this Narrative the idea of drawing up an account of the last campaign with Tippoo Sultan, from journals and other authentic documents, while the events were recent in his memory. Several officers, passengers in the same ship, who had been employed on different parts of that service, considerably aided the undertaking by the information of which they also were possessed; and the assistance of Major Rennell, particularly in constructing the maps, has since been very essential in promoting the publication of this work.

Notwithstanding those, and other advantages, the Author is sensible that his Narrative is still imperfect, and that, in the operations of the several armies, all the interesting circumstances which occurred, cannot have come to his knowledge; but, deficient as he considers it in several respects, he is induced to hope it may not be unacceptable, at a time when a complete history of this important war cannot have been prepared for the information of the Public.

INTRODUCTION.

The climate in the centre of the Peninsula of India, especially in the high country of Mysore, is temperate and healthy to a degree unknown in any other tract of the like extent within the tropics. The monsoons, or boisterous periodical rains, which, at two different seasons, deluge the countries on the coasts of Coromandel and Malabar, have their force broken by the Ghauts or mountains; and from either side extend to the interior provinces in frequent showers, which, though sometimes heavy, are seldom of long continuance; and preserve both the verdure of the country, and the temperature of the climate, almost throughout the year: insomuch that the British main army, called in India the grand army, was constantly in the field in tents, and never went into cantonments during the whole war.

The late military operations in India come, therefore, to be divided into campaigns, not so much from the change of season, as from the periods of the accomplishment or failure of the several plans of attack carried on against the enemy. Thus the war with Tippoo Sultan may be divided into three campaigns.

The first campaign, directed towards the southern part of the Peninsula, in order to relieve the Rajah of Travancore, whose country had been attacked by Tippoo Sultan, commenced the middle of June, 1790. Having been employed in the reduction of Tippoo's rich southern provinces below the Ghauts, by the main army, commanded by General Medows; and of his valuable western country below the Ghauts, as far as the Biliapatam river to the north, by the Bombay army, commanded by General Abercromby; it terminated with the year 1790, when the main army returned to Tritchinopoly, and was ordered from thence to Madras.

The second campaign, carried into the heart of Tippoo's dominions by Earl Cornwallis, was distinguished by the siege and capture of the important fortress of Bangalore, which fixed the seat of war in the enemy's country, and was decisive of its success; although the campaign closed in an unsuccessful attempt against Seringapatam, and the destruction of the greatest part of the battering train, and equipment of both the main army and the Bombay army, which were under the necessity of retiring from the capital; an event that took place towards the end of May, 1791.

The third campaign may be said to have commenced immediately after the failure in the last object of the former campaign, when the Mahratta armies arriving unexpectedly, enabled Earl Cornwallis to begin his arrangements for a second attempt on the enemy's capital; which, in March 1792, terminated the war by an advantageous and glorious peace.

The following Narrative contains a detail of the transactions and operations as they occurred, and were generally known in the army, during the last campaign; to which, in a concluding chapter, some farther information and remarks are added, that may be useful in forming an idea of the important consequences of the war, and of the present prosperous state of affairs in India.

CONTENTS.

PART FIRST.

TRANSACTIONS AND OPERATIONS PREVIOUS TO THE SIEGE OF SERINGAPATAM.

PAGE

CHAPTER I.

Retrospect to the Conclusion of the former Campaign—Subsequent Junction of the Mahrattas, and an Account of their Armies - - - 1

CHAPTER II.

March of the Allied Armies from Seringapatam to Bangalore—Arrangements for refitting the British Army, and Disposition of the Confederate Forces till after the Monsoons - - - 15

CHAPTER III.

Reduction of Oussoor, Rayacotta, and the Forts which com-

PAGE

mand the Policode Pass—Junction of the first Convoys from the Carnatic - - - 29

CHAPTER IV.

Reduction of the Hill Forts to the North-East of Bangalore —Siege of Nundydroog—Tippoo's Movement towards Chittledroog—Detaches Cummer-ud-Deen Cawn against Coimbetore, and sends a Reinforcement to Kistnaghery 41

CHAPTER V.

Position of the Army to cover the Convoys from the Carnatic—Lieutenant-Colonel Maxwell's Expedition to the Baramaul—Arrival of Lieutenant-Colonel Geils with the Battering Train at Bangalore—Cummer-ud-Deen Cawn's Success at Coimbetore - - - 55

CHAPTER VI.

Siege of Savendroog—Escalade of Outredroog—and Capture of other Hill Forts between Bangalore and Seringapatam - - - - - 66

CHAPTER VII.

Siege of Gurramcondah—State of the Cavalry in the Carnatic—Difficulties in collecting and bringing forward the last Convoy—Relief of Gurramcondah by Hyder Saib—

PAGE

Colonel Floyd's Arrival with the Convoy at Bangalore—State of the Country; and Arrangements of Earl Cornwallis for subsisting the Army - - 79

CHAPTER VIII.

The Bombay Army re-ascends the Ghauts—Description of the Poodicherrim Ghaut—Account of the Courga Rajah and his Country—Strength of the Army, and March to the Mysore Frontier - - - - 89

CHAPTER IX.

Operations of Purseram Bhow's Army—Escape of Mr. Drake and three other Prisoners from Chittledroog—Capture of Hooly Onore and Bankapoor—Battle and Reduction of Simoga—Expedition to Bidenore - 99

CHAPTER X.

Tippoo detaches Cummer-ud-Deen Cawn against Purseram Bhow—Incursion of a Party of the Sultan's Horse to Madras—Junction of Colonel Floyd's Convoy, and of Colonel Duff with the Battering Train from Bangalore, and of the Nizam's Army from Gurramcondah - 110

PART SECOND.

MARCH OF THE ALLIED ARMIES TO, AND SIEGE OF SERINGAPATAM.

PAGE

CHAPTER I.

Review of the British Army by the Nizam's Son and Hurry Punt—March of the Allied Armies to Seringapatam - 119

CHAPTER II.

Position of the Confederate Army, and Description of Tippoo's fortified Camp—Retrospect to the Proceedings of the Confederacy against Hyder Ally in 1767 - 128

CHAPTER III.

Orders for, and the Attack of, Tippoo's fortified Camp, and the Island, on the Night of the 6th February—Operations of the Right Division—Of the Centre Division; and of the Left Division—General Success of the Attack - 135

CHAPTER IV.

Operations of the 7th of February—Position on the Island—Defence of the Sultan's Redoubt.—Advanced Position of the Camp—Final Repulse of the Enemy on the Island 168

PAGE

CHAPTER V.

Consequences of the Victory—Return of Cannon taken—Of the killed, wounded, and missing, in the English Army, and some Account of the Enemy's Loss - 178

CHAPTER VI.

Arrangements and Preparations for the Siege—Description of the Island—Tippoo's Overtures towards a Negotiation for Peace - - - - 185

CHAPTER VII.

Attempt to cut off Lord Cornwallis—Junction of the Bombay Army—Plan of Attack and Arrangements for opening the Trenches - - - - 191

CHAPTER VIII.

Diversion made to draw the Attention of the Enemy to the South Side of the Fort, while the Trenches were opened on the North Side—Description of the Ground and Work done during the Night—The Bombay Army crosses the River, and invests the South-West Face of the Fort - 201

CHAPTER IX.

Progress of the Attack—Operations on the Island—Admis-

PAGE

sion of Tippoo's Vakeels—His Action with the Bombay Army on the 22d of February - - 210

CHAPTER X.

Farther Progress of the Siege—Prospects of Success—Tippoo's Situation—His Submission to the Terms demanded, and Cessation of Hostilities - - 218

PART THIRD.

TREATIES OF PEACE; AND REVIEW OF THE CONSEQUENCES OF THE WAR.

CHAPTER I.

Preliminary Articles of Peace—Arrival of the Hostages—Their Reception, and some Account of Tippoo's Sons - 225

CHAPTER II.

Adjustment of the Definitive Treaty—Difficulties with respect to the Country of the Coorga Rajah, and the Exchange of the Money to be paid by Tippoo—Preparations for the Recommencement of Hostilities—The Sultan's final Submission, and the Delivery of the Definitive Treaty by the Princes - - - - - 233

PAGE

CHAPTER III.

Retrospect of the Military Transactions in India since the former Peace, and a short Statement of the general Consequences of the late War. - - - 249

APPENDIX - - - - 275

GLOSSARY - - - 293

DIRECTIONS FOR PLACING THE PLATES.

No.		PAGE
I.	View of Seringapatam to face the Title Page	
II.	Map of the Campaign, to face - - - -	1
III.	Group of Mahratta Horse - - - -	4
IV.	Order of Battle of the Bombay Army - - -	89
V.	Order of Battle of the Main Army - - - -	119
VI.	Plan of the Attack of Tippoo Sultan's fortified Camp at Seringapatam	135
VII.	Plan of the Siege of Seringapatam - - - -	185
VIII.	Sketch of the Peninsula of India, shewing the ceded Countries -	225
IX.	Tippoo Sultan's Great Seal, Appendix, No. III. - -	286

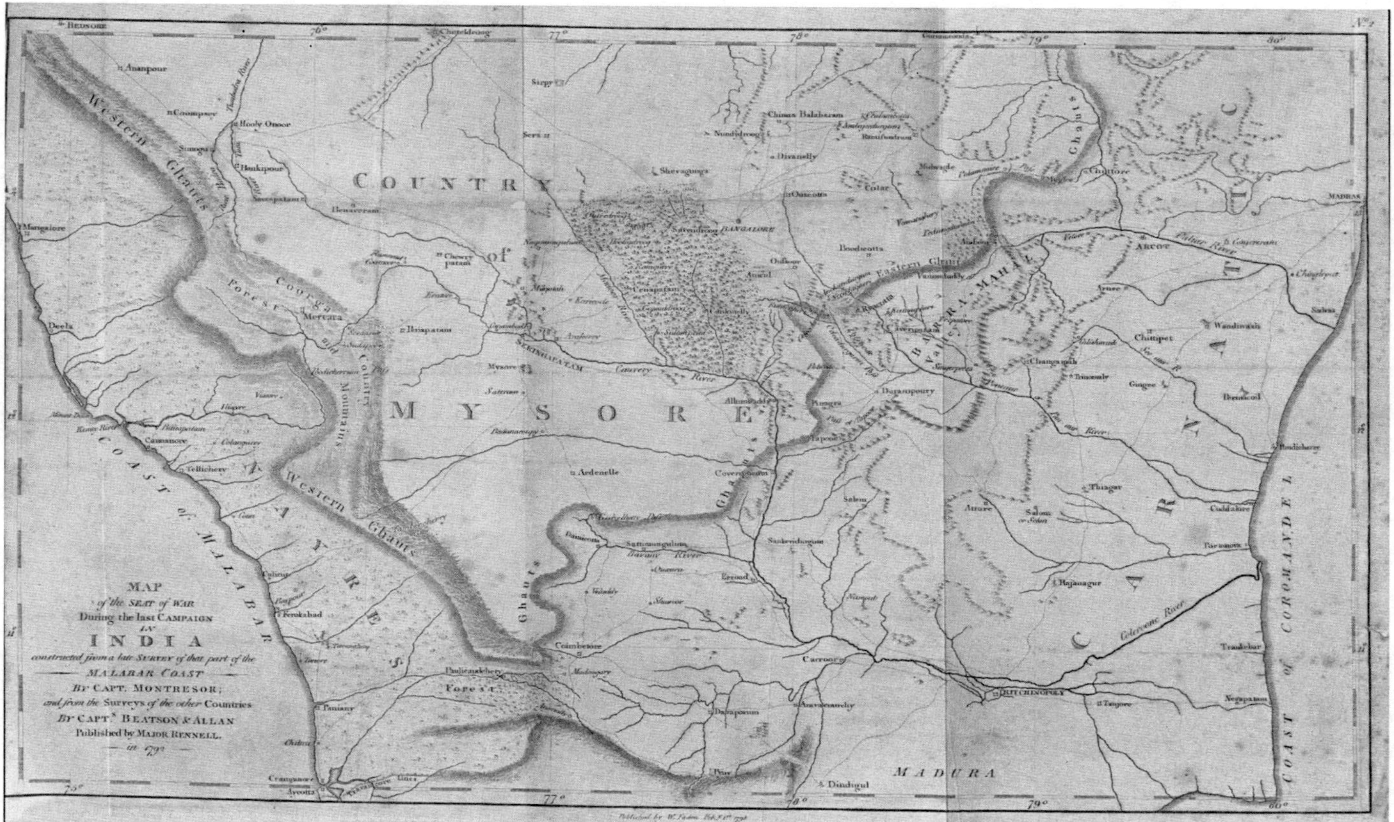
MAP
of the SEAT of WAR
During the last CAMPAIGN
IN
INDIA
constructed from a late SURVEY of that part of the
MALABAR COAST
By CAPT. MONTRESOR;
and from the Surveys of the other Countries
By CAPTS. BEATSON & ALLAN
Published by MAJOR RENNELL.
in 1792
COUNTRY of MYSORE
CARNATIC
BARRA MAHAL
MADURA
COAST of MALABAR
COAST of COROMANDEL
Western Ghauts
Eastern Ghauts
Coorga Forest
Country and Mountains
BANGALORE
SERINGAPATAM
ARCOT
MADRAS
TRITCHINOPOLY
Cauvery River
Coleroon River
Mangalore
Tellichery
Cannanore
Coimbetore
Dindigul
Tanjore
Negapatam
Tranquebar
Pondichery
Cuddalore
Chittore
Colar
Oussoor
Mysore
Mercara
Ossoor
Ardenelle
Chinna Balabaram
Nundidroog
Sheragunga
Chingleput
Anapour
Hooly Onoor
Paulicatcherry
Caroor
Erroad
Sattimungulum
Salem
Attore
Thiagar
Chillambrum
Porto Novo
Dharmapoory
Ryacotta
Changamah
Trinomaly
Wandiwash
Vaniambady
Amboor
Vellore

A

NARRATIVE, &c.

PART FIRST.

TRANSACTIONS AND OPERATIONS PREVIOUS TO THE SIEGE OF SERINGAPATAM.

CHAPTER I.

Retrospect to the Conclusion of the former Campaign—Subsequent Junction of the Mahrattas, and an Account of their Armies.

THE Mahratta armies having advanced to Seringapatam in May, 1791, later than the appointed period, their delay, and other unfortunate circumstances, reduced Earl Cornwallis to the necessity of destroying his battering train, after having defeated Tippoo Sultan on the 15th of that month in a pitched battle; and obliged his Lordship to lead back his victorious army, leaving the siege of the enemy's capital to be the object of another campaign.

The Bombay army, commanded by Major General Abercromby, had, with infinite labour, formed roads, and brought a battering train, and a large supply of provisions and stores, over fifty miles of woody mountains called Ghauts,* that immense barrier which separates the Mysore country from the Malabar coast. Part of General Abercromby's train also fell a sacrifice to the necessity of the times; and his army, who thought they had surmounted all their difficulties, had the mortification to find their exertions of no utility, and had to return, worn down by sickness and fatigue, exposed to the incessant rains which then deluged the western coast of the Peninsula.

Lord Cornwallis had advanced to Caniambaddy, eight miles above Seringapatam, with a view to form a junction with the Bombay army, which the swoln state of the Cavery, and the unexpected badness of the ford, rendering impracticable, his Lordship remained some days on the banks of the river, to cover their march, as they retired from Periapatam to the Ghauts, and began to move himself towards Bangalore on the 26th of May. The army had suffered exceedingly from the inclemency of the weather, from wounds, and from extreme fatigue in bringing on the battering train and stores, which had required much assistance on the march from Bangalore to Seringapatam; and, from thence to Caniambaddy, had been dragged almost entirely by hand. The season of the year was unfavourable to the cattle; they were infected with an epidemic disorder, which killed them in vast numbers, and rendered the greater part of what remained of little service. The scarcity of grain was such, that the lower class of followers were reduced to the necessity of subsisting chiefly on the putrid flesh of the dead bullocks; and, to add to this scene of distress, the small-pox unfortunately raged in the camp.

* For an explanation of Indian terms, see the Glossary.

The public store of rice being nearly exhausted, and the loss which had taken place from the negligence or embezzlement of the bullock drivers on the march, having decreased the original stock in a most alarming degree, it became necessary to issue to the troops the greater part of what remained, as the only means of securing it for their subsistence. The fighting men were thus provided at the rate of half their usual allowance, with a quantity sufficient to support them till the army might by easy marches reach Bangalore; the followers depending chiefly on the casual supply, which, by taking a new tract, would be found in the adjacent countries. The distress of the officers was still more severe than that of the soldiers; for having given part of their private carriage (cattle and carts) to the public departments, to assist in transporting shot and stores from Bangalore for the siege of the capital, and disappointed in the supplies they expected from the Bombay army, they were now in want of every thing; and many were under the necessity of requesting permission to draw the same allowance as the private men. The tents and the clothing were nearly worn out; the arrack as well as the rice was almost expended; and, in this situation, the assistance of the troops was necessary to carry back part of the intrenching tools, which it might be difficult to replace; and to drag the field-pieces and tumbrels attached to their corps; a task to which the surviving cattle were unequal, in their weakly state. Great part of the horses of the cavalry were so reduced by want and fatigue, that they could no longer carry their riders; and many, unable to march, were now shot at their picquets. The ground at Caniambaddy, where the army had encamped but six days, was covered, in a circuit of several miles, with the carcasses of cattle and horses; and the last of the gun-carriages, carts, and stores of the battering train, left in flames, was a melancholy spectacle, which the troops passed, as they quitted this deadly camp.

The army had not completed the first day's short, but dreary and tedious, march of six miles, when a party of horse rode in unexpectedly on the baggage flank. Their appearance was that of enemies, but they soon proved to be most welcome friends; an escort of Mahrattas, that accompanied Mr. Uhtoff, the paymaster of the Bombay detachment, with Purseram Bhow's army. He brought the glad tidings of that army being at hand, followed by another, commanded by Hurry Punt; the first, consisting of twenty thousand horse and foot, and two battalions of Sepoys, commanded by Captain Little (part of a detachment which had assisted the Bhow in the reduction of Darwar); the second, of twelve thousand horse, which had advanced from Poonah, by way of Gooty. The Bhow, Mr. Uhtoff said, had ample supplies for our army, and was near enough to join on the next day, if required. He was astonished to hear of what had happened in consequence of their delay, and to find that all the messengers they had dispatched had been intercepted by the vigilance of the enemy, and that they now brought the first news of their own approach.

No longer under the necessity of continuing the march from the want of supplies, the army moved only two miles on the 27th of May, and encamped opposite to Seringapatam, in front of the French Rocks; the ground from which we had marched on the 19th, in advancing to Caniambaddy, and since rendered more memorable by the events of the ensuing campaign.

No. 3

Sketch of the advanced Guard of the Mahratta Army, coming to join Earl Cornwallis, near Seringapatam 26th May 1791.

Copied by permission from the Plate published by Major Rennell.

Tippoo had fired a salute on the 26th from the fort, in the sight and hearing of our camp; which some of our people, who made their escape from Seringapatam, said was in consequence of Syed Saib's having brought in some prisoners and baggage, which he took at Periapatam, belonging to the Bombay army. We learned from them also, that Tippoo had given a reward to his army, and published some orders, in which he now, for the first time, praised their conduct on the 15th of May; saying, "that "the valour of his troops, and the effect of his artillery, in that "battle, had made such havock in the English army, as had "obliged them to destroy their battering guns, and abandon "the siege; and concluded by exhorting his officers and men "to continue strict in their discipline, and firm in their alle-"giance."

Though surrounded with enemies, Tippoo thus triumphed in his fortunate relief from immediate danger, while the approach of the Mahratta armies diffused as general satisfaction in our camp. We were convinced that the Sultan had obtained but a reprieve from fortune, and that his ruin, though suspended, was now inevitable. He was himself not insensible of what might await him, and, seeing his enemies active and firm in their union, endeavoured to conclude a peace with Lord Cornwallis before he should meet the Mahratta chiefs.

With this view, Tippoo sent out a flag of truce on the 27th, accompanied by a numerous retinue of servants, with baskets of fruit, and letters to his Lordship, in which it was said he solicited earnestly for peace. The Sultan's secretary, in a note to Lord Cornwallis's Persian interpreter, which was delivered with the fruit, signified that he had his royal master's permission to send it for the use of Lord Cornwallis, or something to that effect, to provide against the chance of the refusal of a present offered immediately from the Sultan to his Lordship.

The flag and the fruit were returned next morning (a sight which gave pleasure to the army), with an answer, acquainting Tippoo, that the English nation would agree to no peace which did not include their allies; and if he meant to negotiate he must, in the first instance, deliver up all the British subjects who were prisoners in his dominions, and consent that a truce should take place, until his proposals could be considered, and the terms adjusted. The fruit was returned in the same manner as it had been sent; not as an insult, but merely to shew that his Lordship declined even the appearance of friendly intercourse with the Sultan.

The correspondence that passed between Lord Cornwallis and Tippoo Sultan on this occasion, and during the whole of the transactions of the war, will, if ever made public, be no doubt highly interesting, and reflect as much honour on his Lordship's wisdom and firmness, as every other part of his conduct. In the army it was understood, that Tippoo, finding he could not treat separately with the English, and seeing he had another season to try his expedients for disuniting the confederacy, as well as to prepare for his defence, replied to his Lordship, by asserting, that he had no British subjects detained prisoners in his country since the former war, and that he would not agree to a truce.

On the 28th of May the army fell back a few miles from the capital, towards Milgottah, where the Mahratta armies were to encamp; and, to prevent discussion and delay on points of ceremony, Lord Cornwallis proposed to meet the Mahratta chiefs next day, at tents to be pitched midway between the Mahratta and the British camps.

Lord Cornwallis, accompanied by General Medows, their staff, and some of the principal officers of the army, went to the tents at the hour appointed, which was one o'clock; but the chiefs, who consider precision as inconsistent with power and dignity, did not even leave their own camp till three, though repeated messages were sent that his Lordship waited for them. They at length mounted their elephants, and, proceeding as slow and dignified in their pace as they had been dilatory in their preparation, approached the place of appointment at four o'clock; escorted by several corps of their infantry, a retinue of horse, and all the pageantry of eastern state. The chiefs, on descending from their elephants, were met at the door of the tent by Lord Cornwallis and General Medows, who embraced them, and, after some general conversation, retired to a private conference in another tent.

Hurry Punt, about sixty years of age, a Bramin of the first order, and the personage of greatest consequence, is said to be the third in the senate of the Mahratta state. His figure is venerable, of middle stature, and not corpulent; he is remarkably fair, his eyes grey, and his countenance, of Roman form, full of thought and character.

Purseram Bhow, aged about forty, stands high in military fame among the Mahrattas. He is an active man, of small stature, rather dark in his complexion, with black eyes, and an open animated countenance, in which, and his mien, he seemed desirous to shew his character of an intrepid warrior. His antipathy to Tippoo is said to be extreme; for the Sultan had put one of his brothers to death in a most cruel manner, and Hyder's conquests to the northward fell chiefly upon the possessions of his family, which he lately recovered by the reduction of Darwar.

Hurry Punt was destined to be the chief negotiator on the part of his nation; each commanded a separate army, but the Bhow was to be employed more immediately in the active operations of the field.

The chiefs themselves, and all the Mahrattas in their suite, and indeed all their people, were remarkably plain, but neat, in their appearance. Mild in their aspect, humane in their disposition, polite and unaffected in their address, they are distinguished by obedience to their chiefs, and attachment to their country. There were not to be seen among them those fantastic figures in armour so common among the Mahommedans, in the Nizam's, or, as they style themselves, the Mogul army; adventurers collected from every quarter of the East, who, priding themselves on individual valour, think it beneath them to be useful but on the day of battle, and, when that comes, prove only the inefficiency of numbers, unconnected by any general principle of union or discipline.

The Mahrattas of every rank seemed greatly rejoiced in having effected this junction, and considered it an happy omen, that this event should have taken place at Milgottah, a spot so renowned in their annals for the signal victory gained by Madharow in 1772, in which he completely routed and dispersed Hyder's army, and took all his cannon. Many of the chiefs and people who had served with that general were now in these armies; but they had since felt the superiority of the forces of Mysore, and were impressed with such an idea of Tippoo's discipline, and his abilities in the field, that they were not a little pleased in having joined the British army, without having occasion to try their fortune singly with the Sultan. They all shewed great eagerness to hear the news, and to know the reason of our having burst our great guns. On being told of the victory of the 15th of May, and of the subsequent necessity of destroying the battering train, from want of provisions, and not knowing of their approach, they partook in the joy and grief we had experienced on those events; and seeing that we considered the late defeat of Tippoo as a matter of course, and that we looked forward with confidence to the capture of the capital, they expressed themselves to the following effect: "We have "brought plenty—do you get more guns—we will feed you, and "you shall fight."

The conference between the generals and the chiefs broke up between five and six o'clock, apparently much to the satisfaction of both parties.

The famished followers of our army now ran to the Mahratta camp in thousands, and were happy to purchase grain at any rate. Luckily the want of money was none of our difficulties, else we should have profited little by this supply; for the chiefs, being the proprietors of the grain, which they had brought from their own, or collected as plunder in the enemy's, country, did not permit their joy to operate to the prejudice of their interest, and sold every thing at the most exorbitant rates. Three seers (quarts) of rice, and six of raggy, or gram, for a rupee, was the common, and, in general, the lowest price; so that the wages of the black servants could not provide them with grain, and the pay of a subaltern would scarcely feed his horse. But grain was now worth its weight in gold; and, while this lasted, there was no hesitation in making the exchange.

The Mahratta supplies, consisting chiefly of raggy, a coarse grain, which grows in more abundance than any other in the Mysore country, it became necessary to serve it out to the troops, giving rice only to the sick. To prevent discontent the raggy was issued to them *gratis*; but being a very heating, unwholesome food for men not accustomed to it, fluxes prevailed in camp; and the weather, damp and cold at night, though without much rain, if not the first cause, contributed greatly to increase the sickness.

The Mahratta camp was at the distance of about six miles from ours, and, on approaching it, had the appearance of a large irregular town; for the chiefs pitch their standards, and take up their ground around their general, without order; and their tents being of all sizes, and of many different colours, at a distance resemble houses, rather than canvas. The streets, too, of their camp, crossing and winding in every direction, display a variety of merchandize, as in a great fair. There are shroffs jewellers, smiths, mechanics, and people of every trade and description, as busily employed in their occupations, and attending as minutely to their interest, as if they were in Poonah, and at peace. The Bombay detachment, advanced always at some distance in their front, served as a picquet to their camp; and they had some outposts of their own, established more with a view to cover the supplies coming in to their army, than to guard against a surprise from the enemy.

The park of artillery, where all their guns are collected, made an extraordinary appearance. The gun-carriages, in which they trust to the solidity of the timber, and use but little iron in their construction, are clumsy beyond belief; particularly the wheels, which are low, and formed of large solid pieces of wood united. The guns are of all sorts and dimensions; and, having the names of their gods given to them, are painted in the most fantastic manner; and many of them, held in esteem for the services they are said to have already performed for the state, cannot now be dispensed with, although in every respect unfit for use. Were the guns even serviceable, the small supply of ammunition with which they are provided has always effectually prevented the Mahratta artillery from being formidable to their enemies.

The Mahratta infantry, which formed part of the retinue that attended the chiefs at the conference, is composed of black Christians, and despicable poor wretches of the lowest cast, uniform in nothing but the bad state of their musquets, none of which are either clean or complete; and few are provided with either ammunition or accoutrements. They are commanded by half-cast people of Portugueze and French extraction, who draw off the attention of spectators from the bad clothing of their men, by the profusion of antiquated lace bestowed on their own; and if there happens to be a few Europeans among the officers and men, which is sometimes the case, they execrate the service, and deplore their fate.

The Mahrattas do not appear to treat their infantry with more respect than they deserve, as they ride through them without any ceremony on the march, and on all occasions evidently consider them as foreigners, and a very inferior class of people and troops. Indeed the attention of the Mahrattas is directed entirely to their horses and bazars, those being the only objects which immediately affect their interest. On a marching day, the guns and the infantry move off soon after day-light, but rarely together; the bazars and baggage move nearly about the same time, as soon as they can be packed up and got ready. The guns and tumbrels, sufficiently unwieldy without farther burden, are so heaped with stores and baggage, that there does not seem to be any idea of its ever being necessary to unlimber, and prepare for action on the march. As there are no pioneers attached to the Mahratta artillery to repair the roads, this deficiency is compensated by an additional number of cattle, there being sometimes a hundred, or a hundred and fifty bullocks, in a string of pairs, to one gun: the drivers, who are very expert, sit on the yokes, and pass over every impediment, commonly at a trot. The chiefs remain upon the ground, without tents, smoking their hookers, till the artillery and baggage have got on some miles; they then follow, each pursuing his own route, attended by his principal people; while the inferiors disperse, to forage and plunder over the country.

A few days after the junction of the Mahratta armies, an irregular fire of cannon and musquetry was heard in their camp between nine and ten at night. The troops immediately turned out in our camp, and stood to their arms, thinking that Tippoo had certainly attacked the Mahrattas; but it proved to be only the celebration of one of their ceremonies, in which they salute the new moon, on its first appearance.

Another circumstance occurred soon after, also characteristic of their customs and discipline.

The ground on which our army had encamped at the junction, being bare of grass, and extremely dirty, Lord Cornwallis was desirous of marching; and sent to the Mahratta chiefs, to request they would move next morning, as their camp lay directly in our route. They returned for answer, "that they should be happy "to obey his Lordship's commands; but, as they had halted "eight days, it was not lucky, nor could they, according to the "custom of their religion, march on the ninth day." His Lordship gave way to their superstitious prejudice, and deferred his march.

CHAPTER II.

March of the Allied Armies from Seringapatam to Bangalore—Arrangements for refitting the British Army, and Disposition of the Confederate Forces, till after the Monsoons.

THE allied armies made their first march from the neighbourhood of Seringapatam on the 6th of June, and continued to move occasionally, but slowly; first northward, towards Naggemungulum, where Purseram Bhow had established a post, and depôt of provisions; and from thence eastward, towards Bangalore.

The motives for retiring in this manner, and by this route, were, 1. To enable the Mahrattas to withdraw the posts they had left upon the road, by which Purseram Bhow had advanced to the westward of Chittledroog, maintaining only the safer communication by Roydroog and Sera. 2. To keep Tippoo confined to as small a part of his country as might be practicable, and oblige him to consume the provisions he had laid up for the defence of his capital. 3. To subsist the confederate forces in some measure at the expence of the enemy, and gain time for collecting and bringing forward supplies.

In falling back from Seringapatam towards Bangalore, the Mahrattas, who encamped in the rear of our army, were generally rouzed by our advanced guard several hours after daylight; and we had frequently to halt, till they had cleared the way, or moved off. When joined by the baggage of our army, which, in marching from the enemy, was sent in front, the whole formed an irregular multitude, which, seen from an eminence, covered the country as far as the eye could reach. Our troops, following in several columns, then about fifteen thousand under arms, appeared but as the rear-guard of the united forces.

The Mahratta horse did not, however, remain inactive after their junction, but were constantly scouring the country in parties, in every direction. They took some elephants, and intercepted several small convoys of Tippoo's. They also laid snares for his horse, and attacked them boldly, whenever they could to advantage. This was of material service, as it kept our camp quiet, and prevented our being harassed on the march: for so reduced were the horses of our cavalry from want and fatigue, that the only service they could now render was to walk on slowly with the sick and wounded soldiers on their backs, for whom we were in great want of conveyance; and it was highly pleasing to see the cheerfulness with which the troopers walked by the side of their horses, while their distressed comrades of the infantry rode upon the march.

Lord Cornwallis and General Medows continued, to have frequent conferences with the Mahratta chiefs, who took care to support their dignity by being constantly too late in all their appointments; and his Lordship had occasion to exert all his patience to keep them in humour, and all his talents and diligence to make arrangements for the further prosecution of the war.

Battering guns and stores were easily to be replaced from the different presidencies; there was no great apprehension of the want of money; but the serious difficulty was to provide cattle for the new train, and to collect and find carriage for that immense quantity of provision, which, in the exhausted state of the Mysore country, would be required for the siege of Seringapatam. In short, bullocks and rice, the great sinews of Indian warfare, were objects of indispensable importance; and which, at this late period of the war, required every exertion of power, activity, and arrangement, to obtain and bring forward in sufficient abundance for the interesting service of the ensuing campaign.

Such had been the mortality among the draft and carriage cattle, that the contractors, and the people employed by them, had lost near forty thousand during the last campaign; a number equal to the complete equipment of the public departments of the army, on its leaving Madras in the beginning of February. To repair that loss with the greatest efficacy and dispatch, Lord Cornwallis appointed agents to purchase bullocks on the part of government, in addition to what the contractors could replace; and sent orders to Madras to the same effect, that every possible exertion might be made to recruit this essential department. His Lordship also made an offer of a monthly allowance to the officers of the army, who would engage to carry and provide their own tents for the remainder of the war; and to officers commanding battalions of Sepoys, who would in like manner engage for their men's tents, and for the carriage of the ammunition and stores attached to their corps. The zeal which animated the army induced the officers in general to accede to his Lordship's offers. This measure relieved the bullock department, and the public service, of a most expensive and troublesome detail; and although the competition in purchasing cattle in the Mahratta camp so enhanced the price as to prevent the contractors from recruiting any great number on their own account, yet it had the essential advantage of soon bringing every camel and bullock, the Mahrattas could possibly spare, into the service of our army.

Rice, cattle for slaughter, sheep, salt, and arrack, were the next objects of immediate attention; and chiefly rice, which is the only article issued to the native troops. The quantity of grain captured in Bangalore, although considerable, had been since mostly expended, and we had no public store above the Ghauts. The supplies brought by the Mahrattas were nearly exhausted; it was not to be expected that they could do more in future than support their own armies; and the Nizam's troops had not hitherto made any arrangement adequate even to their own subsistence.

Lord Cornwallis, foreseeing the probable want of this great staple of subsistence in an Indian army, had approved of a plan proposed by Captain Alexander Read, for encouraging the brinjarries, or grain merchants, to bring forward supplies of rice to the army. Captain Read, indefatigable in his exertions, and skilled in the languages and customs of the country, had already collected a convoy of those people, with several thousand bullock load of rice and other grain, in the neighbourhood of Vincatighery, in readiness to meet the army at Bangalore. This channel of supply, by a just and liberal encouragement, soon became more considerable, as will appear in the sequel of this Narrative, and at last furnished grain in such abundance as exceeded all expectation, far beyond what ever could have been procured by any arrangement of public carriage and convoys.

The allied armies moved slowly from Milgottah northward to Naggemungulum, a large mud fort, which was now abandoned, from being to the westward of the line of communication, as already mentioned. From thence the direction of the march was eastward to Hooleadroog, a hill fort, six miles on the east side of the Maddoor river. The route by which the armies marched from Milgottah, was through a bare, stony, and, in general, barren country; but on approaching this river the prospect cleared up; a fertile and charming country was seen to extend on each side of the Maddoor, which, flowing between its high banks, in a wide and beautiful stream, takes a south-east course, passing through the fertile district of Sultan Pettah, till it falls into the rugged channel of the Cavery.

On the 19th of June, the allied armies crossed, and encamped on the east bank of the Maddoor: the chief engineer, Lieutenant-Colonel Ross, having been sent on with the 22d battalion of coast Sepoys, commanded by Captain Oram, to reconnoitre and summon Hooleadroog: and on the next day, the 6th brigade was sent to invest the place, and make an appearance of attack. The fort was inaccessible and impregnable, had the killedar and his garrison chosen to defend it; but luckily they thought their enemies too formidable, and agreed to give it up, on condition of having their private property secured to them, and being sent clear of our camp, with a safe escort. Above six thousand head of cattle, and two thousand sheep, were collected about this place; which, with a quantity of grain in the fort and pettah, afforded a most seasonable aid to the subsistence of the army; for although relieved from want by the supplies procured from our allies, we by no means enjoyed plenty, as the Mahrattas brought forward their provisions with great caution, and very sparingly, to keep up the price.

This place, reckoned too inconsiderable to be kept by our army, was offered to the Mahrattas, as a post that might be useful to them as a halting place for their convoys; but they also declining to possess it, orders were given to destroy it so far as might prevent its being again occupied by the enemy.

Between the river Maddoor and Bangalore there is a tract of country full of hills, and very woody, extending all the way from Shevagunga to the north bank of the Cavery, and forms a very strong barrier between Bangalore and Seringapatam. Through this difficult country there are three roads, or defiles; one to the southward, by Cankenelly; a middle road, by Cenapatam; and a northern road, by Savendroog, Outradroog, and Hooleadroog. On each of these roads, and throughout the whole extent of this tract of country, many of the hills are fortified, and were formerly the castles and possessions of rajahs and polygars, the petty princes and chiefs of the Gentoo people; but they are now all subject to Tippoo, and garrisoned by his troops.

Lord Cornwallis had advanced against Seringapatam by the southern road, on account of its approaching the Cavery, and of its promising a more immediate junction with the Bombay army; he now retired by the northern route, to cover the Mahratta supplies, and in hopes of finding more forage and grain in this quarter than he had done on the southern, or could expect in the middle road, where Tippoo had laid waste the country, and driven off the inhabitants.

The allied armies left Hooleadroog on the 22d; and, to avoid the closest part of the country above described, made their first march up the valley to the north, and directing their next march through the hills to the eastward, they encamped on the 25th of June before Outradroog.

While the army halted on the 23d, accounts were received from Captain Read, at Vincatighurry, that his convoy of brinjarries had been attacked by a body of horse; and as it was known that Tippoo had detached Cumer-ud-Deen's son with two brigades of infantry, to Savendroog, a detachment of three battalions of Sepoys, under Captain Archibald Brown, was immediately sent off from the army to join Captain Read, and bring on his convoy to Bangalore.

The chief engineer, on being sent to reconnoitre and summon Outradroog, received the following answer from the killedar: "I have ate Tippoo's salt (received his pay) for twenty years, "and will not give up my post till you first take Seringapatam." The upper fort was defended by several high walls, at different distances, on the only side that was accessible, to attack which would require time and battering cannon; and the lower fort not appearing to contain many cattle, or any thing to compensate the loss which might be sustained in taking it by assault, the faithful killedar was for the present left in quiet possession of his post.

The armies passing eastward, through a narrow defile, from Outradroog, entered a rich, beautiful, and varied country, where Savendroog, the prominent feature of the landscape, towered like an elephant amidst the lesser hills which encircle this romantic district.

On the 28th of June the armies encamped at Magré, a large town in the centre of this valley, about six miles from Savendroog. Two lofty ancient pagodas, of elegant structure, and smaller pagodas in every village, and swamey houses (Hindoo temples), on every eminence, even on the pinnacles of the Droog, bear testimony, as do also the numerous large tanks that water the adjoining country, to its having been formerly a rajahship of great note; and where the monuments of the Hindoo worship are still held in veneration by the remaining Bramins, and people of that religion. At present, the town of Magré, and surrounding villages, were deserted; the people having retired, with their cattle and effects, to Savendroog.

On the 28th and 29th of June, the chief engineer, and the officers of his corps, were employed in reconnoitering the Droog. It was found to be surrounded by a forest of natural wood, or jungle, several miles in depth, thickened with clumps of planted bamboos, to render it every where as impenetrable as possible. The road, winding through it, was defended by different barriers, and at other places by trees felled to obstruct the passage. The enemy, however, did not attempt to oppose the troops sent on this service, otherwise than by firing cannon shot occasionally from the fort; which, coming from a great elevation, buried themselves as they fell, and luckily did no hurt. The place, in the course of two days, was closely reconnoitered on the west and south faces; the east face was also seen in profile; and it appeared so strong, that there could be little hope of assailing in those quarters with success: the lower fort, which occupied a range of separate hills, covered the town or pettah, which lay between it and the great mountain. These hills, which appeared low only from the proximity of the huge mass behind them, were not, however, so steep but that they might be carried by assault, the walls being of great extent, and in some places in ruins: the lower fort might therefore be taken, the pettah sacked, and the jungle partly swept of the cattle that were drawn into it from the country; but the immense hill itself seemed to deserve the fame it had obtained of being the most impregnable fortress in India. To invest or blockade Savendroog closely was impossible; for the rock itself forms a base of from eight to ten miles in circumference, and with the jungle, and lesser hills which surround it, includes a circle of twenty miles, through the various pathways of which the garrison might always find means to keep up the communication with the country.

The advantage to be gained by any attempt on Savendroog not appearing to be an object, compared with the loss and delay it would occasion in the present distressed state of the army, Lord Cornwallis proceeded again on the 2d of July; first marching to the northward, to avoid the closest part of the country, and afterwards eastward, towards Bangalore.

In marching to the eastward, the armies of the allies encamping in the rear of our army, then fronting Savendroog, were not disturbed in the mornings by our march: and having sometimes, to pass beyond our camp to their ground, it was highly entertaining to see them in motion the whole day; the chiefs in different groups, Moguls and Mahrattas alternately, themselves and their principal attendants mounted on elephants, distinguished by their state-flags and nagars, also borne on elephants. They were surrounded by cavalry, with their various standards, and preceded by their bards, and bands of music, who sung the praises of their masters, and the heroes of their nation. Group succeeding group; elephants, camels, pikemen, standard-bearers; horsemen innumerable, armed with sword and shield, with lances, bows and arrows, and every variety of ancient and modern arms and armour; tilts and tournaments for exercise, and a continual discharge of pistols and carabines, displayed the jubilee of their march. A spectacle so wild and irregular, yet so grand and interesting, resembled more the visions of romance, than any assemblage that can be supposed to have existence in real life!

On approaching Bangalore, which the army looked forward to as their home, the following articles of interesting intelligence were received:

1. That Captain Read, with his convoy of brinjarries of ten or twelve thousand bullock loads of grain, had arrived safe.

2. That Gunjicottah, which had been besieged for some time by the Nizam's troops and the Madras detachment, surrendered on the 12th of June; which gave his Highness possession of an extensive valuable district, and would enable that army to advance their operations to the siege of Gurramcondah.

3. That accounts had arrived from England of the vote of parliament in approval of the war, and of Lord Cornwallis's conduct; that five hundred thousand pounds in specie was to be sent out this season by the Company, to enable his Lordship to carry on his operations with vigour and effect; that an augmentation had been voted to the establishment of the King's regiments in India, which would be completed by the ships of this year; that a detachment of the royal artillery might also be expected; and that every exertion was making to send out recruits for the Company's service.

4. That one hundred elephants had arrived at Vellore from

Bengal; and that the contractors had engaged to have twenty-eight thousand bullocks, the number lately ordered, in readiness by the 8th of August.

These circumstances, which afforded the fairest prospect of the army being soon refitted, and enabled to advance again in full force, were not less agreeable to us than to the allies; and the communication being open with Bangalore and the Carnatic, thousands of coolies were coming in daily with supplies, that relieved all present wants. The private letters were also now sent on that had arrived from Europe, and from the presidencies in India; which was no small gratification after so long an interval. All hardships were forgotten, and the army looked forward with confidence to the event of the ensuing campaign.

The Mahrattas having disposed of all their grain and spare cattle to our army, and got all our money in exchange, it became necessary that these multitudes should separate, both to facilitate their subsistence, and to prosecute the measures agreed upon, as preparatory to their assembling again for the attack of the enemy's capital.

Previous to the separation of the armies, it was meant that the Mahratta chiefs should see our line under arms, and orders were given for the troops to be in readiness on the 7th of July; but on being informed that it would be necessary they should come on horseback, as the Nizam's chiefs had done, in order to see the troops to advantage, and that Lord Cornwallis and General Medows, who never rode on elephants, could not otherwise accompany them, they declined the offer, and rather chose to forego the satisfaction of a sight that might be thought so interesting to them, and the honour of being received by the British army with all military distinction, than come in a style which they conceived to be derogatory to their own dignity.

On the 8th of July, Lord Cornwallis proceeding to Bangalore, Purseram Bhow, with his army, and the Bombay detachment, commanded by Captain Little, directed his march towards Sera, a quarter favourable to the subsistence of his army, and a position which would cover his supplies, and prevent Tippoo from advancing into the country; as the Sultan durst not make any material movement against either army, without incurring the risk of being intercepted in his return to his capital.

The greatest part of the Nizam's horse was sent, under Assud Aly Khan, to join the other forces of his Highness at Gunjecottah; a few of the best only remaining under the Rajah Tiege Wunt, who was at first both commander in chief and minister plenipotentiary on the part of the Nizam; but having proved himself very unequal to either station, had been lately superseded in the last office by a more able negotiator, Meer Alum, formerly the Nizam's vakeel to the government of Bengal. Hurry Punt, as plenipotentiary of the Mahratta state, also remained with his army along with Lord Cornwallis.

The regiments of cavalry under Colonel Floyd being sent soon after to recruit in the Carnatic, there remained only with our army the two troops which formed the body guards attached to Lord Cornwallis and General Medows; and which, freed from the duties of the line, but employed equally on every service of danger, were, much to the credit of the officers who commanded them, Lieutenants Turner and Grant, still in such order as to enable them to keep the field.

Colonel Duff, the commanding officer of the artillery, who had commanded in Bangalore after its capture, and had with great diligence and ability refitted the battering train used in that siege, and carried on from thence to Seringapatam, was again appointed to the command, that he might get ready such guns, ammunition, and stores, as the place would afford, for another train; and on the colonel's reporting what the arsenal and magazines of Bangalore could furnish, Lord Cornwallis sent orders to forward the remainder from the presidencies of Bengal and Madras.

The sick, now very numerous, were sent into Bangalore, and the recovered men, who had been left in the hospitals, were ordered to join their corps. The half of the camp equipage that had been left behind, was got out; the officers supplied themselves with every thing at a moderate rate from the stores lately brought forward by the sutlers from Madras, and the soldiers had again their allowance of arrack, which, from repeated losses on the march, had been expended for some time, and the want of it severely felt in the damp weather.

It was highly satisfactory to see how much Bangalore had recovered during these last two months; several thousands of the inhabitants had returned to their habitations in this extensive town, or pettah; the gardens afforded a variety of vegetables and roots, and the markets abounded with many of the necessaries of life. The inhabitants of several of the villages had also returned, and the recommencement of cultivation proved that the neighbouring country was recovering rapidly from the desolation occasioned by the inhuman policy of Tippoo, who had laid it waste on the first approach of the British army.

CHAPTER III.

Reduction of Oussoor, Rayacotta, and the Forts which command the Policode Pass—Junction of the first Convoys from the Carnatic.

THE disposition of the confederate forces having taken place for the period of the monsoons, it will be necessary to detail separately in what manner each army was employed until the beginning of the year 1792, when they again assembled, to attack the capital of Mysore.

The operations of the grand army were first directed to the great object of establishing a secure and easy communication with the Carnatic, in order to bring forward the battering train and supplies for the service of the ensuing campaign.

It is here necessary to premise, that the Muglee pass, by which the army had ascended the Ghauts, in advancing to the attack of Bangalore, is too far to the northward, and not sufficiently connected with posts, to secure it as a line of communication with the Carnatic; and the Pednaigdurgum pass, between Amboor and Vencatigherry, which had since been opened, had the disadvantage of being of very difficult ascent.

The Policode pass, the most immediately connected with Bangalore, by which the Mysore armies have always invaded the Carnatic, and the only open and easy ascent between these countries, was still in the possession of the enemy. This road leads through an open country from Bangalore, for twenty-eight miles, to Oussoor; and from thence descending gradually among the hills which separate Mysore from the Baramaul, is defended by various hill forts, till it reaches Caveripatam, in the middle of the valley. From thence several roads branch off, which, passing through the hills on the east side of the Baramaul, are called passes, into the Carnatic, of which the principal are three.

1st. The Amboor pass, defended by the hill fort of Amboor, within the boundary of the Carnatic.

2d. The Changama pass, within the boundary of the Baramaul, where there are various openings between the hills, without any obstruction or defence, the principal roads leading to Trinomaly and Gingee, or by Caliswauk to Arnee.

3d. The Atore pass, defended by a hill fort of that name, also within the precincts of the Baramaul, is the road leading by Thiagar to Pondicherry, and used by the French in their communication with Mysore.

But those passes, while they facilitated the operations of Hyder when invading the Carnatic from the Baramaul valley, were not attended with similar advantage in any projected invasion of his country from that quarter; for, as the only roads practicable for an army unite in the Policode pass, which leads to Oussoor, he had but one entrance to defend, into the Mysore country.

It became an object of great importance to dispossess the enemy of this pass, not only to check their inroads to the Carnatic, which was now open to them from Seringapatam, by Cankanelly and Oussoor, but also to facilitate the bringing forward the supplies for our army, by the easiest and best channel.

The army being in some measure relieved from its late distress, Lord Cornwallis prepared to move against Oussoor, and the hill forts which command the Policode pass; and, with this view, lodging half the tumbrels of the field artillery in Bangalore, to lighten the army of an unnecessary incumbrance, ordered out four heavy iron guns, two twenty and two eighteen-pounders, which had been prepared as part of the battering train, but were, luckily, not carried with the army to Seringapatam. These, with four iron twelve-pounders, which had been reserved for field service when the heavier guns were destroyed, made a train of eight battering guns, which was judged fully adequate to the present service.

On the 15th of July, the army moved from the neighbourhood of Bangalore, and marched towards Oussoor, through a fertile varied country, beautified with chains of tanks for the culture of the low grounds, and with numerous villages and small forts; which, surrounded with trees, crowned and adorned every eminence. The inhabitants, hitherto undisturbed, had continued the cultivation of their fields. The verdure of a new crop, the proximity of the mountains, and the cool temperature of the climate, resembled more a peaceful country in Europe, in the midst of spring, than the seat of war in the height of summer between the tropics in India!

The 7th brigade, commanded by Major Gowdie, having been sent a march in front of the army, reached Oussoor on the 15th of July.

The enemy were preparing to abandon the place, but, dilatory on all occasions, the unexpected approach of this brigade forced them to a precipitate retreat. They spiked the guns, burnt the carriages, and as they went off fired a mine, which blew up one of the bastions; but a train they had laid to the magazine, luckily did not take effect, so that the damage done to the place was not great, and both a quantity of powder and other ammunition, and a considerable store of grain, which the garrison had not time to remove, was found in the fort.

Tippoo, sensible of the importance of Oussoor, had lately made great exertions to improve its defences. The works of the old fort were inclosed within a new rampart, flanked with good bastions, and surrounded by a wide ditch, excavated from the solid rock, which, already filled on three sides, would soon have been completed also on the fourth to such depth as to be filled with water from a large tank which covers the south side of the fort. Protected by another tank on the north, and on the east by an extensive tract of low rice fields, which are watered by those tanks, it can only be attacked with advantage on the west side, where its defences would be such, when the present plan should be completed, as would enable it to stand a regular siege.

Luckily the Sultan's engineer had left the weakest part of the fort to be the last strengthened; and having only begun to excavate the ditch opposite to the south-west angle, they considered the place as untenable, and had blown up that bastion to prevent our possessing it as a post.

There is a hill beyond the tank on the south side of Oussoor, which has been said to command the fort, but the distance is very great (several thousand yards); and although the ground rises gradually from the tank and pettah, which may afford some advantage to an enfilading battery, yet the place cannot suffer materially from an attack on that side.

Captain Welch, with five companies of his battalion of Bengal Sepoys, and a detachment of artillery, was appointed to garrison Oussoor; and the four battering guns, and two of the iron twelve-pounders, destined for its reduction, were sent in for its defence. A party of pioneers, under an engineer, was also ordered to build up the breach in the bastion, which would render it perfectly defensible, by our troops, against any attempt that could be made upon it by the enemy.

In one of the storehouses in the fort (a kind of laboratory, where the military stores were kept), there was a little journal found, in English, by which it appeared that some Europeans had been confined here, and mentioned the work the person who wrote it had done as a carpenter. Some poor people, who remained in the pettah, said there had been three Europeans, one of them called Hamilton, prisoners at this place; who were all very much respected, and regretted by the inhabitants; that they were alive till after the capture of Bangalore, when Tippoo sent orders to put them to death; that the killedar, who was a man of great humanity, evaded the first order, but the second came by a messenger who was instructed to see it carried into execution. They shewed the place where the unfortunate men were beheaded and buried; and, on digging up the graves, the heads were found severed from the bodies, and, from the appearance of the hair, and some remnants of their clothes, no doubt remained of the truth of this murder; which is one of the many

Tippoo appears to have committed, to prevent his false assertions being detected, of there having been no British subjects detained by force in his country, since the last war. Some have fortunately made their escape; but wherever the tyrant suspected they might fall into our hands, he has always ordered them to be put to death.

Another act of barbarity was discovered in one of the villages in this neighbourhood, which had lately been committed by the inhabitants, without any orders from their inhuman master. Having caught two soldiers, who had gone beyond the picquets in search of grain, they were not contented with putting them to death, but, adding insult to cruelty, hanged a dog on the same tree, and threw the carcass along with their bodies into a grain-pit, where they were found. Two old people, who remained in the village, gave this account of their fate.

From Oussoor, Major Gowdie, with his brigade, was ordered to proceed to Rayacotta, and arrived before it on the 19th of July.

The killedar refusing to surrender, the major next morning attacked the lower fort, which incloses the pettah. He soon carried it by assault, and, pursuing the fugitives, got possession of the two first walls, which form a sort of middle fort, between the lower fort, and that which defends the summit of this stupendous rock. The place was known to be too strong by nature to be reduced, if the garrison were resolute in its defence; Major Gowdie was therefore directed to return to the army, if it was not given up on the first attack; but having made a lodgement on the hill, where the troops were covered from the fire of the upper fort, and having reason to think the garrison were intimidated, he requested leave to continue the attack. A battalion, with the two other iron twelve-pounders, was sent on the 22d of July to join his brigade, and enable him to breach another of the walls, which was within his reach. The major's spirited measures were also enforced by a movement of the army at the same time, towards Rayacotta, when the killedar proposed a parley, which soon ended in his giving up the place, on condition of security to private property, and his being permitted to go with his family to reside in the Carnatic.

The hill forts of Anchittydurgam, Neelagheri, Rutnagheri, Oodeadurgam, and Chinraydurgam, several of which lie nearer to the pass than Rayacotta, but, though strong, are of less importance, either gave up on being summoned, as the army moved down towards Rayacotta, or were taken after a slight resistance.

In the attack of Rayacotta, Lieutenant Crie, of the engineers, a very zealous, promising officer, was killed; one soldier, and one Sepoy, were also killed, and several wounded: one havildar was killed, and several Sepoys wounded, at the other forts.

Rayacotta was found to be amply supplied with guns, ammunition, and provisions, for its defence. Two hundred French and English firelocks, belonging to a reinforcement of regular infantry, sent in when Tippoo returned from the Carnatic, and a number of country arms, were also delivered up with the place. Several tanks, or reservoirs, that fill during the rains, supply it with excellent water; and so strong and complete in all respects was this lofty, spacious fort, that it ought to have yielded only to famine and a tedious blockade.

On the 29th of July the army returned above the pass from

Rayacotta, and continued in the neighbourhood of Oussoor, to cover the convoy from Amboor, now ordered to come up by this route. The 7th coast battalion, commanded by Captain Chace, was left to garrison Rayacotta, Oodeadurgam, and Anchitty-durgam: the three other hill forts which have been mentioned were destroyed, as not being necessary to the defence of the pass.

Captain Rattray, of the Bengal establishment, with his own, the 22d, and 23d battalions of coast Sepoys, commanded by Captains Oram and Campbell, had been detached to bring up the convoy from Amboor, at the time Colonel Floyd returned with the cavalry to the Carnatic.

This important convoy left Amboor the 2d of August, and, proceeding by Tripatore and Caveripatam, marched through an open and well cultivated country to Rayacotta, which leaving a few miles to the north, they proceeded by a gradual ascent, passing under the smaller hill forts that have been named, and in eight easy marches joined the army on the 10th of August, then encamped near Oussoor.

One hundred elephants, marching two abreast into camp, all loaded with treasure, on the foremost of which was displayed the British standard, was a sight fit to have graced an eastern triumph; and accompanied by six thousand bullocks with rice, one hundred carts with arrack, and some thousands of coolies with trunks and baskets of private supplies, formed such a convoy as never before joined any army of ours in India.

The supplies having been delivered to the proper departments, and lodged partly in Oussoor, this noble reinforcement of elephants, the bullocks, carts, &c. were dispatched on the 14th of

August, with a proper escort, under Captain Williamson, to bring forward another lading from Amboor. He was directed to go from Rayacotta by Kistnaghery, as a nearer road, which the pioneers had lately been sent to repair, and Captain Oram, who had been left with his own, and half the 15th battalion, to watch the enemy at Kistnaghery, was directed to meet him in that neighbourhood.

The road by Kistnaghery, which passes under the guns of Rayacotta, winds through the hills and woods that lie directly between these forts, and was not found to be so near as the apparently more circuitous route by Caveripatam. Besides the inconvenience of the wood or jungle, where a convoy gets on with difficulty, and bullocks go astray, and are lost, there is a great want of water on that road; and it has the farther disadvantage of passing within the range of the guns of Kistnaghery, which, fired from the summit of that immense rock, reach to a great distance, and did the convoy some damage. This route, however eligible for a small detachment to avoid an enemy, was on every account given up as unfit for an army, or any large convoy; and it was evident that Kistnaghery, although the principal fort in the Baramaul valley, being thus retired from the best road, does not merit the estimation in which it has been held, and that Rayacotta may be more justly styled the key to the Mysore country.

About this time, the middle of August, a vakeel from Tippoo arrived at Oussoor, in consequence of the Sultan's having agreed to address the confederate powers jointly on the subject of peace. This vakeel, named Apagy Row, a Mahratta, had been employed in negotiations with our government during the former war, and was considered as a person not likely to be entrusted by Tippoo with full powers to make the concessions expected by his enemies. He proposed such conditions, with respect to the forms of his reception, and opening the negotiation, as shewed that he was merely an instrument of intrigue and delay; and as he said he was not authorized to dispense with those forms, he was sent back to his master, without being permitted to enter the camp.

So little respected was this ambassador by the people of his own cast and nation among our allies, that he was openly insulted by the Mahrattas, and under the necessity of requesting to have a guard of our troops to protect his person. His dismission soon relieved them of this irksome charge, and was a subject that afforded general satisfaction to the confederate armies.

The second convoy from Amboor, consisting of camp equipage, rice, and stores, left that place early in September, and, proceeding by the same route the first had marched, joined the army about the middle of the month, when encamped near Bangalore.

Lord Cornwallis had been pleased to desire that Mr. Thomas Cockburn, of the Company's civil service at Madras, would take this opportunity to come up to the army, for the final arrangement of the bullock department, and other business connected with the supplies for the ensuing campaign. Mr. Cockburn was one of the contractors for providing the army with draft and carriage cattle, and the person by whose exertions and abilities this important department had been conducted with such unexampled success during the late war. His colleagues in that line, the late Lieutenant Colonel Moorhouse and Captain Campbell, had seconded his able arrangements, by conducting the detail of the business, with equal zeal and honour, with the army. The loss sustained by the contractors, and the black people employed under them, who furnished the cattle, had been so heavy during the last campaign, that, in the exhausted state of this resource in the Carnatic, it was doubtful if the exertions of any individuals, at the stated low rate in a contract, were equal to furnish the supplies (greater than ever) that would be required for the service of the campaign. By Mr. Cockburn's activity, aided by the support of Sir Charles Oakely and the Madras government, the number of bullocks lately ordered (twenty-eight thousand) had been provided in the Carnatic for the use of the grand army; and ten thousand more collected in the southern countries, were sent across the Peninsula to assist in the re-equipment of the Bombay army. This main spring of all military movements in India was again in complete repair, but required constant attention to preserve it in force.

Lord Cornwallis had always been of opinion, that a department so immediately connected with the operations of the army, and which must be supported at every risk and expence, ought not to depend on the performance or failure of a contract, but be conducted by agents under the immediate controul and direction of government. The cattle that had been lately purchased from the Mahrattas, or collected by the army, were under the management of agents on that footing; but the agents not having been able to engage servants in the field, were under the necessity of requesting the contractors to allow them to employ their people. In this manner the bullock department had become extremely complicated, and it was necessary that the business should be conducted solely either by agents or the contractors. Mr. Cockburn and Captain Campbell, the two remaining contractors, desirous to second his Lordship's wishes, and wearied of the trouble and anxiety, which had not been compensated by the advantages of the contract, agreed to give it up; and his Lordship, whose objection was to the system, not to the persons employed, was pleased to secure the services of Mr. Cockburn, and testify his approbation of his conduct, by appointing him to continue at the head of that department, as the principal agent on the part of government.

CHAPTER IV.

Reduction of the Hill Forts to the North-East of Bangalore—Siege of Nundydroog—Tippoo's Movement towards Chittledroog—Detaches Cummer-ud-Deen Cawn against Coimbetore, and sends a Reinforcement to Kistnaghery.

THE bullock department, and other important affairs arranged, the next object that engaged the attention of the commander in chief was the reduction of several hill forts to the north-east of Bangalore; which, situated between that fortress and Gurramconda, interrupted the communication with the Nizam's army, and the supplies which might be collected from that quarter, or brought from the Carnatic by that route.

The forts that occasioned this embarrassment were Raymanghur, Ambajee-Durgum, Chillum-Cottha, Nundydroog, and Calarumconda, or Cumeldroog, in the neighbourhood of China-Balaporam, a very fertile district, through which the army had passed in going to join the Nizam's troops in April, 1791, after the reduction of Bangalore.

Major Gowdie's brigade having returned from Rayacotta, was sent also on this service, reinforced by a detachment of artillery under Major Montagu, with four iron twelve-pounders, and two small mortars, and by the detachment of infantry under Captain Alexander Read, consisting of the 4th and part of the 3d and 15th battalions of coast Sepoys, which had been employed with him in protecting and bringing forward the convoys of brinjarries to Bangalore.

On the 14th of September Major Gowdie was joined by Captain Read, within nine miles of Raymanghur, and immediately proceeded to reconnoitre and summon the place.

The killedar refusing to surrender, the plan was immediately fixed on for the siege. On the 17th the batteries, constructed within a few hundred yards of the walls, were ready to open, when the killedar, alarmed at the rapidity and vigour of the attack, proposed to give up the place on terms, which being refused to him, the batteries opened on the afternoon of the 17th, when a few rounds of shot and shells determined him to surrender at discretion; and in the evening the major, without having sustained any loss, was put in possession of a place of great strength and importance.

On the 18th of September, Captain Read having been sent with a detachment against Ambajee-Durgum and Chillum-Cottha, the former five, the latter ten miles from Raymanghur, both surrendered to him on the first summons.

Major Gowdie was now ordered to proceed to the attack of Nundydroog, before which he arrived on the 22d of September. This detachment, reinforced by the 19th Bengal and 10th coast battalions of Sepoys, under Captain Macleod, with two heavy guns, and two large mortars, consisted in all of one regiment of Europeans, and six battalions of Sepoys, with six battering guns, and four mortars.

Nundydroog, the capital of a large and valuable district, is built on the summit of a mountain about one thousand seven hundred feet in height, three-fourths of its circumference being absolutely inaccessible, and the only face on which it can be ascended protected by two excellent walls, and an outwork which covered the gateway, and afforded a formidable flank fire. The foundation for a third wall had been dug, but, in the state of many of the other forts, the suddenness of the war had not given the Sultan time to complete the plan. This fort, however, in point of strength, ranked after Savendroog, Chittledroog, and Kistnaghery, and stood a siege worthy of the garrison which Tippoo had placed in it for its defence.

The first object was to cut and form a road to the top of a hill adjoining to the mountain, upon which a battery was erected, and guns brought up with infinite labour. This done, it was expected the place might be immediately breached, and carried by assault; but unfortunately the hill, which seemed so favourably situated to bring the siege to a speedy termination, was found to be too distant, and the battery was not effectual in even taking off the defences of the fort.

There was no alternative, but to abandon the attack, or attempt to work up the face of this steep and rugged mountain, to within breaching distance of the fort. This arduous undertaking was adopted, rather than leave a post of such consequence in the possession of the enemy, and encourage them by an instance of our troops being foiled in the attack of a fortified place, which had not yet happened during the war.

The exertions required to form a gun-road, and erect batteries on the face of this mountain, surpassed whatever had been known in any former siege in India; and such was the steepness of the ascent, that the battering guns could not have been drawn up without the assistance of elephants; whose strength, sagacity, and patient docility, can only be known to those who have seen them employed in the Indian armies.

During a fortnight that the troops were employed in this last arduous work, a continual fire was kept up on them from the fort. The cannon shot, directed from so great a height, seldom took effect; but they were severely annoyed by ginjall, or wall pieces, which are in general use among the native powers in the defence of forts, and throw a bullet of considerable size, with much accuracy, to a great distance.

The batteries formed, two breaches were made; one on the re-entering angle of the outwork, the other in the curtain of the outer wall; but the inner wall, at the distance of eighty yards, could not be touched by our shot.

On the place being breached, Major Gowdie summoned the bukshey to surrender; who refusing in firm but polite terms, the major, with great humanity, made him an offer to send out the women, and those persons who did not carry arms, that they might not suffer in the assault. Of this offer the killedar said he would avail himself, but which he unaccountably neglected.

The breaches being reported practicable, Lord Cornwallis, on the 17th of October, detached the flank companies of the 36th and 71st regiments to lead the assault; and General Medows having, with his usual zeal, made offer of his services, went to command the detachment that was engaged in this important enterprize.

On the 18th of October Lord Cornwallis, with a view to intimidate the garrison, encamped with the army within four miles of Nundydroog; and having examined the breaches, directed, in order to render them more practicable, and to take off some adjoining defences, that the firing should be continued from the batteries till night, when the rising of the moon should be the signal for the assault.

It was determined to storm the breaches, and attempt to carry the inner wall by escalade; but if the attempt should not meet with that success which the boldness of the measure deserved, it was at least thought practicable to make a lodgment behind a cavalier between the walls, and proceed from thence in the regular attack of the inner wall.

The trench dug for the foundation of the third wall, within a hundred yards of that which was breached, having been formed into an advanced parallel, the flank companies had been lodged in it before day-break on the morning of the 18th, that they might be in readiness to advance early in the evening; but it was afterwards judged more expedient to defer the assault till towards midnight, when the garrison would be probably less prepared, and the assailants have the advantage of a clearer moonlight.

Captain Robertson, the senior officer of the flank companies, was to lead the grenadiers of the 36th and 71st regiments to the breach in the curtain. Captain Burne, of the 36th, the next senior officer, declining to quit his grenadier company, at the head of which he had distinguished himself during the war, the light companies were to be led by Captain Hart to the breach in the outwork. The flank companies of the 4th European regiment, commanded by Captain Doveton, were to follow with ladders, for escalading the inner wall.

The disposition above stated, and every preparation, having been made for the assault, the time had almost approached, when some person unthinkingly mentioned, in the hearing of the troops, that a mine was reported to be near the breach. General Medows, with that promptitude which marks his character, replied, "If there be a mine, it must be a mine of gold." The orders being given, the troops moved out from the right and left of the parallel, and rushed forward to the assault.

The vigilance of the enemy soon discovered the assailants.— The fort was instantly illuminated with blue lights, and a heavy fire of cannon, musquetry, and rockets, opened from the works. The fire from the garrison was luckily ill-directed, but the large stones which were thrown down from the hill, acquiring great velocity as they bounded from the rock in their descent, were extremely formidable, and attended with more certain effect. The storming party, however, soon mounted both the breaches, and pursued the enemy so closely, as to prevent their effectually barricading the gate of the inner wall. This was forced open with some difficulty, and the troops entered the body of the place.

The carnage which must have ensued in clearing the fort of the enemy, was prevented partly by a number of the garrison escaping by ropes and ladders over a low part of the wall; but chiefly by the exertions of Captain Robertson; who, seeing the place was carried, turned all his attention to preserving order, and preventing the unnecessary effusion of blood. To his humanity the bukshey and killedar owed their lives; and of the garrison there were only about forty men killed and wounded.

The flank companies, which formed the storming party, had two men killed, and twenty-eight wounded; the latter chiefly from bruises by the stones thrown from the rock. The loss during the siege was, in all, forty Europeans, and eighty Sepoys and pioneers killed and wounded. Captain Read, who had exerted himself with great success, was severely, but not dangerously wounded, in carrying on the approach up the face of the hill. Brigade Major Cranston, and Lieutenant Hill of the Bengal artillery, were also slightly wounded.

Nundydroog, defended by seventeen pieces of cannon, chiefly iron guns, of a large calibre, improved by its late works, and well garrisoned, was thus taken by regular attack in the course of three weeks, although of such strength that it was not yielded to Hyder by the Mahrattas till after a tedious blockade of three years!

Cummeldroog, or Calarumconda, the other hill fort near to, and dependent on, Nundydroog, although a place of great strength, gave up on the first summons, after the fall of the greater fort.

GENERAL AFTER ORDERS.

" *Camp, 19th October,* 1791.

" Lord Cornwallis having been witness of the extraordinary " obstacles, both of nature and art, which were opposed to the "detachment of the army that attacked Nundydroog, he cannot "too highly applaud the firmness and exertions which were ma-"nifested by all ranks, in carrying on the operations of the "siege; or the valour and discipline which was displayed by the "flank companies of his Majesty's 36th and 71st regiments; "those of the Madras 4th European battalion, the 13th Bengal "battalion of native infantry, and of the 3d, 4th, 10th, 13th, "and 27th battalions of Madras native infantry, that were em-"ployed in the assault of last night, and which, by overcoming "all difficulties, effected the reduction of that important fort.

"His Lordship is highly sensible of the zealous and meri-"torious conduct of Major Gowdie in the command of that "detachment, both at the attacks of Raymanghur, and in car-"rying on the arduous operation of the siege of Nundydroog, for "which the major will be pleased to accept his best acknow-"ledgments. The whole of the officers and soldiers who com-"posed that detachment appear likewise to be justly entitled to "the strongest expressions of his approbation; and he parti-"cularly desires that his warmest thanks may be presented to "Major Montagu, for his successful efforts in bringing the ar-"tillery into the batteries, and for the ability with which it was "afterwards served.

"To Captain Robertson of the 71st regiment, who com-"manded in the European flank companies, that led the assault, "and to Captain Macleod, who supported the Europeans with "the flank companies of the native regiment, for the gallantry "and judgment with which they discharged the duties of their "respective situations. To Captain Read, for his almost un-"exampled perseverance in carrying on an approach, and estab-

"lishing a parallel near to the enemy's works on the ascent of "the hill, which was calculated to facilitate the success of the "assault.

"To Captain Kydd, his Lordship's aid-de-camp, for the zealous "and able professional assistance which he gave as engineer; "and to Lieutenant Mackenzie, the senior engineer upon duty, "for the skill and indefatigable industry which he uniformly "exerted, both at Raymunghur, and during the whole of this "siege. Although the services of pioneers are less brilliant "than those of the troops, they are of peculiar value in all such "operations; and his Lordship thinks himself called upon, in "justice to Lieutenant Dowse, and all the non-commissioned "officers and men of the pioneer corps, as well as to Ensign "Stokoe of the engineers, who assisted with so much ability "in directing their labours, to declare that their behaviour on "this occasion has deserved his highest commendation.

"Lord Cornwallis cannot sufficiently express the sense of "his obligation to General Medows; but he requests that he "will be assured that he considers the handsome manner in "which the general undertook the temporary command of a "detachment so inadequate to his rank, and the conduct of the "assault, both as a mark of personal friendship to himself, and "as an additional proof of his earnest desire to promote the "honour and interest of his country."

The principal people, and fighting men, taken in Nundydroog, were sent prisoners to Vellore. The women, Bramins, &c. were conducted by a guard beyond the picquets, and proceeded in safety to a small hill fort, at the distance of six miles, where they supposed the part of the garrison that escaped had taken refuge.

The bukshey, an old and very respectable man of sixty, had been above forty years in Hyder's and Tippoo's service, and was one of the ambassadors whom the Sultan had sent to Constantinople. On his talking, some weeks after, on the subject of Tippoo's affairs, he did not seem to think them desperate. He allowed little merit to his own defence. He said that Bangalore had been taken by surprise, and that we must expect to meet with a very different degree of resistance at Seringapatam. It was his opinion we should not be able to remain long enough before it to take the place; and if his master's sentiments might be judged of from the conversation of this old servant of the family, the Sultan's hope of extricating himself from his troubles were founded not less in a confidence of protracting the siege of his capital, than from a knowledge of the resources of the Company, which he imagined would not support another campaign. The bukshey allowed it would be prudent in the Sultan not to hazard the event; but, impressed with an idea that the English aimed at subjecting him to their government, and depriving him of his authority as an independent prince, he said that Tippoo would never consent to a peace, unless he could conclude it with honour to himself; and that we mistook his character, if we imagined he would ever agree to give up his sovereignty, and solicit a pension to get fat upon, like an old woman (such was his expression), for the rest of his life.

During the siege of Nundydroog, it was reported that Tippoo had taken that opportunity to move out to the northward against

Purseram Bhow, who was then with his army in the neighbourhood of Chittledroog, raising contributions in the country, and protecting the supplies that were coming forward from the Mahratta states, and from the provinces he possessed by the reduction of Darwar.

Tippoo would no doubt have been eager to attack the Bhow, but he probably did not deem it safe to advance so far to the northward, and it appears that his movement was intended merely to cover a large convoy he expected from Bedenore, the only country from which he could draw any considerable supply, and that having effected his object, he returned to the neighbourhood of his capital.

The Sultan had, some time previous to this movement, sent a detachment to attack Coimbetore, and a party to raise contributions, and endeavour to collect supplies in that country.

Lieutenant Chalmers had been left in the command of Coimbetore at the close of the first campaign, with a small force, consisting of a company of Topasses (black Christians), and a battalion of Travancore Sepoys, commanded by Monsieur Lecomb, a French officer in the service of the Rajah. The place was so weak, that only a few bad guns, not worth removing, with a small quantity of ammunition, was left in it; and Lieutenant Chalmers was directed to fall back to Palgautcherry, in case the enemy should appear in considerable force.

The detachment sent against Coimbetore was not of such magnitude as to obiige Lieutenant Chalmers to quit his post. They however breached the place after a siege of some duration, and on the 11th of July attempted to storm. The Travancore troops were extremely turbulent; but the zeal of their commandant inspired them with confidence, and ably seconded the exertions of Lieutenant Chalmers. The assault was repulsed with great loss, above three hundred of the enemy were killed in the fort and ditch; and the rout of the detachment was completed by Major Cuppage, who, advancing with great expedition from Palgautcherry, took the two battering guns with which they had breached the place, and pursued the remains of the enemy till they crossed the Bowanny, opposite to Damicotta.

Tippoo no sooner returned from the movement he made to the northward, than he shewed his perseverance in whatever object he undertook, by detaching Cummer-ud-Deen Cawn, his second in command, with a much larger force, to retrieve the disgrace of his arms at Coimbetore.

The Sultan had also other objects in view in this expedition to the countries below the Ghauts. A light party, chiefly horse, separated from Cummer-ud-Deen, after descending the Gudzelhatty pass, and crossing the Cavery, came through the Tapoor pass, and with great secrecy and rapidity conducted a killedar of more trust, with a reinforcement, to Kistnaghery, the only place of consequence he now possessed between Bangalore and the Carnatic. Part of this detachment returned with a sum of money which had been collected in the districts, while part, remaining in the Baramaul, began to ravage that country, and threatened interruption to our convoys.

Leaving the account of the farther operations in the Coimbetore country to be related hereafter, it is here necessary to mention that the ships of the season had by this time brought out all the draughts and recruits for the King's and Company's troops, as well as the expected supply of money and military stores. In the last ship which arrived at Madras, on the 10th of October, were two companies of the King's artillery, commanded by Major David Scott, a very fine detachment, which landed in perfect health.

The Court of Directors, in addition to the reinforcements from England, had the precaution to order a detachment of three hundred seasoned troops to be sent from St. Helena; a measure suggested by the zeal of Mr. Brooke, their governor at that settlement. Disciplined and inured to military duty in a temperate climate within the tropics, this detachment arrived in perfect health; and being less subject to sickness than the men sent immediately from England, they fully evinced the expediency of the measure, and how important St. Helena may be rendered as a nursery for troops intended for the service in India.

The Honourable Mr. Stuart, and the Members of the Supreme Government in Bengal, whence the war had been hitherto chiefly supported, continued to use every exertion to give efficacy to the measures of their governor general. Large supplies of rice and money had been constantly forwarded from Calcutta. The guns and stores ordered from thence to complete the new battering train, had also arrived, together with a number of draughts, and a supply of clothing for their artillery and Sepoy battalions, serving with the army.

Sir Charles Oakely, and the Government of Madras, nearer to the scene of action, were still more constantly employed in seconding the zeal of their governor, and the measures for the success of the war; and the presence of General Musgrave at that presidency, was of great importance in all the arrangements necessary for completing and forwarding the various supplies required for the service of the ensuing campaign.

The draughts and recruits from Europe having also arrived at Bombay, General Abercromby had gone thither himself, for the dispatch of public business, and to forward the arrangements for refitting his army. Having returned early in November to Tellicherry, with the reinforcements and a new battering train, he was preparing to re-ascend the Ghauts with renewed vigour, and in greater force.

The preparations were now completed on both sides of the Peninsula, and it only remained to bring forward those supplies in safety to the scene of action.

CHAPTER V.

Position of the Army to cover the Convoys from the Carnatic—Lieutenant-Colonel Maxwell's Expedition to the Baramaul—Arrival of Lieutenant-Colonel Geils, with the Battering Train, at Bangalore—Cummer-Ud-Deen Cawn's Success at Coimbetore.

After the reduction of Nundydroog, Lord Cornwallis hastened towards the passes, to cover the convoys that were coming forward from the Carnatic. His Lordship remained with the army to the eastward of Bangalore, between the two great roads that come by Ouscotta and Oussoor from the Carnatic; and hearing of the depredations in the Baramaul, sent a detachment to clear it of the enemy, and to prevent their giving annoyance to the convoys.

This detachment, commanded by Lieutenant-Colonel Maxwell, left the army on the 21st of October, on its moving from Nundydroog, and consisted of the 74th regiment, and three battalions of Sepoys, with their field-pieces; one of which joined him as he passed Rayacottah.

The enemy's force, which had been greatly exaggerated, decreased, by the accounts the colonel received of it as he advanced, and were at last said to be a party of fifteen hundred irregular horse, commanded by Bunker Saib, son to Budderul-Zeman Cawn, the late killedar of Darwar. They had plundered Tripatore, whence the 22d battalion found it necessary to retire, to protect the public cattle sent from Amboor to graze at Vaniambaddy; and they had desolated the country, and swept every thing towards the passes to the southward.

Colonel Maxwell, finding that these plunderers harboured chiefly at Penagra, a strong mud fort at the south end of the Baramaul valley, hastened there by forced marches, and arrived before it on the 31st of October.

The fort fired from some Malabar guns, on seeing a battalion move towards it; and a flag of truce, sent to summon the place, being also fired upon repeatedly, although beckoned to from the walls to advance, orders were given to surround the fort, and attack it by assault. A six-pounder was brought up, and fired several times at the gate, without bursting it. Scaling ladders were then applied to the only part of the wall that was accessible, and ascended by the flank companies of the 74th regiment, by which means the outer gate was gained. The wall of the second gate was gained in the same manner with equal success; and the rampart communicating with that of the third gate, both were opened by those who first entered, for the admission of the rest of the troops.

The resistance of the enemy was feeble, and they hung out the flag for quarter in the midst of the assault. It was too late: they had violated the rules of war; the troops had closed with them; and out of three hundred men that composed the garrison, one hundred and fifty were put to the sword. The aumildars, or managers, of the districts of Oudengery and Darampoury were killed; and Mahommed-Fakeer-ud-Deen, the aumildar of the district, and several other managers, and people of consequence, were made prisoners, with the remainder of the garrison; but the party of horse that had been here, made their escape on the approach of the detachment.

On our side there were only seven men slightly wounded.

The powder found in the fort was employed for its destruction; and the cattle which had been collected round the place, too much dispersed to be driven off by the detachment, could not be easily recovered by the enemy.

Colonel Maxwell having scoured the Baramaul to the southward, returned towards Caveripatam, and encamped within five miles of Kistnaghery, on the 7th of November. The lower fort was to be attacked, and the pettah destroyed, in order to leave as little cover and encouragement as possible for the enemy's predatory parties to remain in that quarter.

Seeing the inhabitants, who had fled from the country, crowding with their effects to the upper fort, the colonel determined to lose no time in making the attack. He marched from his camp, at ten o'clock that night, in three divisions. The right and left divisions, sent by a circuitous route, to avoid the enemy's guards, were directed to attack the lower fort on the western and eastern sides; while the centre division advanced slowly towards the front wall, to sustain the other attacks.

The divisions sent out to the right and left, approached close to both sides of the lower fort before they were discovered, and escalading the walls, got possession of the gates, and entered without much resistance. The enemy formed within, but were soon broken; and finding they were attacked on both sides, fled to the upper fort.

The original object was gained; but, from the confusion of the enemy, it was highly probable that our troops might enter the upper fort with the fugitives; and Captain Wallace, who commanded the right division, which first charged the enemy, determined not to lose so favourable an opportunity. His party rushed up, made themselves masters of a work defended by a gun, near the foot of the steps; and, notwithstanding the length and steepness of the ascent, his advanced party followed the enemy so closely, that they had barely time to shut the gateway. The standard of their regulars, taken on the steps of the gate-rewarded the rapidity of the pursuit. Unfortunately the ladders were not brought forward so speedily as to enable our troops to escalade the wall at this critical period of the attack. The enemy recovered from their panic; and having recourse to the same tremendous means by which a like gallant attempt was repulsed in a former war, hurled down showers of rocks and stones into the road, broke the ladders, and crushed those that carried them under their ponderous weight. During two hours, repeated trials were made to get the ladders up the small part of the road that was overhung by the rock, and thus powerfully commanded from above; but unluckily a clear moonlight discovered every motion to the enemy, and at length the ladders being all destroyed, and many officers and men crushed in carrying them on, Colonel Maxwell found it necessary to desist from the assault.

The retreat of the men who had reached the gate, and of the

rest of the troops, was conducted with such regularity, that a party who sallied from the garrison to harass them in going off, was received by the covering platoon; which, facing about, gave them so close and well directed a fire, that not one of the enemy escaped.

On returning from the rock, the pettah was set fire to; but the rains which had fallen prevented its being burned so completely as was intended. The troops were withdrawn before daylight, and returned to their camp.

The loss of the enemy appeared to have been considerable, from the number of dead bodies found in the streets of the pettah. The prisoners said that two hundred regular Sepoys, and a body of Polygars, were below, and one thousand men above, for the defence of the place.

The loss on our side, in this partly successful, and partly unsuccessful, but brilliant enterprize, was very considerable. Two lieutenants, one serjeant, and five privates, of the 74th regiment, killed; and three officers, and forty-seven non-commissioned officers and privates, wounded. Of the rest of the detachment, one Sepoy, and one gun Lascar killed; two officers, a native officer, and twelve Sepoys, wounded.

The officers killed were Lieutenants Forbes and Lamont, of the 74th regiment, both exceedingly regretted. The officers wounded, were Captain Agnew, aid-de-camp to Lieutenant-Colonel Maxwell; Captain Wallace, Lieutenants Mackenzie and Ayton, of the 74th regiment, and Lieutenant Bird, of the 7th Bengal battalion.

Colonel Maxwell having executed his orders in the Baramaul, was further directed to reduce several small forts in the district of Oussoor; which having also done, and put friendly Polygars in possession of them, he rejoined the army on the 30th of November.*

EXTRACT OF GENERAL ORDERS.

" *Camp, Kingery,* 1*st December,* 1791.

" Lord Cornwallis returns his best thanks to Lieutenant-" Colonel Maxwell, for the zealous and able manner in which he " has executed his general instructions, to dislodge and drive out " the detachments that the enemy had sent into the Baramaul, " and the district of Oussoor.

" The good conduct and gallantry which was manifested at " the assault of Pinagra, reflects great credit upon Lieutenant-" Colonel Maxwell, and the corps under his command; but his " Lordship considers the spirited and judicious attempt which, " after surprising and carrying the pettah and lower fort, was " made upon the upper fort of Kistnaghery, as highly ho-" nourable to all the officers and soldiers who were employed " on that occasion, and justly deserving his warmest ap-" plause."

During this time, several convoys of grain and stores were brought forward by the Pednaigdurgum pass; which takes its

* The account of the operations of this detachment, is taken chiefly from a narrative which appeared in the Madras Courier, supposed to have been written by Captain Agnew, an officer of great merit, who distinguished himself with his usual zeal and gallantry in this attack.

name from a small hill fort near the top of it, and is only seven miles north from Amboor.

This pass, which ascends to the Table Land of Mysore, just beyond the northern extremity of the Baramaul valley, was used in the war of 1769, with Hyder Ally; and in April last was opened by Captain Alexander Read, when he commanded at Amboor, as being the safest and best communication for bringing up the supplies from the Carnatic. He had at the same time reduced Vencatigherry, a fort situated on the verge of the open country beyond the pass. This had also the advantage of being connected by the posts of Colar and Ouscotta, and is by much the nearest road to Bangalore.

Lieutenant-Colonel Geils, of the artillery, who had been sent to collect the battering train from Madras and Vellore at Amboor, proposed its being brought up the Pednaigdurgum pass, which had not been thought practicable for heavy guns, in preference to going through the Baramaul valley, by the Policode pass; which, although a better road in dry weather, is at all times a circuitous route; and at this season, from its being flooded by the rains, would be more impracticable than a short though difficult ascent into the high country.

This proposal met with approbation, and was attended with success. The road up the Pednaigdurgum pass was farther opened and repaired; and although the first mile be extremely steep, where it was necessary to drag up the guns entirely by hand, yet the difficulty to be surmounted was small to what the colonel would have had to encounter in attempting to drag such cannon through a tract of low country in the wet season. Even by this route the guns were greatly retarded by the heavy rains and bad roads, but at length arrived at Bangalore on the 29th of November, without other loss than great part of the draft and carriage cattle, which always die in vast numbers when exposed to rain and fatigue.

Lieutenant-Colonel Ross, the chief engineer, who had gone to the presidency to make the necessary arrangements in his department, also rejoined the army by the end of November.

Having mentioned the proceedings of the party which Tippoo sent into the Baramaul, it remains to relate the success of the detachment employed under Cummer-ud-Deen Cawn, for the reduction of Coimbetore.

The Cawn arrived before this wretched, but gallantly defended fort, towards the end of October, with a force said to consist of five hundred regular cavalry, and eight thousand regular infantry, with six pieces of cannon; besides a body of irregulars, both horse and foot. He met with as determined opposition as the disgraced commander of the former detachment had done, and laid siege to it in vain for three weeks. Lieutenant Chalmers, reinforced by the two heavy guns taken from the first detachment, and by Lieutenant Nash, with a company of regular Sepoys from Palgautcherry, was not of a disposition to decline the defence of his post, even against this formidable force; and expecting Major Cuppage to advance again to his relief, resolved to hold the place to the last extremity.

The major had sent supplies of musquet ammunition repeatedly to Lieutenant Chalmers by Sepoys, who contrived to get into the fort at night, but was, from various circumstances, prevented from advancing himself, with his detachment, till the 22d of October, when he marched from Palgautcherry with three battalions of Sepoys, and six field-pieces, and two of the Rajah of Travancore's battalions, without guns.

The three corps of our Sepoys were the 5th and 16th coast, and 12th Bombay battalion, commanded by Captains Hope, Vigors, and Oakes.

Cummer-ud-Deen, confident in his superior numbers, and with the advantage of a numerous body of cavalry, determined to meet the major, and prevent his throwing a reinforcement into the place.

On the 23d of October, just as the detachment had come to its ground, near Madagery, within six miles of Coimbetore, the Cawn advanced with great boldness, and made a formidable appearance. The camp was struck, and the detachment drawn out to give him battle. This he appeared to decline; but making a movement to the right of the detachment, he pressed Major Cuppage on that flank, and brought him to a decision either to force his way to Coimbetore, leaving the pass open to Palgautcherry, or to fall back for the security of that more important post.

It had been necessary to bring out as many men as possible from the garrison, in order to oppose the Cawn with effect; and it might not be an easy matter for Major Cuppage to force his way back again, if the enemy got possession of the strong and narrow defile through the woods and mountains that separate Palgautcherry from Coimbetore. But the major's greatest embarrassment arose from the large convoy of bullocks for the Bombay army; which, sent across from Dindigul, were now on their way beyond Animally, and might be certainly intercepted by the enemy, if they got between him and the pass. Although anxious to save Coimbetore, it was of no material importance to the success of the war; and he determined not to risk the loss of the greater, for the chance of giving security to the lesser object.

Cummer-ud-Deen, on seeing the detachment begin to retreat, pressed on rapidly to the attack: showers of rockets were thrown to break the detachment, while his cavalry advanced boldly to the charge. They were received by the flank companies of the three battalions which formed the rear-guard, and repulsed repeatedly, with great loss. The flank companies, supported by the 12th and 16th battalions, continued the action with the enemy till the baggage and the head of the column had moved off, when the troops engaged also followed in regular order, and covered the retreat.

Three officers were wounded, and seventy Sepoys killed and wounded, on our side. The loss on the part of the enemy, particularly in the body of cavalry which charged with so much boldness, must have been very considerable.

Cummer-ud-Deen, having effected his intention, proclaimed a victory, and returned to prosecute the siege.

The powder and cannon-shot for the few guns in the place were nearly expended. The fort was breached, and there being no farther hopes of relief, Lieutenant Chalmers was under the necessity to capitulate on the 2d of November. The terms agreed upon were, that the garrison should march out with the honours of war, have their private property secured, and be immediately sent to Palgautcherry, with leave to go from thence to the Carnatic, to remain on their parole during the rest of the war. They were sent into the pettah, where they were detained, under pretence that Tippoo's approbation was necessary for the ratification of the treaty. This the Sultan refused, and ordered the Cawn to return with his detachment, and bring his prisoners to Seringapatam.

CHAPTER VI.

Siege of Savendroog—Escalade of Outredroog—and Capture of other Hill Forts between Bangalore and Seringapatam.

LORD CORNWALLIS had long regarded Savendroog as an obstacle of most serious inconvenience to the reduction of Seringapatam. Situated eighteen miles west of Bangalore, and a place of immense strength, and great extent, it afforded such harbour to the enemy, that there was scarcely a possibility of a convoy passing it unmolested. Indeed the brinjarries, who undertook to bring forward large quantities of grain to Bangalore, declared they could not possibly supply the army at Seringapatam, if Savendroog remained in the possession of the enemy.

The battering train, which required the most immediate protection on the march, had reached Bangalore; but there being still a large convoy to come on from the Carnatic under Colonel Floyd, Lord Cornwallis determined to employ the interim in attempting, if possible, to reduce this fortress, which stood so immediately in the way of his success.

Savendroog has already been described as a vast mountain of rock, and is reckoned to rise above half a mile in perpendicular height, from a base of eight or ten miles in circumference. Embraced by walls on every side, and defended by cross walls and barriers wherever it was deemed accessible, this huge mountain had the farther advantage of being divided above by a chasm which separates the upper part into two hills, which, having each their defences, form two citadels capable of being maintained independent of the lower works, and, affording a secure retreat, should encourage the garrison to hold out to the last extremity.

The chief engineer was now sent to reconnoitre the Droog on the north side, where it had not been closely examined. There it also presented a most stupendous appearance, although not altogether so strong and inaccessible as it had appeared to be on the other sides. A single wall, but of great strength, extended along the north side, near half way up the mountain, which might be approached under the left or eastern hill; but the works on that hill were also to be surmounted; and when in possession of it, the western hill, too distant to be breached from the other, was defended by works of such strength as would require a second attack.

The siege of Nundydroog had taught what boldness and perseverance might achieve, and favourable opinions were now formed of this enterprize. Lord Cornwallis reckoned, besides, on the impression which the reduction of the other would make on the minds of the enemy in the defence of this fort, and determined to make the attempt.

Lieutenant-Colonel Stuart, who commanded the right wing of the army, and, in the first campaign, had been employed in reducing the important forts of Dindigul and Palgautcherry, was destined to command at the siege of Savendroog, and pitched his camp, on the 10th of December, within three miles of the north side of the rock, the quarter from which the chief engineer had proposed to carry on the attack. The force sent with Colonel Stuart consisted of the 52d and 72d regiments, commanded by Lieutenant-Colonel Nesbitt, and three battalions of Sepoys. Major Montagu, in command of the detachment of artillery, had a park of four iron eighteen, and four iron twelve-pounders, and two howitzers, besides the field-pieces of the corps.

Lord Cornwallis having not only to support the attack, but also to cover the important convoy which was still to arrive from the Carnatic, made the following disposition of the army during the siege.

The main body was encamped on the north of the fort, five miles in the rear of Colonel Stuart's detachment. Lieutenant-Colonel Cockerell, with his brigade, was detached towards Shevagunga, on the north road; Captain Welch, with two battalions, took post on the middle, or Chinapatam road; and Captain Alexander Read, with his detachment, on the south, or Cankenelly road; so that the enemy could not pass unobserved any where through the defiles that lead from Seringapatam towards Bangalore, and the passes to the Carnatic.

The first operation of the siege was to cut a gun-road from the encampment of the detachment, and to transport the artillery to the foot of the mountain; a work of incredible labour, over rocky hills, and through a thick forest. To give an idea of the exertions of the troops on this service, it is only necessary to say, that in many places they were obliged to drag the battering guns over rocks of considerable height, and nearly perpendicular; and the labour of opening a road through a forest of bamboos, can only be known to those who are acquainted with the nature of that tree, which, growing in clumps, even from the crevices of the rock, resists more than any other the axe and fire.

This stupendous fortress, so difficult of approach, is no less famed for its noxious atmosphere, occasioned by the surrounding hills and woods, than for its wonderful size and strength; and is said to have derived its name of Savendroog, or the Rock of Death, from its fatal climate.

The Sultan, sensible of its advantages, was reported to have congratulated his army on the infatuation of the English in having engaged in an enterprize that must terminate in their disgrace; as half the Europeans, he was pleased to assert, would die of sickness, and the other half be killed in the attack.

The garrison which the Sultan had placed in Savendroog also considering the attempt to reduce it as madness, luckily trusted more to its strength than to their own exertions for its defence, and, except by the fire of their cannon, made but little opposition to the erecting of the batteries.

On the 17th of December two batteries opened, one at a thousand, the other at seven hundred yards distance, by which the defences of the wall were much damaged; but the difficulty of making a breach was greater than expected, the wall being built of immense stones, the lower tier of which is rivetted to the rock by iron clamps.

On the 19th a battery opened, which it had been found necessary to advance to within two hundred and fifty yards of the wall, and, in the course of that and the succeeding day, made a practicable breach.

The forest, through which the troops had cut their way with

such infinite labour, became an advantage in the cover it afforded in the closer approaches of the attack; and the natives in India, who generally surround their forts with a hedge of this bamboo jungle, and have great reliance on it for their defence, had planted it close up to the wall on this side of Savendroog. The rock is so extremely steep, that without the assistance of this jungle, it would have been extremely difficult to have ascended to the assault; but under cover of it, and of crevices and rugged parts in the rock, a lodgment was made for the troops within twenty yards of the breach.

The flank companies of the 71st and 76th regiments having been sent from camp to join the detachment, and every thing being in readiness, the morning of the 21st of December was fixed for the assault.

Lord Cornwallis had directed this time, as probably the least expected by the enemy; and came himself, accompanied by General Medows, to witness the success.

The storming party, commanded by Lieutenant-Colonel Nesbitt, was directed to four different attacks.

Captain Gage, with the grenadiers of the 52d, and flank companies of the 76th regiment, to gain the eastern hill to the left; the Honourable Captain Monson, with the light company of the 52d, to scour the works towards the western hill, on the right; the Honourable Captain Lindsay, and Captain Robertson, with the flank companies of the 71st regiment, to separate, and attack the works or parties they might discover in the chasm or hollow between the hills; the 52d and 72d regiments were to follow the flank companies; and parties were detached under Lieutenant-Colonel Baird, and Major Petrie, round the mountain, to draw the attention of the enemy from the main object, and to endeavour to prevent their making their escape.

At eleven o'clock, on a signal of two guns being fired from the batteries, the flank companies, in the order described, followed by the 52d and 72d regiments, advanced to the assault; the band of the 52d regiment playing, *Britons, strike home!* while the grenadiers and light infantry mounted the breach.

A large body of the enemy had been seen coming down from the western hill, in the morning, for the defence of the breach; but on the appearance of the Europeans advancing to the storm, they were seized with a most unaccountable panic, and fled. Our troops advanced as rapidly as the ruggedness of the rock and the steepness of the hill would permit; and the eastern hill, immediately above the breach, was carried by Captain Gage, without meeting, or even overtaking, the enemy.

The other division, and main body of the enemy, endeavoured to gain the western hill, which, had they effected, the siege must have recommenced; that part of the mountain being defended by several walls and barriers, as already mentioned, and in most places of a giddy steepness. The hopes were not sanguine of immediately getting possession of it; and Captain Monson was left to his discretion, either to advance, or to take post where the ground might favour a lodgment for attacking those works.

The road, or pathway, from the breach to the western hill being not only extremely steep, but narrow, the fugitives impeded each other, and a few well directed shot from the batteries, at that moment, did execution, and increased their confusion. Captain Monson, with his own light company of the 52d regiment, and a serjeant and twelve grenadiers of the 71st regiment, pressed so hard, that they entered the different barriers along with the enemy, and killing a number of them, among whom was the second killedar, gained possession of the top of the mountain, where the head killedar was made prisoner. So close and critical was the pursuit, that the serjeant of the 71st regiment, when at some distance, shot the man who was shuting the first gate.

Above a hundred of the enemy were killed on the western hill, and several fell down the precipices in escaping from the assailants. The prisoners were few, who said the garrison had consisted of one thousand five hundred; but that many had deserted during the siege.

Thus, in less than an hour, in open day, the stupendous and hitherto deemed impregnable fortress of Savendroog, was stormed without the loss of a man, only one private soldier having been wounded in the assault!

GENERAL AFTER ORDERS.

22d December, 1791.

"Lord Cornwallis thinks himself fortunate, almost beyond
" example, in having acquired, by assault, a fortress of so much
" strength and reputation, and of such inestimable value to the
" public interests, as Savendroog, without having to regret the
" loss of a single soldier on the occasion. He can only attri-
" bute the pusillanimity of the enemy, yesterday, to their asto-
" nishment, at seeing the good order, and determined coun-
" tenance, with which the troops who were employed in the

" assault entered the breach, and ascended precipices that have " hitherto been considered in this country as inaccessible. But " although the resistance was so contemptible, he is not the " less sensible that the behaviour of the grenadiers and light in- " fantry of the 52d, 71st, 72d, and 76th regiments, who led the " assault, and who must have made the decisive impression upon " the minds of the enemy, reflects the most distinguished honour " upon their discipline and valour.

" The vigour and alacrity which was shewn by the officers " and men of Lieutenant-Colonel Stuart's detachment, in sup- " porting the labours and fatigues of the siege, entitle them to " the highest commendation; and his Lordship desires that " Lieutenant-Colonel Stuart will accept of his warmest acknow- " ledgments for the zeal and judgment which he manifested, " both in directing the efforts of the troops under his command " during the siege, and in making arrangements for the as- " sault.

" His Lordship also returns his best thanks to Lieutenant- " Colonel Ross, chief engineer, for the judicious choice which " he made in selecting proper situations for the batteries, and for " the great attention which he paid to the other duties of his " station; and to Lieutenant-Colonel Nesbitt, for the able and " officer-like manner in which he conducted the troops to the " assault; and the greatest praise is due to Major Montagu, for " his laborious and successful exertion to overcome the infinite " difficulties that occurred in placing the guns in the batteries, " and for his professional skill in directing their fire."

On the 23d of December Lieutenant-Colonel Stuart's detachment marched against Outredroog, about twelve miles west from Savendroog; and next day, the 24th, Lord Cornwallis followed with the army, and encamped at Magré, between these two forts.

The Colonel, on his arrival before Outredroog, sent a party to summon the place. The killedar, who, when summoned last year, had answered that he would not surrender his post till we first took Seringapatam, seemed still determined in that intention, and, to avoid any communication, fired on the flag of truce.

In consequence of this conduct, Colonel Stuart made his disposition to attack the lower fort and pettah next morning. Captain Scott, of the Bengal establishment, with four battalion companies of the 52d and 72d regiments, and his own battalion of Sepoys, was sent on this service; while another body made a feint, and opened some guns on the opposite side of the fort.

Captain Scott carried the lower fort by escalade so rapidly, that the killedar sent to request a parley. While this took place, an appearance of treachery was observed in the upper fort, and that the garrison were employed in moving and pointing guns to bear upon the assailants. Fired at this sight, and impatient of the delay, the troops again rushed on to the assault. Lieutenant M'Innes, of the 72d regiment, led the storm with part of the Europeans and the pioneers, commanded by Lieutenants Dowse and Macpherson, supported by Captain Scott, who followed in more regular order with the rest of his force. Some of the gateways were broké open, others escaladed; till passing five or six different walls, which defended this steep and difficult rock, the troops at length gained the summit, and put the garrison to the sword. So infatuated were the enemy, that whenever they saw a single European above the walls they fled; and although such was the steepness and narrowness of some parts of the road in the ascent, that a few resolute men might have defended the place against an army, it was only at the last gateway that they attempted any resistance, and that only by firing a few musquet shot, by which two soldiers were wounded. The killedar was made prisoner: a number of the garrison were killed; and many, terrified at the approach of the Europeans with their bayonets, are said to have precipitated themselves from the rock.

The killedar mentioned, that on the appearance of the detachment before the place, his garrison had mutinied, and four hundred had deserted during the night.

GENERAL AFTER ORDERS.

Camp at Magrè, 25th December, 1791.

" Lord Cornwallis has received, with the highest satisfaction,
" a report from Lieutenant-Colonel Stuart, that the strong and
" important rock of Outredroog was carried yesterday forenoon
" by assault, by a detachment consisting of two companies of
" the 52d, and two companies of the 72d regiments, and the
" 26th Bengal battalion, without the loss of a man on our side.
" The judgment with which Lieutenant-Colonel Stuart made the
" general disposition for the assault, reflects the highest credit

"on him as an officer; and his Lordship desires that Captain "Scott, of the Bengal infantry, who commanded the assault, will "accept his warmest acknowledgments for the spirit and good "conduct which he manifested in availing himself of the con-"sternation of the enemy, according to the instructions given him "by Lieutenant-Colonel Stuart. His Lordship likewise desires "that his thanks may be communicated, in general, to the other "officers and soldiers who composed the detachment, for their "gallantry and steadiness on that occasion; and that it may be "particularly signified to Lieutenant M'Innes, of the 72d regi-"ment, who led the European company; and to Lieutenants "Macpherson and Dowse, who conducted the European and "native pioneers that were employed in carrying the scaling "ladders to break open the gates; that, from Lieutenant-Colonel "Stuart's report, he considers their behaviour and services as "highly meritorious."

The joy excited by this last spirited assault was kept up by farther accounts of similar important success.

Captain Welch, after the fall of Savendroog, was ordered to advance, and summon the hill forts of Ram Gurry and Sheria Gurry, which command the middle road upon which he was stationed. The first of these refusing to surrender, he immediately attacked and carried the lower fort and pettah by assault. The rapidity of the attack alarmed the garrison, and the killedar instantly gave up the place, which was followed by the surrender of Sheria Gurry, without any resistance.

Ram Gurry was found to be a place of considerable strength, and lately improved by new works. It was also well provided with guns, provisions, and stores, which had been chiefly removed from Chinapatam, on that fort being dismantled the former year.

GENERAL ORDERS.

" *Camp at Magré, 27th December,* 1791.

" Lord Cornwallis has been highly satisfied with the report " that Captain Welch of the Bengal infantry has made, of the " reduction of the important forts of Ram Gurry and Sheria " Gurry by the detachment under his command.

" The detachment was sent before those forts on the 22d " instant, without being provided with any means to reduce " them by force, but with the expectation that the garrison " would be found so much intimidated by the fall of Saven- " droog on the preceding day, as to be disposed to surrender; " and his Lordship is sensible that the complete success of the " plan is principally to be attributed to Captain Welch's judi- " cious conduct, for which he desires that he will accept of his " best acknowledgments."

The capture of Savendroog, preceded by that of Nundydroog, had made such an impression on the minds of the enemy, that in no other of the hill forts, however inaccessible, did they attempt to resist our troops. The strong hilly country between Bangalore and Seringapatam, which, studded with hill forts, had opposed such serious inconvenience to the operations of the army, now increased the security of the convoys, and gave the most promising hopes of success in the attack of the last and main object of the war.

The only fort not in our possession in this tract of strong country was Gopauldroog, beyond Cankenelly. Remote from the tract of our convoys, it was not thought of sufficient consequence to send a detachment for its reduction; nor need it be mentioned, were it not to give due merit to a party of brinjarries, who, animated with the spirit of enterprise that prevailed in the army, went secretly against that hill fort. Provided with arms, which they carry for the defence of their cattle and grain, this party surprised the lower fort of Gopauldroog; and had even the boldness to attempt the upper fort, but were beat back with some loss. The plunder, however, of the pettah, with which they loaded their cattle, amply rewarded their spirit; and they returned to the army in great triumph.

CHAPTER VII.

Siege of Gurramcondah—State of the Cavalry in the Carnatic—Difficulties in collecting and bringing forward the last Convoy—Relief of Gurramcondah by Hyder Saib—Colonel Floyd's Arrival with the Convoy at Bangalore—State of the Country; and Arrangements of Earl Cornwallis for the subsistence of the Army.

THE army of his Highness the Nizam had hitherto effected but two objects during the war, the reduction of Copaul and Gunjicotta, neither of which would have been accomplished without the aid of the Madras detachment of two battalions of native infantry, which, according to agreement, had been sent to act with his troops. The fall of Copaul, which was the place of chief strength, had, like that of Darwar, been rather a consequence of the reduction of Bangalore, than occasioned by the operations carried on against it in the siege.

This division of the confederate forces had, ever since the month of August, been employed in the attack of Gurramcondah; but depending on the Nizam's train of artillery for their success, had not been able to breach the lower fort, till the guns which had been employed at Nundydroog, with a supply of ammunition from Bangalore, were sent to them for this service.

A battery of two twenty-six, and two eighteen pounders, was now constructed within four hundred yards of the east face of the fort, and in two days made a practicable breach.

Captain Andrew Read, who commanded the Madras detachment, seeing that the enemy were still determined to defend the place, formed his disposition for the assault, which was made at eleven o'clock on the night of the 7th of November.

The small party of artillery were the only European troops with this detachment; who, after breaching the place, quitted their guns, to have the honour of also leading the assault.

A forlorn hope of eight men, commanded by Mr. Nixon, conductor, followed by the rest of the detachment of artillery, and the flank companies of the two battalions of Sepoys, formed the storming party, supported by six battalion companies.

Measures having been taken which drew off the attention of the enemy, the assailants advanced, and with little opposition mounted the breach. Having cleared the obstacles with which it was barricaded, they proceeded along the rampart till they met a body of the enemy, who made a stand at the second bastion. The artillery charged them with such spirit, that they instantly gave way, and were pursued with such vigour, that they did not dare again to face the assailants.

Of the enemy one hundred and twenty were killed, and double that number wounded, or made prisoners. The remainder had gained the upper fort, which was too steep and impracticable to be attempted by assault.

Of the detachment, three Sepoys were killed; Lieutenant Hall, one serjeant, one matross, of the artillery, a subedar, and twenty-three Sepoys, wounded.

Next morning Captain Read delivered the lower fort into the possession of the Nizam's troops, and in it there was a considerable quantity of grain, which afforded an important supply to his army.

Soon after this event, a large reinforcement arrived from Hyderabad, under the command of the Nizam's second son, Secunder Jaw, who was accompanied by the minister Musheer-ul-Mulk, lately dignified with the higher title of Azeem-ul-Omrah, and by Sir John Kennaway, the British resident at the Soubah's court.

The prince, or rather his mentor, the minister, finding that the upper fort of Gurramcondah, which was said to be well supplied with provisions, could be reduced only by a tedious blockade, left one of his best generals, Hafez Jee, with a body of troops, in command of the lower fort for that purpose, and about the middle of December advanced himself, with the main body of his forces, and our detachment, to the neighbourhood of Colar, in concert with other measures taken by Lord Cornwallis, to cover the convoy which he still expected from the Carnatic, with the remainder of the ammunition and stores for the siege of Seringapatam.

Colonel Floyd, under whose command this convoy was to be forwarded to the army, had arrived at Madras early in August. The several regiments of cavalry were placed in different stations, to enable them to forage to advantage; and the colonel's exertions particularly directed to the care and refitting of his own corps.

A sufficient number of horses not having been procured to remount the whole of the cavalry, Lord Cornwallis directed that the horses of the other regiments should be draughted into the 19th dragoons, and the two native regiments, commanded by Majors Stephenson and Orr, for the service of the ensuing campaign.

The 19th dragoons, which, under their gallant leader, had made so powerful an impression on the minds of the enemy during the war, was again completely remounted; and, with the addition of the draughts and recruits that had arrived from England, was in nearly as great force as when it first took the field. This favourite corps was reviewed by General Musgrave at the Mount in the beginning of October, when it shewed near four hundred mounted, both men and horses in perfect order.

Major Stephenson's regiment was also completed to its establishment. Zeal and disinterested exertion united to bring this corps also into the field again in full force; and having been ordered up as part of the escort for one of the first convoys, ascended the Ghauts before the commencement of the monsoon in the Carnatic.

The remainder of the horses, and such of the sick horses as recovered after completing those two corps, were draughted into the regiment commanded by Major Orr, but did not amount to above two hundred; and being the weakest horses of the whole, and later formed, could not be in the same state of strength and discipline. But the three regiments, together with the two troops of body guards, which had continued with the army, would in all amount to about twelve hundred effective cavalry; a very formidable body to Tippoo, in the reduced state of his horse.

While the interesting operations that have been detailed were carried on in the high country of Mysore, without any material interruption from the change of season, it had been extremely difficult to collect and forward the last great convoy from Madras, under the heavy rains, which, setting in earlier than usual, and with uncommon violence had flooded the Carnatic.

The powder captured in Bangalore not having proved of so good a quality as was at first expected, an additional quantity was ordered from Madras, which, with farther supplies of other stores that were from time to time also ordered, did not all arrive at Amboor till the middle of December. The heavy rains, and depth of the rivers, had not only impeded the different parts of this convoy in marching through the Carnatic, but parties of the enemy's horse having come through the Baramaul towards Pondicherry, it was necessary to proceed with caution on that account. The cattle, suffering extremely from being exposed to the cold and rain, died in such numbers, that the greater part was replaced repeatedly, which added to the other causes that detained the convoy.

The detachment of the royal artillery, which had arrived in perfect health, having come out late in the season, suffered exceedingly from the necessity of taking the field immediately, and being exposed to the heavy rains. The draughts and recruits sent out for the 19th dragoons were also sickly; and the horses of the cavalry, from being constantly exposed to the inclemency of the weather, were much reduced from the excellent state they were in before the setting in of the monsoon.

From Amboor, where the convoys were collected, the stores were arranged and forwarded by Captain Cuppage, who succeeded Captain Read in the command of that post, and had great merit from the zeal and activity with which he executed this important duty. The corps of pioneers, which had repaired the pass for the battering guns, remained to assist in bringing up the store carts; and a detachment, consisting of a battalion and a half of native infantry, commanded by Captain Oram, was stationed on the high ground beyond Vencatigherry, to receive and protect the stores, as they arrived from Amboor.

On the 24th of December the last of the convoy, and the escort, ascended the Ghauts. The rains having ceased, the men and horses recovered rapidly, and, from the great attention paid to them, were in surprising good health and order, after all they had suffered from the severity of the season.

On the 26th of December, Colonel Floyd proceeded from Vencatigherry towards Bangalore, and had but just got his detachment and convoy in motion, when a harcara met him with a letter from Sir John Kennaway, containing the following intelligence.

That Hyder Saib, Tippoo's eldest son, had made his appearance at Gurramcondah, with a light army of twelve thousand horse and foot, without guns, and had on the 21st taken the Nizam's general, Hapez Jee, who, ignorant of the magnitude of his force, had pushed out with two hundred horse, to save some Mahratta vakeels, who were in danger; and that young Hyder had afterwards advanced, and taken the lower fort, with the rest of the detachment, and all their baggage. Sir John added, that the minister had determined to march back immediately to Gurramcondah, which they should reach the next day, the 23d; and that Hyder Saib might then possibly attempt to pass them, and go round by Vencatigherry, with an intention to harass or intercept the convoy.

Colonel Floyd had already taken every precaution for the security of his convoy. His detachment was respectable; but, from the report, the enemy's force was very numerous, and it would be difficult to guard so long a line from annoyance on the march. The colonel, therefore, made every exertion to pass the open country, where he was most liable to annoyance; and in two days march, the last, a very long and fatiguing one, reached Colar.

There was nothing so probable as that Tippoo had it in view to intercept this convoy; for unless he could do so, or cripple it materially, he could have no other hope of retarding the allied armies from advancing to the siege of his capital. But the force under Hyder Saib had been magnified, and it either was not his intention to attempt intercepting this convoy, or he had seen that the risk would be too great, were he to commit himself amidst the allied armies. Satisfied with throwing some succour into Gurramcondah, and taking out the families of some principal people from the upper fort, he went back by the same northern route to Seringapatam.

The Nizam's army, on returning to Gurramcondah, were again put in possession of the lower fort by the Madras detachment, who retook it after a slight resistance.

Colonel Floyd having halted a day at Colar, was met beyond that place by a reinforcement to his escort; and proceeding by Ouscottah, arrived near Bangalore on the 22d of January, without having met with any interruption, or even seen a party of looties on the march.

At this time the country between Vencatigherry and Bangalore was completely resettled and under cultivation, and appeared to be as quiet as any part of the Carnatic. The inhabitants had every where returned to their villages, and seemed highly pleased with their change of government. They all praised Captain Read, who was intrusted with the management of those districts; and having just heard of the fall of Savendroog, they thought there could no longer be any doubt of our success, and their continuing under their new masters.

As this detachment advanced with the convoy, they were constantly meeting or passing large parties of brinjarries, plying to and from the army, without any protection, except the arms they carried for their own defence. They had great pleasure in telling the news; said that the road was quite open, and shewed their tickets from Lord Cornwallis. They spoke highly in his Lordship's praise; and said, "he always kept his word with "them; and that they never went to him ill received, nor came "away disappointed."

Lord Cornwallis had by this time engaged brinjarries in the service of the army, who had passes for above fifty thousand bullocks, and were constantly bringing forward supplies to an extent that could never have been accomplished by any arrangement of public carriage. In general, those people purchase grain, and other articles of consumption, wherever they can to advantage, and come to sell their merchandize, either at a price fixed by contract, or for what it will bring in the public bazars, or markets, of the camp. But the great and indispensible object being to procure supplies for the army, without too scrupulous a regard to expence, at so interesting a period of the war, Lord Cornwallis had encouraged the brinjarries beyond all former example. The resources of the upper country being nearly exhausted, and what they might be able to collect or purchase being uncertain, his Lordship gave them orders to receive rice from the granaries in the Carnatic at a low rate, sixteen seers for a rupee; and if, at their return to the army, they could not instantly dispose of it to their satisfaction in the bazars, he took their rice immediately for the public stores, at such rate as amply satisfied them; generally at four or five seers for a rupee; and either paid them in ready money, or gave them orders for more rice in the Carnatic, so that they returned without delay for another cargo.

Thus, by protecting the inhabitants, and encouraging the grain-dealers, the resources of the enemy's, as well as of our own country, were brought forward with full effect, and, instead of decreasing, were augmenting daily, from the industry and emulation excited amongst every class and description of the people. It was only by such measures that the myriads that composed and followed the allied armies could possibly have been supported for so long a period, in a country poor by nature, and which, if ravaged, would have been soon exhausted.

So different also appeared to be the state of our treasury to that of Tippoo's at this period, in consequence of the state of public credit, and the large sums lately sent out from England; at least so superior was the policy of Lord Cornwallis to the Sultan's, that several of his principal brinjarries had lately brought in their grain to our camp; as he, they said, would only give them ineffectual orders on the collectors of his revenues (some of which they produced), and not ready money; for their supplies.

This abundance of specie in our army, so unusual in former wars, also enabled his Lordship to economize the grain, which was of still more value; and instead of giving the native troops their full allowance of rice, for which they would have paid the customary stoppage, half allowance was issued to them gratis; which, considering the price paid to the brinjarries, was not only an advantage to the Sepoys, but a considerable saving to the public. The soldiers, in the same manner, received only half their allowance of arrack, and were paid for the other half. The Sepoys bought coarser grain with the money they received for the half of their allowance of rice; and the soldier who preferred more liquor to the money, might buy it in the bazars; so that, without murmur or hardship, the public stores of grain and arrack were made to last double the time by this arrangement.

No. 4

ORDER of BATTLE of the ARMY Commanded by MAJOR GEN.^L ABERCROMBY

16.th January 1792.

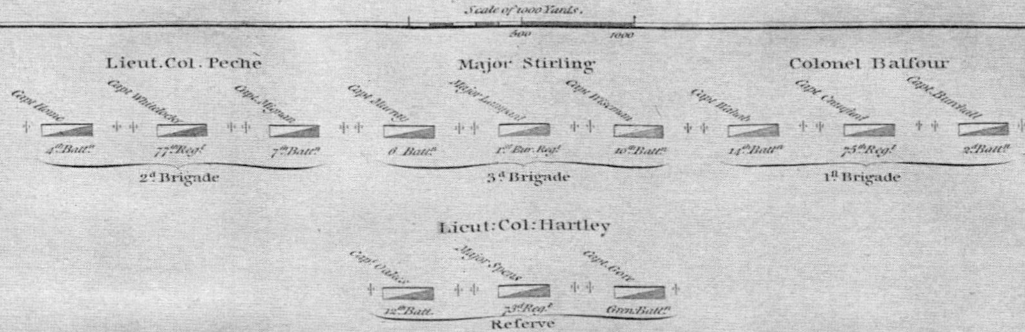

GENERAL STAFF

Commander in Chief M:G: Abercromby.	
Mil. Secy. & Pay Mr. to the Kings Troops	Capt. Auchmuty
Aids de Camp	Capt. Hall; Lts. Sandiford, Wilson, Abercromby
Dep: Adjt. Genl.	Majr. Sinclair
Dep. Quar. Mar. Genl.	Lt. Col. Hartley
Chief Engineer	Majr. Sartorius
Commissary	F.W. Pemberton Esq:
Pay master	Edw. Galley Esq.
Surgeon Genl.	Doctr. Clugston

BRIGADE STAFF

1st Brigade	Col. Balfour
Brigr. Major	Lieut. Erskine
Brig. Qr. Master	Lieut. Gordon
2d Brigade	Lt. Col. Peche
Brigr. Major	Lieut. Hooke
Brig. Qr. Master	Lieut. Stewart
3d Brigade	Major Stirling
Brig. Major	Lieut. Weston
Brig. Qr. Master	Lieut. Manly
Reserve	Lt. Col. Hartley
Brig. Major	Lieut. Woodington
Brig. Qr. Master	Lieut. Brittan

ARTILLERY

Commanded by Major Jones.

	Brass 6 Pounrs.	Brass 10 I. How.	Brass 8 I. How.	Brass Total	Iron 18 Pounrs.	Iron 12 Pounrs.	Iron Total	Total
Field Artillery	20	-	-	20	-			20
Battering Train	-	1	1	2	10	4	14	16
Total	20	1	1	22	10	4	14	36

ABSTRACT of the ARMY

	No. Corps	European Troops	Native Troops	Total
Artillery	1	216	500	716
Infantry	12	2,810	5,432	8,242
Total	13	3,026	5,932	8,958

Published by W. Faden Feb. 1. 1793.

CHAPTER VIII.

The Bombay army re-ascends the Ghauts—Description of the Poodicherrim Ghaut—Account of the Coorga Rajah, and his Country—Strength of the Army, and March to the Mysore Frontier.

GENERAL ABERCROMBY returned to Tellicherry from Bombay early in November, and brought with him the draughts and recruits for completing the corps; a new battering train, and all the necessary supplies of ammunition and stores for the service of the ensuing campaign. His army, refitted in their clothing and necessaries, and recovered in their health, quitted their cantonments, and assembled at Cananore on the 23d of November.

Earl Cornwallis having ordered this army to act again from the same quarter, as in the preceding campaign, they marched on the 5th of December towards the Poodicherrim Ghaut, and crossed the river at Iliacore on the 7th in boats, it not being fordable in consequence of late rains, which had fallen unexpectedly at that season, and had been attended with much inconvenience.

This river, which falls into the sea at Biliapatam, about five miles north from Cananore, is navigable for above twenty miles, to within two miles of Iliacore, and was so far useful in facilitating the conveyance of the guns and stores to that post.

The first operation of the army was to repair the road from Iliacore to the top of the Ghaut, which in many parts was exceedingly broken by the torrents of rain which had fallen during the last monsoon.

Viewing this immense range of mountains from below, in height a mile and a quarter from the sea, covered with forest, their tops often hid in the clouds, they appear to form an insurmountable barrier between the Mysore country and the Malabar coast.

From Iliacore to Poodicherrim the distance is twenty-six miles, through woods, and over lesser hills; but in many parts the road is exceedingly steep and difficult, till passing Stony river, twenty miles from Iliacore, the ascent commences up the great hill, which is particularly called the *Ghaut*, the pitch or steepest part of which is the last two miles to the summit. The trees, of an uncommon size, are very difficult to fell, and clear from the road; but without the aid of the forest, which every where affords a hold for the ropes and tackles for hoisting and lowering the guns, it would be impossible to pass these mountains with artillery.

The Stony river, precipitating itself from amidst the mountains at the back of the Ghaut, falls in a cascade, and bursts through a chasm, or narrow rugged valley, which separates this from the other mountains; and, winding round the foot of the Ghaut, takes its course to the sea, forming a branch of the Biliapatam river. At a distance it seems as if one of the most impracticable mountains had been chosen for this road, to render the entrance into the country as difficult as possible; but on examination it was found to be the only part of this steep range that could be passed for many miles along this part of the Malabar coast.

From Poodicherrim the hills and forests continue, with intermediate valleys, for thirty miles farther, to the Sedaseer Ghaut, whence the descent is gradual, for two miles, to the foot of the mountain; but the woods continue, though decreasing gradually, to the neighbourhood of Periapatam, six miles from the foot of the Sedaseer Ghaut, making in all near sixty miles of forest and mountains from Iliacore.

Looking from the Poodicherrim Ghaut, on the one side, down upon Tellicherry, and the Malabar coast, and from the Sedaseer Ghaut, on the other side, down upon Periapatam, and into the Mysore country, and seeing the rivers take their course, in different directions, to the east and west, these mountains have less the appearance and character of an ascent into a high country from the Malabar coast, than of an immense ridge, which, ranging from north to south, seems to divide the Peninsula in its whole extent, and, drawing continual moisture from the heavens, gives birth to the rivers that fertilize the countries on either coast.

The portion of these mountains which is called the Coorga country, is considered to extend from the Tambercherry pass, on the south, to the confines of the Bidenore country, on the north. Periapatam was formerly its capital; but of late years the village of Mercara, situated among the mountains, twenty-five miles north of Poodicherrim, has been the residence of the Rajah's family.

The Coorgs are said to be a division of the Nair cast, a

Hindoo race of great eminence. Like the Rajahpoots, in a different part of India, leaving the arts of peace to the other classes of people that also inhabit the country, their only occupation is that of arms; and they are a more active, animated, and warlike people, than perhaps any on the Peninsula. Hyder attempted in vain to subdue these mountain Nairs, till a dispute on the succession arising between the present Rajah's father and brother, he took that opportunity to offer his interference; and, by the destruction of the one family, and making the other prisoners, got possession of the country. The elder brother's family was cut off; and the present Rajah, son to the younger brother, was a prisoner in Seringapatam from his infancy till the year 1785, when he effected his escape.

Tippoo's policy, and zeal for his religion, appear to have led him to expect that these warlike Hindoo tribes might be subdued like wild animals, and tamed by violence; and, by subjecting the Coorgs and Nairs to the rites of his religion, he thought to alienate them from their own cast, and attach them to his service. The rank of the young Rajah did not save him from this shameful treatment: he was made a Mussulman, and enrolled among the Chelas (corps of slaves); and, though strictly guarded, had the nominal command of a battalion at the time he made his escape.

During the Rajah's servitude, his country had been a continual scene of devastation and bloodshed, occasioned by the discontent and insurrections among his people. They now flocked round their prince to avenge the cause of their country; and one of their first exploits was the total destruction of a brigade of

Tippoo's troops, returning with a convoy from the Malabar coast. Their bones and their accoutrements, scattered on the Poodicherrim Ghaut, bear witness to their recent defeat.

Soon after this event, and previous to the commencement of the war, the Rajah came down to Tellicherry, to solicit the friendship of our government. Although he understood that he could not then be assisted, he knew that Tippoo was considered as the common enemy, and on the first breaking out of the war immediately offered his services, of which he gave an earnest by sending down supplies of bullocks for the service of the army. Reduced by the stern policy of his Mahommedan conqueror, who had used artifice as well as violence to enthral and remove his people, the force he could levy consisted of no more than four thousand, instead of twelve thousand Coorgs, that had been in arms during the former war. His other resources were also small, in the desolated state of his country, but whatever he promised was executed with the utmost punctuality; and his exertions were in many instances of infinite service, in promoting the success of the army from the Malabar coast. Bred in adversity, and obliged to submit to the duties of a religion which was foreign to his cast, the Rajah's mind was enlarged beyond the prejudices which generally fetter the natives in India: he was desirous of seeing, and being instructed; went on board the ships at Tellicherry; was fond of conversing with our officers; of making himself acquainted with our discipline; and on many occasions, particularly on horseback, adopted the English dress. But the Rajah's character will be better understood from the following circumstances.

At the time that the Bombay army was first ascending the Ghauts, the Rajah, after clearing the greater part of his country of the enemy, was employed in the blockade of Mercara, which Tippoo had fortified with cannon, and maintained as a post in the heart of his country. A detachment sent from Seringapatam to relieve it was surrounded, and summoned to lay down their arms. The officer who commanded this corps having been friendly to the Rajah, and particularly instrumental in assisting him to escape from Tippoo's service, made himself known; and having represented to him that he should not only be dismissed from the Sultan's service if he did not execute his orders, but that his master's vengeance would be wreaked upon his innocent family, the Rajah allowed him both to send in his provisions, and return safe with his detachment.

Fearful what appearance this transaction might have to his friends the English, the Rajah explained the whole matter in a letter to General Abercromby, and said, that his allowing the provisions to be thrown into the place was of no consequence, and would only protract the siege a few weeks.

The general, fully convinced of the Rajah's sincerity, and struck with his conduct, offered to send a detachment to assist him in recovering Mercara from the enemy. This, with many expressions of gratitude, he declined; saying, he should in time be able to effect the object himself, and was determined to regain his capital with his own troops.

The Rajah's generosity to his friend in the Sultan's service, and his magnanimity in prosecuting the siege with his own people, were soon rewarded by the surrender of his capital, which, with the spirit of a Spartan, he dismantled of its defences; resolved to leave no harbour for his enemies, and that his Coorgs should depend solely on their own bravery for the defence of their country.

To complete the description of the Rajah's dominions, which are no less distinguished by their local situation, and natural advantages, than he appears to be by his elevated mind and character, these mountains, while they shelter innumerable elephants and tigers in their forests, afford not only the sandal and most valuable woods in India, but teem also with the spontaneous production of all the richest spices of the East. Enjoying a fertile soil and temperate climate, his mountainous country is a fund of wealth that requires only peace and commerce to render inexhaustible. It is a beautiful scene to contemplate; a delightful journey to the traveller: but a most arduous march, and formidable barrier, to an invading army!

The repair of the road completed, and the field train brought across the river, four brigades began to ascend the last and most difficult stage of the Ghaut on the 17th of December. Although a distance of only two miles, such is the difficulty of the ascent, that two days were required to drag and hoist twenty field-pieces (light six-pounders), with their tumbrels, to the summit of this steep and rugged mountain.

The arduous work of bringing up the heavy guns and stores was still to be accomplished, for which ropes and tackles were provided, and every preparation made which experience had suggested, to facilitate their transport to the summit of the mountain.

The brigade, commanded by Major Stirling, had been left at Iliacore for the purpose of forwarding the battering train across the river to the foot of the Ghaut, whence the guns, &c. were brought up by working parties sent down from the other brigades.

Three weeks of constant hard labour were employed to bring up fourteen heavy guns, none larger than an eighteen-pounder, and two mortars, with their tumbrels, stores, &c. to the top of the Ghaut. These, with four iron eighteen-pounders, that were buried last year upon the Ghaut, formed the battering train.

On the 18th of January, the whole of the artillery, amounting in all to eighty-six carriages, with the usual proportion of powder, cannon shot, musquet ammunition, and a provision of forty days rice for the fighting men, carried on bullocks, was above the Ghaut, and formed the equipment of this army, besides camp equipage and private baggage.

The number of bullocks required for the service of the Bombay army was twelve thousand; one half for the artillery and military stores, the other half for the victualling department.

The bullocks provided by the Madras government, and sent across from the Carnatic, arrived at Iliacore on the 8th of December, in charge of the two battalions sent to meet them at Palgautcherry. They had been ten thousand, but were reduced by the fatigue of the long march to eight thousand, of which a great proportion was in so weak a state, as to be unfit for service.

Luckily a supply of very fine cattle had been provided on the Malabar coast, most of them from Bancoote and Guzerat, enough for the transport of the artillery and stores. They were procured, chiefly through the influence of Sir Charles Mallet, from the Mahrattas, and, attended by drivers engaged in that country, were embarked and sent by sea to Tellicherry. Supported at the expence of government, and fed regularly with grain, they continued in good order; while the Carnatic bullocks, engaged by contract, without any allowance or stipulation for grain, which it is not customary to give to bullocks in the Carnatic, soon gave way to the fatigue, and the want of forage.

These circumstances evince how precarious the success of an army is in India; for had not General Abercromby taken uncommon precaution, great difficulty must have arisen from the unexpected failure of so large a portion of the cattle provided for this service.

Rice, the other great staple of supply, had been sent in abundance from Bengal, whence it must always come for the subsistence of an army on the Malabar coast.

Besides the forty days rice carried with the army, arrangements were made for establishing a large depot on the top of the Ghaut; and other depots were formed by the Coorga Rajah, between the Ghaut and the Mysore frontier.

The Bombay army, on its ascending the Ghaut, consisted of four European regiments, four companies of artillery, and eight battalions of Sepoys, in four brigades, amounting to eight thousand four hundred effective men.

This army, in high order, and provided with the battering train, and supplies that have been stated, made their first march towards the Mysore country on the 22d of January, when orders were received from Lord Cornwallis to leave or send back their battering train, and to advance only with their field artillery. The heavy guns, and their stores, were in consequence sent back to the top of the Ghaut, where they were placed in batteries judiciously constructed for the defence of the pass, and left under the command of Lieutenant-Colonel Peche, with a detachment of three hundred men.

Besides this detachment, the 4th native battalion, commanded by Captain Home, was stationed at Iliacore and Biliapatam, to furnish escorts, and keep open the communication with the coast.

The minister of the Rajah of Travancore, with a party of horse, and two battalions of infantry, was encamped a few miles beyond the Ghaut, and furnished the escorts from thence to the army. The Rajah's battalions are commanded by European officers; and though his Sepoys cannot be compared with ours in discipline, they are, however, well armed, and well clothed, and supported in a style infinitely superior to the infantry of our other allies. The old Rajah's aid in men and money, and supplies of every sort, has been as ample as his means would afford, and furnished with all the zeal that might be expected, in a war first undertaken for his protection.

In consequence of Colonel Peche's being left in command on the Ghaut, the two corps of his brigade, besides the 4th battalion, were ordered to do duty in the other brigades; and the army, relieved from the incumbrance of the battering train, proceeded towards the Mysore side of this range of mountains, and encamped on the Seidasur Ghaut, until the time appointed should arrive for advancing to co-operate with the grand army.

CHAPTER IX.

Operations of Purseram Bhow's Army—Escape of Mr. Drake, and three other Prisoners, from Chittledroog—Capture of Hooly Onore, and Bankapoor—Battle and Reduction of Simoga—Expedition to Bidenore.

The Mahratta army, commanded by Purseram Bhow, and the Bombay brigade of three native battalions, which acted with it, commanded by Captain Little, separated from the grand army, in the neighbourhood of Bangalore, on the 8th of July, as before mentioned, and proceeded towards Sera and Chittledroog, as a station favourable for its subsistence, and for distressing the enemy, while it faclitated the collections in the provinces he had conquered, and covered the supplies sent on from the Mahratta states.

So fully engaged had Tippoo been in opposing the grand army, that the only check which the Mahrattas had hitherto met with, was from Cummer-ud-Deen Cawn, who cut off a detachment of theirs about this time, under one of their chiefs named Bulwant Rhow, near Mudgurry.

On approaching Chittledroog, the Bhow sent off his sick to Hurry Hier, a post of considerable strength on the southern bank of the Tumbudra; which, on his advancing to Seringapatam, he had reduced, and established as an hospital. The sick arrived on the 23d of August, at this place, which had also proved a most fortunate asylum for some of our countrymen, who had made their escape from Chittledroog.

Mr. Drake, midshipman of the Hannibal, and three private men belonging to his Majesty's navy, who regained their liberty on this occasion, were of the few that remained of the five hundred prisoners of war, who were delivered over by Monsieur Suffrein to Hyder Ally in August 1782, in consequence of a difference that arose between him and the Madras government, on the subject of the subsistence and exchange of prisoners. Their account of the fate and sufferings of their fellow-captives, excites no less indignation against the policy which delivered them into the hands of the tyrant, than revenge for his cruel and shameful conduct. Of these, as well as of the other unfortunate men who fell into his hands during the late war, he detained such as were bred artificers, or whom he thought most likely to be useful in his service; and treated them, not as prisoners of war, but as slaves, and with a degree of severity that slaves never before experienced in any age, or in any quarter of the globe.

On the 1st of September, the Bhow attacked and got possession of Kincoopy, a hill fort which lies eighteen miles north-east from Chittledroog, which also added to his security in that district. He reconnoitered the Droog, and made some attempts to gain over the garrison to his interest, in which he did not succeed, and found the place was too strong to be attacked with a probability of success.

The country on the west of Chittledroog and Chinroypatam,

between those places and the sea coast, including the rich provinces of Bidenore and Mangalore, was the only part of Tippoo's dominions, of any consequence, that was not either in the possession of his enemies, or had been laid waste during the war.

In order to secure his communication with that quarter, whence he must draw his supplies, he had detached the Nabob Reza Saib, his cousin, and one of his generals, with a large force, to take post at Simoga, and keep up the communication with Bidenore and the coast.

The Bhow continued in the neighbourhood of Chittledroog till towards the end of December, when the time approached that had been fixed for his junction with General Abercromby; which he might effect with safety by crossing the Cavery to the westward of Chinroypatam, at such distance as might prevent Tippoo from moving out to oppose his march.

With a view to employ the intermediate time to advantage, this active chief determined to undertake the reduction of Simoga, and other forts on the rivers Tum and Budra, which would give him possession of a fertile district; an acquisition extremely desirable, as his army became distressed for forage, in the neighbourhood of Chittledroog.

Hooly Onore, situated at the conflux of these rivers, from the junction of which the great river they form takes the name of Tumbudra, was the first object of attack. Captain Little, to whom the enterprize was entrusted, finding the garrison determined to hold out, took up his ground before it on the 19th of December, and in the course of that day opened a battery of a few guns against one of the angular bastions. In the course of the succeeding day it was breached, and that night carried by storm with very little loss, in consequence of judicious feints that were successful in drawing the attention of the enemy to the gateways, and other parts of the fort. It was garrisoned by between three and four hundred men, who threw down their arms, and saved themselves in the pagodas, where they took shelter on finding the assailants had forced the breach. A few horses, and some private plunder, taken by the Sepoys, appear to be all that was found in the place.

Bankapoor, which lies ten miles to the southward of Simoga, about the same distance that Hooly Onore does to the northward of it, was the next object. Alarmed on hearing of the assault of the former place, the garrison of this fort surrendered at the first summons, on the 24th of December.

The forts, which thus lie to the eastward of the rivers having been reduced, the army proceeded to the main object, and crossed the Budra, a little above Hooly Onore, on the 25th of December, and next day crossed the Tum, about five miles below Simoga, which lies on the western bank of that river.

Captain Little, accompanied by the Bhow's son Appah Saib, having been employed in reconnoitering Simoga, found that a line of intrenchment, with redoubts in front of it, was abandoned, and that the main body of the enemy's troops, to the amount of seven thousand infantry, provided with artillery, and eight hundred horse, had taken post some miles to the westward, in the woods, with a view to attack the Bhow's army, as soon as he should engage in the operations of the siege.

Knowing both the enemy's design and position, the Bhow determined to dislodge them, if possible, previous to his commencing the siege; and having, on the 29th of December, made a circuit of about ten miles, and encamped between them and the fort, gave orders to attack them on the same day. They were drawn up in an open space in the jungle, behind a deep ravine; had their right flank to the river, and in their front a thick jungle, which also covered their left, and extended to the hills. To force a large body, with artillery, from a position of such strength, was an arduous task, especially as the nature of the ground would not permit the Mahratta cavalry to assist essentially in the attack.

Captain Little, leaving two of his field-pieces and eight companies, by the Bhow's desire, to guard the camp, advanced with the other four guns, and the rest of his men (about a thousand), joined by Appah Saib, with five hundred of their infantry, and three thousand horse.

This force entered the jungle at one o'clock; which, though tolerably open for the first half mile, became extremely thick and difficult towards the front of the enemy's line, which, on being approached about two o'clock, opened upon them with grape, musquetry, and rockets.

The enemy's position being strongest in front, where they had parties in the ravine, it became necessary to attack them on the right and left; but the closeness of the jungle, also on both their flanks, afforded them such advantage, that our troops forced their way with infinite difficulty, and penetrating only in small numbers to the open space in their front, were repeatedly repulsed. Part of the Mahratta infantry charged at times, when they saw the enemy appearing to give way, but were always beat back, and returned in such disorder as greatly increased the difficulty in forming and leading on our Sepoys; while the greater part of their infantry, or corps of 300 topasses, on being directed by Captain Little to advance, declared their unwillingness to take their share in the action, and that they had come out entirely unprovided with ammunition. The contest continued hot and bloody for two hours, when at length a successful impression was made on their left, where three guns being taken, the enemy began to retreat.

Captain Little, whose conduct had excited general admiration throughout the whole of the action, pursued with such force as he could collect. There was but one road through the jungle; and so closely did he follow the enemy, that, in the course of five miles, he came up with seven more of their guns, which completed the capture of all their cannon. A bukshey and a sepadar (two officers of high rank) were taken, together with great part of the baggage; and, but for the approach of the night, their general would probably have been also numbered among the prisoners. The victory, as it was, did not require this circumstance to render it one of the most brilliant actions in the war.

The Mahratta cavalry had, from the nature of the country, but little opportunity of coming forward in the battle; but in the pursuit, they secured about 300 of the enemy's horses, and 600 of the artillery bullocks, which they cut from the yokes and carried off without regard to the security of the guns and tumbrels. Next morning they continued the pursuit, and in the village of Mungaody, ten miles in the jungle, captured a great quantity of baggage.

Reza Saib made his escape to the hill fort of Coolydroog, thirteen miles from Bidenore, with 400 horse and 1500 foot, which, with thirteen loaded elephants, that were sent off the morning of the action, was all he saved of his force or baggage after this defeat.

The loss sustained by Captain Little's detachment amounted to four officers and fifty-five Sepoys killed and wounded.

The officers were, Lieutenant Ross, major of brigade, killed, when bravely exerting himself in encouraging the Sepoys in the heat of the action Lieutenants Bethune, Doolan, and Moor, all severely, but none of them mortally, wounded. Of the Sepoys, forty-four were of the 8th, Captain Little's battalion, which led the attack.

The army, now at liberty to prosecute the siege, that operation was also intrusted to Captain Little, assisted by Captain Thompson, who commanded the artillery of the brigade.

A battery of five guns, constructed opposite to the gateway, was opened on the 2d of January, and by noon the following day had made a breach nearly practicable, when the garrison agreed to give up the place, on condition of their private property being secured to them, and the capitulation guaranteed by the English detachment. The Bhow overlooked the distrust indicated of his nation, and empowered Captain Little to conclude the terms.

Simoga was found to be well supplied with cannon and military stores. Six of the iron guns were so particularly good, that the Bhow exchanged them for others in his battering train. There was nothing else of much value in the place, the Nabob having taken out a lack of pagodas, lodged in it a few days before, which he had carried off on his elephants.

The reduction of Simoga, which added a very valuable district to the countries that had been conquered by Purseram Bhow's army, would consequently continue to raise his pretensions and influence in the Mahratta state. His brilliant success, and the broken state of the enemy's forces in that country, induced him to think of another enterprize that promised still greater advantage to himself, which he had the imprudence to undertake at the risk of the general success of the war; and, instead of proceeding to join the Bombay army, according to the plan agreed upon, he marched in the contrary direction, towards Bidenore, of which the consequences will be hereafter related.

In addition to the operations carried on by the confederate armies on the western side of the Peninsula, the enemy also suffered much from the activity and vigilance of his Majesty's squadron on the Malabar coast.

Commodore Cornwallis, although he had not any naval force of the enemy's to oppose, had contributed essentially to the success of the war, in aiding the operations of the army. Captain Byron, in command of the Phœnix, had assisted most zealously in the attack of Cananore, and several of the forts on the Malabar coast, during the first campaign; and an expedition had lately been sent by the commodore against *Fortified Island*, situated within a mile of the coast, and nearly opposite to Onore.

Captain Sutton, of his Majesty's ship Minerva, joined by the Thames and Vestal frigates, commanded by Captains Troubridge and Osborne, approached *Fortified Island* on the 11th of October. The ships were run close in, and anchored within musquet shot of the fort. The killedar refusing to surrender, a party of marines was instantly landed, and, uniting threats with stratagem, carried a point that, if disputed, must have cost many lives.

This small island, about a mile in circumference, is strong by nature, and has been fortified at a great expence. The only landing place is at the gateway, which is defended by strong works. The garrison consisted of two hundred men, and had thirty-four pieces of cannon for its defence, with an ample supply of ammunition, and provisions to have stood a siege.

Besides the military stores, three hundred bags of pepper, twenty tons of iron spikes for ship building, with almost the whole of the iron work for a ship of sixty guns, and some lesser naval stores, were found in the fort. The ship, for which this preparation had been made, was nearly completed, but had been scuttled and sunk in the river at Onore, on the commencement of the war.

The Mahratta cruizers had lately plundered both Onore and Cundapore; but having kept neither as a post, *Fortified Island* was of material importance as a check to the enemy's receiving the supplies of military stores which were said to be expected from France.

The commodore continued on the Malabar coast, with his squadron, in order to intercept the store ships; and towards the end of November, when at anchor in the road at Tellicherry, seeing a French frigate, which proved to be La Resolu, of thirty-six guns, come out from Mahé in convoy of two merchantmen, and steer towards Mangalore, he ordered the Phœnix and Perseverance frigates, each of thirty-six guns, commanded by Captains Sir Richard Strachan and Smith, to chase and bring to the merchantmen, and examine their cargoes. On coming up with the French ships, Sir Richard fired a shot, to give notice of his intention of stopping them; and while Captain Smith sent boats on board the merchantmen, he dispatched an officer to the frigate for information, and to acquaint the French captain with his orders. The officer was returning, but had not got on board the Phœnix, when a broadside was poured into her from the Resolu, which, followed by a second, killed seven men, and wounded many more; among the latter, Lieutenant Findlay, of the marines, received a mortal wound. Sir Richard immediately manœuvred his ship, so as to bring her under the stern of the French frigate, which he raked, and carried away her rudder and ensign staff. Her colours were instantly displayed in the mizen shrouds, and the engagement continued till her bowsprit being carried away, and the Perseverance also joining in the action, which had lasted about half an hour, the French Captain struck. He had twenty-one men killed, and forty-four wounded, among whom was the captain. The loss of men on board the Phœnix was confined to the two first broadsides of the enemy.

The two merchant ships were not found to contain any warlike stores, and were permitted to proceed on their voyage; but the frigate was taken possession of, and carried into Tellicherry. The commodore sent her to Mahé, with an account of what had taken place. She was received after some hesitation, and the second captain was dispatched to France by the first opportunity, to represent what had happened. It is said that the first captain, on being asked an explanation of his conduct, asserted that he had merely acted in conformity to his orders.

The French commodore, Monsieur St. Felix, an officer of distinction, who it appears had given the orders to the captain of La Resolu, arrived at Mahé from the Mauritius, with two frigates, soon after this affair; and thinking the dignity of his nation hurt in the transaction, declared that he would attack the English commodore wherever he should meet him in equal force; but this rash resolution, which might have involved the two countries in a war, was thwarted by a declaration from the crews of his ships, that they would not fight, as the nation was not at war with the English.

Although these merchant ships were not laden with military stores, there was no doubt of ships having sailed from France with such cargoes for Tippoo; and this might have been an experiment, to see if the British squadron would search and seize them, in case of their being forwarded to Mangalore.

CHAPTER X.

Tippoo detaches Cummer-ud-Deen Cawn against Purseram Bhow —Incursion of a Party of the Sultan's Horse to Madras—Junction of Colonel Floyd's Convoy, and of Colonel Duff, with the battering Train, from Bangalore; and of the Nizam's Army, from Gurramcondah.

TIPPOO, alarmed at the late success of Purseram Bhow's army, and probably still more at the direction of his march towards Bidenore, detached Cummer-ud-Deen Cawn instantly with a considerable force to that quarter.

The forts of Cumpsey and Ananpore had surrendered to the Bhow's army as he advanced, and he penetrated without opposition to Futipet, where he arrived on the 28th of January, within a few miles of Bidenore.

The Bhow, whether from hearing of the approach of Cummer-ud-Deen Cawn, who had retaken Simoga, or in consequence of letters he had received from Lord Cornwallis and Hurry Punt, requiring him to return immediately; or, perhaps, influenced by the operation of these circumstances united, desisted from his projected attack on Futipet and Bidenore, and prepared, though late, to move forward to co-operate in the siege of Seringapatam.

Cummer-ud-Deen Cawn continued to watch the motions of the Mahratta chief, but does not appear to have been in force sufficient to attack him; and although the Bhow's ill-judged expedition to Bidenore was likely to deprive Lord Cornwallis of his assistance at the siege, it had the effect of drawing off a large detachment from the Sultan's army, under his best general, which would considerably weaken his means of defence.

It might be imagined that the Sultan's troops had now sufficient employment in the neighbourhood of his metropolis; and that the Carnatic, which had been so little disturbed during the war, would have remained more quiet than ever. To the astonishment and consternation of the inhabitants of Madras, a party of horse made their appearance at the Mount about the middle of this month, cut and robbed some people, burnt one of the villages, and advanced within three or four miles of Madras. Horses were immediately furnished by the gentlemen of the settlement to mount a party of troopers, who were sent out under Major Pater, and a party of infantry under Major Wynch was also sent to the Mount. Luckily none of the families, who were in their country houses, nor any of the inhabitants at the Mount, where a detachment of artillery was stationed, had fallen into the hands of the enemy; who, disappointed in the plunder they had expected, went off again in the course of the day. Although the mischief done by this incursion was inconsiderable, yet the uneasiness it occasioned at the Presidency, and the alarm spread throughout the country, where the inhabitants fled from their villages, and left the cultivation of their fields, were consequences that shewed how necessary it is to be prepared to check such attacks; and that, however far removed from the great scene of action, an open country must, in time of war, ever be insecure against the incursions of cavalry.

Tippoo's operations had, however, been no where attended with such success, as to give him hopes of obtaining more advantageous terms by a continuance of hostilities. On the contrary, the fall of the Droogs, the defeat of his troops at Simoga, and the operations on the Malabar coast, all tended to cut off every hope of relief or safety but in peace. He now renewed his request to be permitted to send vakeels to settle all differences; but his messengers were immediately sent back, with an answer, acquainting the Sultan, that no other embassy would be admitted until he released the prisoners taken at Coimbettore, whom he had detained contrary to the terms of capitulation.

The army was at this time encamped near Outredroog, which was fitting up as a general hospital, and as a magazine for the reception of the grain and public stores that could not be immediately carried on with the army. The lower fort was not only strong, but spacious, and contained a number of good houses, which made it particularly suitable for this purpose. The distance was likewise convenient, between forty and fifty miles from Seringapatam.

Colonel Floyd having been directed to send the detachment of Royal Artillery, and the military stores, to join the battering train at Bangalore, arrived in the camp on the 12th of January with the rest of his convoy, which, consisting of grain, was lodged in Outredroog. The battering train, that ponderous and indispensible part of the equipment, was drawn out, and arranged in the highest order on the glacis at Bangalore, from whence it moved on the 9th, and joined the army on the 14th of January.

Eight heavy guns were already in Outredroog, and twenty more, with a proportion of howitzers and mortars, now came with Colonel Duff. Such were the improvements introduced by the colonel, or acquired by experience during the war, that this unwieldy department moved with nearly as much ease as any other part of the army; whereas, at the commencement of the first campaign, eight eighteen-pounders, with their stores, were got on with infinite difficulty, always created delay, and frequently required two days to make the distance of one short march. The chief improvements which effected this change in moving the great guns, were yoking the bullocks four, instead of two abreast, and carrying back the chain to which they are yoked, to the axle of the gun, instead of the axle of the limber, by which the purchase is taken from the heaviest part of the machine, and the chain raised nearer to a level with the yokes. But above all, the use of the sagacious elephants, (rarely employed by us in former wars,) who, marching behind the heaviest cannon, are always ready to shove them on and help them over every difficulty, has proved of such evident and essential advantage, that they will in future be considered of the first consequence in all operations that require a train of heavy artillery.

The great objection to elephants being employed with the army, was the difficulty of their subsistence, as it was supposed they could not live without a very large daily allowance of rice.

This idea, which their keepers are interested and careful to inculcate, necessity and experience have set aside. The elephant is not only the most powerful and most useful, but one of the most hardy animals that can be employed with an army. He carries a load equal to sixteen bullocks, and without risk of loss or damage on the march. He subsists upon the leaves or small branches of trees, on the sugar-cane or the plantain tree: in short, he lives upon forage which horses and bullocks do not eat; any kind of grain will support him, and he will work as long without grain as any other animal. The loss of elephants, although they had their full share of all hardship and fatigue, was inconsiderable in proportion to that of cattle; and far from being an incumbrance, or an expedient of necessity to supply the want of bullocks, they will hereafter be considered as the first, and most essential class of cattle that ought to be provided for the carriage of an Indian army.

There was still one more junction expected; the army of the Soubah or Nizam from Gurramcondah. Having left a stronger force in possession of the lower fort, and for the blockade of the place, the Prince advanced again to join Lord Cornwallis, and detained his Lordship some days longer than would have been necessary in the neighbourhood of Outredroog.

On the 25th of January, Lord Cornwallis having received accounts of the approach of that army, went to meet his Highness the Prince, by appointment, at Magré, about six miles in the rear of his Lordship's camp, accompanied by General Medows, and the officers of their suite, and escorted by Colonel Floyd, with part of the 19th dragoons, and the body guards.

Guns were prepared to fire a salute on the right of the line, and the flank companies of the first brigade, with the bands of music of the 36th and 52d regiments, were ordered to the place where the tents were to be pitched, in order to receive the Prince with every possible mark of distinction. His Lordship, after waiting several hours at Magré, exposed to the sun, rode on some miles farther, to meet the Prince. Repeated messages were brought that he was approaching, and several questions asked as to the form of his reception. At length, after a most tiresome day, the Prince, the Minister, and their principal attendants, on their elephants, arrived, accompanied by a large body of his horse. Hurry Punt, who had gone to meet his Highness, in order to add to his own consequence, undertook the ceremonies of the introduction, and had contributed not a little to the delay. The sun was set before these great men descended from their elephants; there was no time for paying the intended compliments to the Prince, nor even for pitching a tent, which he had with him; so that, after some conversation standing on foot, it was necessary to conclude the conference. Lord Cornwallis had a long way to return to his camp in the dark, and the Prince had to blame his own delay for the inconvenience of having to take up his ground of encampment after daylight.

This young man appeared to be about twenty years of age, not very tall, but extremely corpulent. He had a heavy look; with the appearance, however, of good-nature, and good sense. The Minister, about sixty years of age, who occasionally prompted or spoke for the Prince, is a man of great and established talents. He had all the appearance of a shrewd and able courtier, possessing the firmness and talents that have not only raised him to his eminent situation from a family of inferior rank, but have enabled him to hold his post for a series of years amidst the cabals of the Soubah's court, which, though chiefly directed by the influence of the Mahratta states, has been open to the intrigues of every government in India.

The Confederacy, which thus united the chief powers on the Peninsula for the overthrow of a formidable and ambitious enemy, was also attended by an ambassador, who arrived at this time, with a party of horse, from Madajee Bounselo, the Rajah of Berar. The Peshwa and the Nizam were themselves in the field, on their respective frontiers, and all India looked with anxious expectation to the event of the ensuing campaign.

The Soubah's forces having joined, the army moved the two following days, and, marching through the jungle among the hills, encamped on the 27th of January at Hooleadroog. The enemy had repossessed and repaired this place since it surrendered to our army in June last. A good many shot were fired from it as a reconnoitering party approached, which was sent on from the left wing of the army; but the killedar, on being summoned by Lieutenant Colonel Maxwell, who told him there was no time to deliberate, and if he delayed he should instantly commence the attack, was so intimidated as to surrender without farther resistance. The fort, though small, was, as formerly described, inaccessible to assault; and, from the trouble which Tippoo had taken in repairing the works, it was supposed the new garrison would have made a more resolute defence.

Hooleadroog being garrisoned, was established as an advanced post, being ten miles nearer the grand object than Outredroog, and from which the allied armies, now finally assembled, were to commence their march, for the second attempt upon the enemy's capital.

ORDER of BATTLE of the ARMY Commanded by the Right Honb: Lt. GENERAL EARL CORNWALLIS K:G:

Governor General and Commander in Chief in INDIA &c. &c. &c. — *1st February 1792.*

Second in Command MAJOR GENERAL MEDOWS.

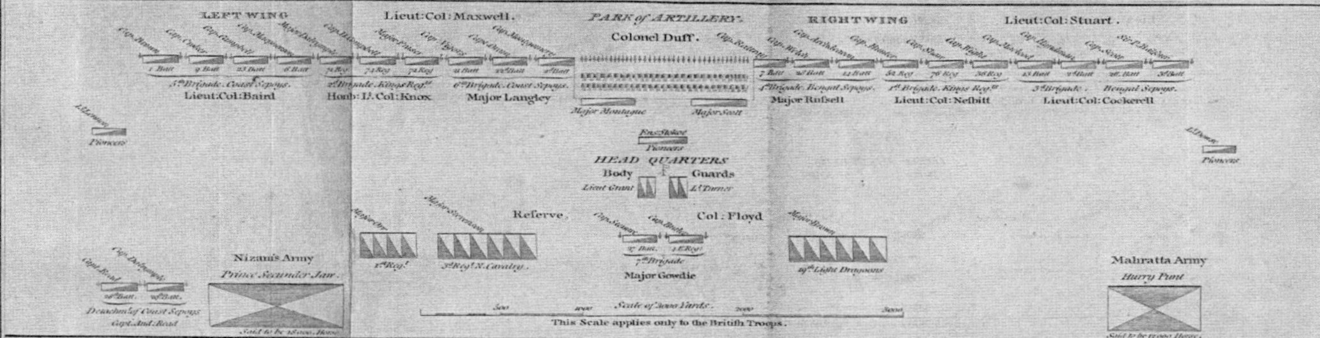

GENERAL STAFF

Commr. in Chief. EARL CORNWALLIS.	
Mily. Secy. & Adj. Gen: K. Troops	Lieut. Col. Ross
Pri. Secy. & Quar. Mr. Gen: … Do.	Maj: Haldane
Persian Interpreter. Cherry Esq. Physician Dr. Laird	
Aids de Camp	Major Skelly, Captn. Madan, Kyd, Robinson, Apsley, Lt. Col. Martin.
Adjt. Gen: Madras Establishment	Lieut: Col: Malcolm
Deputy	Major Close
Deputy Adjt. Gen: K: Troops	Major Dirom
Do. Bengal Estabt.	Major Scott
Qur. Mr. Gen: Madras Establishment	Lieut. Col. Richardson
Deputy	Major Stuart
Captains of Guides	A. Beatson, A. Allan
Intelligence Departmt.	Lieut. Macleod
Baggage Master Lieut: Hay. Dep: Lieut. Evans	
Post Master, Lieut: Grant. Provost. Mr. Mann	
Pay and Provision Department.	
Pay Mr. Gen: Kings Troops	W. Burke Esq.
Paymaster Madras Establishmt.	G. Hoare Esq.
Do. Bengal	Scott Esq.
Commissary of Provisions.	Thos. Kingscote Esq.
Deputy	Lieut. Cunningham
Commissaries of Grain	Cap. Wells & Ln. Morrison
Second in Command.	Major Gen. Medows
Sec. & Aid de Camp	Colonel Harris
Aids de Camp	Major Hart, Captn. Bontes Macauley
Cavalry & Reserve.	Colonel Floyd
Brig: Major	Capt. Dallas
Aid de Camp	Lieut. Forbes
RIGHT WING	Lt. Col. Stuart.
Aids de Camp	Lieut. Hart, Wilkes
LEFT WING	Lt. Col. Maxwell
Aids de Camp	Capt. Agnew, Lieut. Wallace
Artillery	Col. Duff
Brig: Major	Cap. Johnson
Aid de Camp	Lieut: Crunch
Bengal Infantry	Lt. Col. Cockerell
Brig: Major	Capt: Wells
Brig: Qur. Master	Lieut: Dent
Corps of Engineers.	
Chief Engineer	Lieut. Col. Patrick Ross
Aid de Camp	Lt. Colin Mackenzie
Hospital Staff.	
Surgeon General	Doctor Lucas
Secretary	Mr. Fitzgerald
Apothecary	Mr. Bingham

BRIGADE STAFF

1st Brigade	Lt. Col: Nesbitt
Brig: Major	Lieut. Nightingall
2d Brigade	Honb: Lt. Col Knox
Brig: Major	Lt. Sir Geo: Leith Bt.
3d Brigade	Lt. Col: Cockerell
Brig: Major	Capt. Douglas
Brig: Qur. Master	Lt. Mac Donall
4th Brigade	Major Russell
Brig: Major	Cap. Turin
Brig: Qur. Master	Lieut. Graham
5th Brigade	Lt. Col: Baird
Brig: Major	Capt. Grant
Brig: Qur. Master	Lieut. Gibbons
6th Brigade	Major Langley
Brig: Major	Capt. Cosby
Brig: Qur. Master	Lieut. C. Campbell
7th Brigade	Major Gowdie
Brig: Major	Capt. Cranston
Brig: Qur. Master	Lieut. Rand
Detacht. with the Nizams Army.	Capt. A. Read
Brig: Major	Capt. Blair
Brigade in the Coimbetore Country	Major Cuppage
Brig: Major	Capt. Bannerman
Brig: Qur. Master	Capt. Cuppage

ARTILLERY Commanded by Colonel Duff.

Distribution.		Brass Ordnance: Field 6 Pr.	Howitzers 8 In.	Howitzers 5½	Mortars 5½	Mortars 4⅖	Total	Iron: 24 Pr.	18 Pr.	12 Pr.	Total	Total
Right Wing. Bengal Artillery.	Lt. Col: Geils & Maj: Woodburne	20	-	-	-	-	20	-	-	-	-	20
Left Wing. Coast Artillery	Lt. Col: Smith	20	-	-	-	-	20	-	-	-	-	20
Reserve. Coast Artillery	Capt: Saxon	4	-	-	-	-	4	-	-	-	-	4
Battering Train. Royal & Bengal Artillery.	Majors Scott & Montague	2	1	3	4	4	14	4	20	4	28	42
	Total	46	1	3	4	4	58	4	20	4	28	86

ABSTRACT of the ARMY — BRITISH TROOPS

Corps	No. of Corps	European Troops	Native Troops	Total
CAVALRY	4	404	702	1 106
ARTILLERY	4	1 145	3 077	4 222
INFANTRY	24	4482	11 133	15 615
ENGINEERS	1	20	21	41
PIONEERS	3	15	1034	1 049
Total	36	6066	15 967	22 033

Published by W. Faden [illegible]

PART SECOND.

MARCH OF THE ALLIED ARMIES TO, AND SIEGE OF SERINGAPATAM.

CHAPTER I.

Review of the British Army by the Nizam's Son and Hurry Punt—March of the Confederate Forces to Seringapatam.

THE army of the Soubah, or Nizam, having encamped with the Mahrattas a few miles in the rear of the English army, Lord Cornwallis went to pay a visit to the Prince, and invited his Highness and Hurry Punt to see the British troops under arms on the following day.

On the 31st of January the line was accordingly ordered to be drawn out at noon for the reception of the eastern chiefs, when Lord Cornwallis and General Medows went to meet them on the right of the encampment.

Great pains had been taken to explain to the Prince and chiefs the necessity of their coming at the time appointed; and, in order to make the compliment satisfactory to them, who were more desirous of being seen by our army in all their state, than of seeing the troops to advantage, it was agreed that they should come on their elephants.

The chiefs, notwithstanding all that had been said to them on the subject of punctuality, did not approach the right of the line till near three o'clock.

The camp was pitched in a valley close to Hooleadroog, and, from the nature of the ground, could not be in one straight line, but was formed on three sides of a square, with a considerable interval on account of broken ground between the divisions, which were thus encamped each with a different front.

The reserve, consisting of the cavalry, with a brigade of infantry in the centre, formed the division on the right of the line, and the two wings of the infantry formed the two other divisions of the encampment; the battering train being in the centre of the left wing fronting Hooleadroog. The extent of the line, including the breaks between the divisions, was above four miles.

The Prince, the Minister, Hurry Punt, and the tributary Nabobs of Cuddapu and Canoul, who had accompanied Secunder Jau from Hyderabad, were on elephants richly caparisoned, attended by a numerous suite of their best horse, and preceded by their chubdars, who call out their titles; surrounded, in short, by an immense noisy multitude,

The Prince was in front, attended by Sir John Kennaway, on an howdered elephant, near enough to answer such questions as might be asked by his Highness respecting the troops. On his reaching the right of the line, a salute of 21 guns was fired from the park, while the cavalry, with drawn swords and trumpets sounding, received him with due honours as he passed their front. He returned the officers salute appearance , and looked attentively at the troops. The 19th dragoons, of which they had all heard, attracted their particular notice as they passed the corps of the reserve.

Having seen a regiment of Europeans, besides the dragoons in the first division, the chiefs were not a little surprised to find a brigade of three regiments, on proceeding a little farther in the centre of the second division. They had passed the Sepoys at rather a quick pace, but went very slow opposite to the European corps, and seemed much struck with their appearance. The troops all in new clothing, their arms and accoutrements bright and glittering in the sun, and themselves as well dressed as they could have been for a review in time of peace: all order and silence, nothing heard or seen but the uniform sound and motion in presenting their arms, accompanied by the drums and music of the corps, chequered and separated by the parties of artillery extended at the drag-ropes of their guns. The sight was beautiful even to those accustomed to military parade; while the contrast was no less striking between the good sense of our generals on horseback, and the absurd state of the chiefs looking down from their elephants, than between the silence and order of our troops, and the noise and irregularity of the mob that accompanied the eastern potentates.

After passing the right wing, the road leading through some wood and broken ground, the chiefs, on ascending a height, were not a little astonished to discover a still longer line than the two they had passed, and which, in this situation, they could see at once through its whole extent. But for the battering train, which occupied a mile in the centre of this division, at which they looked with wonder; but for the difference of the dress and music of the highland regiments in the 2d European brigade, and the striking difference of size and dress between the Bengal sepoys in the right, and the coast sepoys which they now saw in the left wing; but for these distinctions which they remarked, such was the extent of ground which the army covered, and the apparent magnitude of its numbers, that the chiefs might have imagined a part of the same troops were only shewn again upon other ground, an expedient not unusual among themselves, whenever they have it in view to impress strangers with a false idea of the strength of their forces.

It was five o'clock before the chiefs reached the left of the line, when having expressed themselves highly gratified with all they had seen, they accompanied Lord Cornwallis to his tents. After a short visit, and fixing the time and order of their march for the following day, they returned about sun-set to their own camps.

On the 1st of February, the allied armies commenced their march from Hooleadroog in the following order:

The English army moved off as usual, at day-break, in three columns.

1st. The battering guns, tumbrels, and heavy carriages on the great road, formed the centre column.

2d. The line of infantry and field pieces, on a road made for them at the distance of a hundred yards or more, as the ground required, marched parallel to the battering train, and on its right, that being the flank next to the enemy.

3d. The smaller store carts and private baggage carts marched in like manner, on a road to the left of the battering train, beyond which was the great mass of baggage, carried on elephants, camels, bullocks, and coolies, all the servants of the army, and families of the Sepoys.

This immense multitude on the baggage flank, was prevented from going ahead of the columns by the baggage-master and his guard, and was flanked, giving it a space of several miles which it required, by the part of the cavalry not on other duties, and the infantry of the reserve.

The advanced guard was formed of a regiment of cavalry, the body guards, and the detail of infantry for the picquets of the new camp.

The rear-guard was formed of a regiment of cavalry, and the picquets of the old camp, and did not move till they saw the baggage and all stores off the old ground of encampment.

In this manner the line of march was shortened to one third of what would be its extent if confined to one road; and, from the component parts of the army being thus classed and divided, the whole moved on with as much ease as if the battering train only had been upon the march. The heavy equipment of the army, great guns, store carts, provision and baggage, thus formed a mass of immense breadth and depth, guarded in such manner on all sides, that on no quarter could the enemy approach the stores or baggage without opposition from some part of the troops on the march.

The armies of the allies, which were not mixed in our details, followed, as is their custom, at a later hour, and without any disposition for their defence.

The order of march has thus been particularly described, as

it is one of the most essential improvements which arose from the experience of the late war. At the commencement of the first campaign, the army, as in former wars, marched in one column. The station of the battering train in the first marches was in the rear of the column. It fell so far behind, and wanted so much assistance, that sometimes it did not reach the ground of encampment till the following day. It was then tried in the centre of the column between the wings, which it separated, and still created great delay. Then it was brought to the front, where the heavy guns moved with more advantage, from having the first of the road, and being parked on the leading flank, got off the ground earlier and without interruption from the line. But when the train came to be enlarged, it was found to require the whole of the road; another road was consequently to be made on the flank for the light guns and troops; and when wheel carriages became very numerous, it was necessary to make a third road for the light carts on the baggage flank.

The principle of this order of march, which seems of absolute necessity in the transport of heavy ordnance, was found of essential advantage when the army moved with field pieces only in pursuit of Tippoo. The artillery in brigades, at proper intervals, moved with ease and rapidity along the road without interrupting, or receiving interruption from the troops, who, marching on the flanks, could be immediately formed, while the field pieces were unlimbered and drawn into their stations. By this means the line is at once formed in close order, and the inconvenience of closing up from the rear, avoided; which must otherwise necessarily take place when the troops and artillery intermixed, move on the same road with the guns; and tumbrels occupy a much greater space on the march, than when unlimbered and drawn out for action.

It may seem strange that these improvements had not occurred in former wars in the Carnatic. The reason is, that the army in those times generally marched without any, or with only a very few, battering guns; the force was small compared to the army during the late war, and having few cavalry, it was necessary to march with their line extended to its full length, the better to protect the stores and baggage.

The army, on issuing from among the hills, and approaching the river Madoor, about six miles from Hooleadroog, discovered large parties of the enemy's horse on the opposite side. Mr. Burke, paymaster-general of the King's troops, whose zeal and anxiety for the success of the war, could not be exceeded, being, as usual, with the advanced guard, returned and gave information of this appearance to Lord Cornwallis. It was uncertain if Tippoo might not come forward to dispute the passage of this river; and his Lordship had already taken the precaution to reinforce the advanced guard with the leading brigade of the line. On crossing the river, Licutenant-Colonel Richardson and Major Smart, the quarter-master and deputy-quarter-master-general, accompanied by a few troopers, by Mr. Kingscotte, and some of the brigade quarter-masters and quarter-masters of corps, came suddenly on one of the parties of horse, whom they pursued so closely as to fire some pistols; but they made their escape into a field, where a large body was ready to support them. This body did not attempt to advance, nor was there any line of infantry in their rear; but, finding our army was in motion, and seeing the direction of its march, they dispersed over the country, and, having already driven off the inhabitants and cattle, began their usual employment of burning the villages and forage. The allied armies passed the river without interruption, and encamped on a high commanding ground beyond it, with a rich and open country in their front.

The armies marched again on the 2d of February, about nine miles more to Karricode, the first march having also been about that distance, and halted there on the 3d, in order to repair the old fort which Tippoo had dismantled to prevent its being occupied as a post.

Part of the 9th battalion of coast sepoys commanded by Captain Croker, was left in Karricode; and the remainder of that battalion in another mud fort, nine miles farther, advanced on the ground to which the armies marched on the 4th of February.

The same body of horse, about 1000, continued to attend the confederate armies, or rather only the British army, which was in front, but they durst not risk much, and rather served to amuse than harrass the troops on the march.

The country was hitherto very fertile, and amply supplied with water, in all respects much preferable to the route by Cankinelly and Arakery, by which the army first advanced, and to that by Milgotah and Naggimungulum, by which it had returned from Seringapatam.

The army proceeded on their march with all the confidence that arose from knowing that every difficulty was now foreseen and provided against; and all were sensible that the fatigues they had undergone, and the loss of the few heavy guns that were burst, were amply compensated by the experience gained in the former expedition to the capital. The intermediate countries since reduced, ample forces joined to support the communications, a good season, and the prospect of abundant supplies, seemed to comprise every advantage which could enable the confederate armies to keep the field and prosecute the siege.

The next and last march on the 5th of February, was across the range of barren hills that lies to the north-east of Seringapatam. The view of the city from those heights, and of the Sultan's encampment under the walls of it, was a pleasing but not a new sight to the army. Every circumstance that could be observed was interesting; and, from the Sultan's position, it was evident he meant to defend the place in person, and make this, what we wished it should be, the grand concluding scene of the war.

A larger body of horse attended the army on this march; they endeavoured to harrass the advanced guard, throwing rockets on the flank of the line as it crossed the hills, and were particularly troublesome to the quarter-master-general and his party as they marked out the ground of encampment.

The army having marched about ten miles, arrived on their ground at two o'clock, which, extending across the valley of Milgotah, fronted the Sultan at the distance of about six miles from his camp and capital.

CHAPTER II.

Position of the Confederate Army, and Description of Tippoo's fortified Camp.—Retrospect to the Proceedings of the Confederacy against Hyder Ally, in 1767.

THE encampment of the allied armies, was divided by a small stream, called the Lockany river, which, taking its rise from the lake below Milgotah, runs through the valley into the Cavery.

The British army, forming the front line, its right wing reached from the river along the rear of the French Rocks to a large tank which covered that flank of the line. The park and the left wing extended from the other side of the river to the verge of the hills which the army had crossed on their last march. The reserve, encamped about a mile in the rear, facing outwards, left a sufficient space between it and the line, for the stores and baggage. The Mahratta and the Nizam's armies were also in the rear, somewhat farther removed, to prevent interference with our camp.

The encampment of the confederate army was judiciously pitched at such distance from Seringapatam, and so covered by the French Rocks in front of its right, as to prevent immediate alarm to the enemy, either from its proximity or apparent magnitude.

Tippoo had foreseen where his enemies would probably take up their ground, and having encamped himself very lately in this quarter, had left not only the valley as bare as possible for their reception, but had also cleared the country of every particle of both dry and green forage that might be within their reach. The cattle and horses might be supported for a few days on the roots of grass dug up by their keepers, but there was evidently no sufficient means left for their subsistence, much less for the elephants and camels, which feed on the leaves of trees, there not being even a bush standing that might be useful in forming materials for the siege.

The Sultan, anxious that his enemies should enjoy neither plenty or quiet so near his capital, sent a party of his people with rockets to disturb the camps during the night. Their attention was particularly directed to the Prince, who was encamped in the rear of our left, and was the first inconvenience he had experienced in his military career. But these useless weapons, creating more alarm than damage, were disregarded by our troops.

At eleven o'clock in the forenoon of the 6th of February, a party commanded by Lieutenant-Colonel Maxwell was sent out to the hills in front of the left, to reconnoitre the position of the enemy's camp. He was accompanied by the chief engineer, the quarter-master-general, the captains of guides, and other public officers.

General Medows having sent Major Hart along with that party, went himself, accompanied by Colonel Harris and the rest of his suite, to reconnoitre the ground in front of the right wing between our picquets and the left of the enemy's position.

The party on the hills to the left had a tolerably distinct, though distant view of Tippoo's fortified camp. From what had been seen of the ground after the battle of the 15th of May, from what both the parties now saw, and from the reports of spies, a clear idea was formed of the Sultan's position, which, being afterwards more particularly known, was as follows.

On both sides of the river, opposite to the island of Seringapatam, a large space is inclosed by a bound hedge, which marks the limits of the capital, and is intended as a place of refuge to the people of the neighbouring country from the incursions of horse. On the south side of the river this inclosure was filled with inhabitants, but that on the north side was occupied only by Tippoo's army.

The bound hedge on the north side of the river includes an oblong space of about three miles in length, and in breadth from half a mile to a mile, extending from nearly opposite to the west end of the island to where the Lockany river falls into the Cavery. Within this inclosure the most commanding ground is situated on the north side of the fort; and, besides the hedge, it is covered in front by a large canal, by rice fields, which it waters, and partly by the winding of the Lockany river. Six large redoubts, constructed on commanding ground, added to the strength of this position, one of which, on an eminence, at an ead-gah or mosque, within the north-west angle of the hedge, advanced beyond the line of the other redoubts, was a post of great strength, and covered the left of the encampment.

The right of Tippoo's position was not only covered by the Lockany river, but beyond it by the great Carrighaut hill, which, he had lately fortified more strongly, and opposite to the lower part of the island, defends the ford.

The eastern part of the island was fortified towards the river by various redoubts and batteries, connected by a strong intrenchment with a deep ditch, so that the fort and island formed a second line, which supported the defences of the first beyond the river; and when the posts there should be no longer tenable, promised a secure retreat, as from the outworks to the body of a place.

Tippoo's front line or fortified camp, was defended by heavy cannon in the redoubts, and by his field train and army stationed to the best advantage. In this line there were 100 pieces, and in the fort and island, which formed his second line, there were at least three times that number of cannon.

The defence of the redoubts on the left of Tippoo's position was intrusted to Syed Hummeed and Syed Guffar, two of his best officers, supported by his corps of Europeans and Lally's brigade, commanded by Monsieur Vigie. Sheik Anser, a sipadar or brigadier of established reputation, was on the great Carrighaut hill. The Sultan himself commanded the centre and right of his line within the bound hedge, and had his tent pitched near the Sultan's Redoubt, so called from being under his own immediate orders. The officer is not known who commanded the troops in the island; but the garrison in the fort was under the orders of Syed Saib. The Sultan's army certainly amounted to above five thousand cavalry, and between forty and fifty thousand infantry.

Ever since the junction of the Mahratta armies, Tippoo, seeing he could not continue to keep the field, had employed his chief attention, and the exertions of the main body of his army, in fortifying this camp, and improving his defences in the fort and island. The country had already been laid waste during the former campaign, and the Sultan seemed confidently to rest his hopes on the strength of his works and army for protracting the siege, till the want of supplies, or the approach of the monsoon, should again oblige his enemies to withdraw from his capital.

This plan of defence was the more promising of success, not only from the event of the last campaign, but from its being exactly an adoption of the measures by which his father, Hyder Ally, defeated a similar combination which was formed for the attack of his capital in 1767.

The confederate forces at that time consisted of a great army of Mahrattas, commanded by Mahadurao, and of the Souba's forces, commanded by the Nizam in person, and his brother Bazalet Jung, joined by a detachment of English troops, which the government of Madras had agreed to furnish to the Souba for this enterprize.

Hyder, who had lost many of his countries very rapidly in that war, finding it was the intention of his enemies to attack his capital, determined to risk every thing in its defence, and intrenched himself under the walls of Seringapatam, having first desolated the adjoining country. The position of his camp, defended by redoubts, appears to have been nearly the same with that now adopted by Tippoo; and, with the guns of the fort and on the island, was defended by 300 pieces of cannon.

The proceedings and strength of the confederate armies may be judged of, by the following extract from the history of Hyder Ally, written by a French officer at that time in his service.

" As soon as the two armies (the Mahratta and Nizam's) were " joined, different corps of horse appeared in the plain of Se-

"ringapatam. Many advanced so near as to reconnoitre the "town, and the redoubts in which Hyder's colours were dis-"played: as they met with no interruption from Hyder, they "rode about the plain, and viewed every thing at their ease. "The same ceremony was performed the following day; but "on the third, at nine in the morning, the plain was covered "with cavalry of both armies, with their chiefs at their head on "their elephants: this cavalry was followed by a body of infan-"try, who brought forward about fifty large cannon, that arrived "about noon. The view was grand and striking: the number "of horses was above one hundred thousand; and there were "more than two hundred elephants."

The remainder of the account given by this officer, would be too tedious to quote; but it appears that the confederate forces drew off after receiving the first discharge of cannon from Hyder's lines, and judging it was impracticable to force a position of such strength, they differed on the plan to be adopted for the farther prosecution of the war. The grain brought forward by their brinjarries was soon exhausted; and in want of forage from the desolated state of the country, the Mahrattas were bought off by Hyder, and withdrew from the siege. The Nizam, apprehensive for his safety, also agreed to a separate negotiation, which not only terminated their hostilities, but ended in uniting their forces to exterminate the English from the Carnatic. The Nizam did not continue steady in this alliance, but the consequence was a ruinous invasion of the Carnatic; and although ably opposed by General Joseph Smith, concluded in a disgraceful peace, which Hyder in 1769 dictated to the British government at the gates of Madras.

A retrospect to those events doubtless gave Tippoo confidence in the like posture of his affairs, and may not be an unpleasing digression previous to a detail of the proceedings which now took place in the combination formed by the same powers for the attack of the same capital.

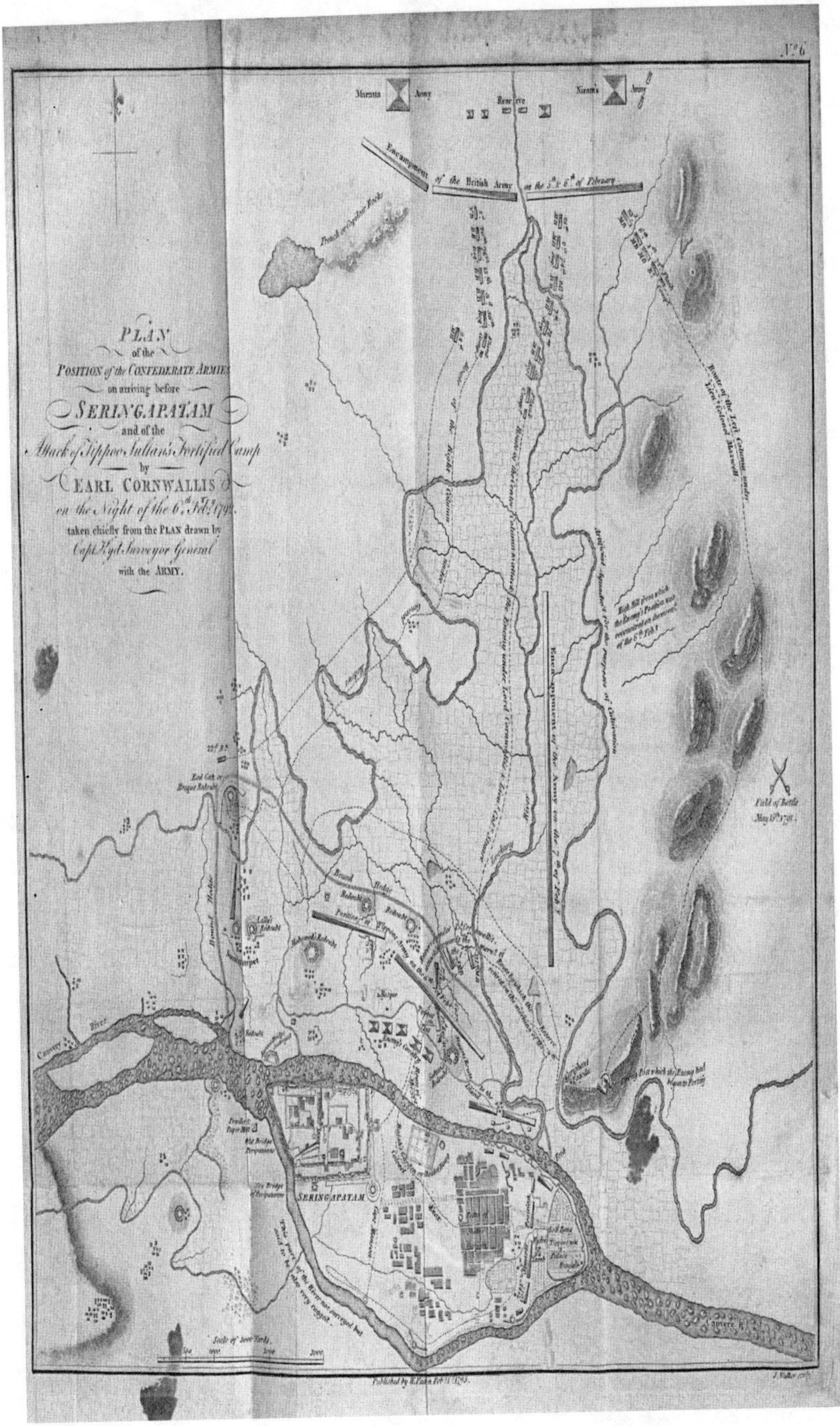
No 6
PLAN
of the
POSITION of the CONFEDERATE ARMIES
on arriving before
SERINGAPATAM
and of the
Attack of Tippoo Sultan's Fortified Camp
by
EARL CORNWALLIS
on the Night of the 6th Feby 1792.
taken chiefly from the PLAN drawn by
Capt. Kyd Surveyor General
with the ARMY.
Maratta Army
Reserve
Nizam's Army
Encampment of the British Army on the 5th & 6th of February
Encampment of the Army on the 7th Feby 1792
Field of Battle May 15th 1791
Cauvery River
SERINGAPATAM

CHAPTER III.

Orders for, and the attack of, Tippoo's fortified Camp, and the Island, on the Night of the 6th February—Operations of the Right Division —of the Centre Division—and of the Left Division—General Success of the Attack.

LORD CORNWALLIS, after receiving the report of the officers who had been sent to reconnoitre, issued the following orders at five o'clock in the evening of the 6th of February.

" Orders to be communicated by officers commanding wings, " to officers commanding brigades and corps only, with the ne- " cessary information to the field officers on picquet."

" The army marches in three divisions at seven this evening " to attack the enemy's camp and lines; picquets to join, field " pieces, quarter and rear guards, and camp guards, to stand " fast."

Right Division. Major General Medows.

36th } 76th } Regiments	Lt. Colonel Nesbitt.
3d Brigade	Lt. Colonel Cockerell.
22d Native Battalion	Captain Oram.

Lt. Lennon's pioneers.

A detail of officers from the engineer corps, and a proportion of scaling ladders.

Centre. Lord Cornwallis.
Lt. Colonel Stuart.

52d, 71st, 74th	Regiments	Lt. Colonel Knox.
4th	Brigade	Major Russell.
2d, 21st	Native Battalions	Major Langley.

Lt. Dowse's pioneers.

A detail of officers from the engineer corps and a proportion of scaling ladders.

Left Division. Lt. Colonel Maxwell.

72d	Regiment	Lt. Colonel Baird.
5th	Brigade	

Ensign Stokoe's pioneers.

A detail of officers from the engineer corps, and a proportion of scaling ladders.

Order of March for the Right Division.

One battalion company from the 36th regiment. Pioneers. Four European flank companies with scaling ladders. 36th regiment. Two Bengal battalions.	Lt. Colonel Nesbitt.

General Medows.
Lieut. Colonel Cockerell.
Engineers.
76th regiment.
Two Bengal battalions.
22d Native Coast battalion.

Order of March for the Centre.

One bat. comp. from the 52d reg.
Pioneers.
Six European flank companies with scaling ladders.
52d regiment.
} Lt. Colonel Knox.

One Bengal battalion.
Lord Cornwallis.
Lt. Colonel Stuart.
Engineers.
71st regiment.
Two Bengal battalions.
74th regiment.
2d
21st } Coast battalions. Major Langley.

Order of March for the Left

One flank comp. of the 72d reg.
One ditto, with scaling ladders.
Pioneers.
One battalion from the 5th brigade.
} Lt. Colonel Baird.

Lieut. Colonel Maxwell.
72d regiment.
Two battalions of the 5th brigade.

" If the right attack is made to the westward of the Somarpett, " the troops of that attack should, after entering the enemy's lines, " turn to the left. But if the attack is made to the eastward of " Somarpett the troops should turn to the right to dislodge the " enemy from all the posts on the left of their position."

" The troops of the centre attack, after entering the enemy's " lines, should turn to the left; the front divisions, however, of " both the right and centre attacks should, after entering, ad- " vance nearly to the extent of the depth of the enemy's camp " before they turn to either side, in order to make room for " those that follow; and such parts of both divisions, as well as " of the left division, as the commanding officers shall not think " it necessary to keep in a compact body, will endeavour to mix " with the fugitives, and pass over into the island with them."

" The reserve, leaving quarter and rear guards, will form in " front of the line at nine this night, and Colonel Duff will re- " ceive the commander in chief's orders concerning the heavy " park, the encampment, and the reserve."

" Young soldiers to be put on the quarter and rear guards at " gun firing, and the picquets to join when the troops march " off."

" A careful officer from each corps to be left in charge of the " camp and regimental baggage."

" Colonel Duff to send immediately three divisions of gun " lascars of fifty men in each to the chief engineer, to carry the "scaling ladders, and the chief engineer is to send them to "the divisions, respectively, along with the officers of his "corps.

"The officers of engineers and pioneers to be responsible that "the ladders, after having been made use of by the soldiers, are "not left carelessly in the enemy's works."

"Surgeons and doolies to attend the troops, and arrack and "biscuit to be held in readiness for the Europeans."

"The divisions to form, as follows, after dark."

"The right in front of the left of the right wing.

"The centre in front of the right of the left wing.

"The left in front of the left of the left wing."

In addition to the troops detailed in the orders, Major Montague of the Bengal, and Captain Ross of the royal artillery, with a detachment of two subalterns and fifty European artillery-men with spikes and hammers from the park, accompanied the centre, and smaller parties the two other columns.

The troops had just been dismissed from the evening parade at six o'clock, when the above orders were communicated; upon which they were directed to fall in again with their arms and ammunition.

By eight o'clock the divisions were formed, and marched out in front of the camp; each in a column by half companies with intervals, in the order directed for their march.

The number of fighting men was at the utmost as follows.

	European Regiments.	Native Battalions.	Total Europeans.	Total Natives.	General Total.
Right division. Major Gen. Medows.	2	5	900	2400	3300
Centre division. Earl Cornwallis. Lt. Col. Stuart.	3	5	1400	2300	3700
Left division. Lt. Colonel Maxwell.	1	3	500	1200	1700
Total	6	13	2800	5900	8700

The officers commanding divisions, on finding that their guides and scaling ladders had arrived, and that every corps was in its proper place, proceeded as appointed at half an hour past eight o'clock.

The evening was calm and serene; the troops moved on in determined silence, and the full moon, which had just risen, promised to light them to success.

The right column was conducted by Capt. Beatson, of the guides, the centre column by Captain Allen, of the guides, and Lieut. Macleod of the intelligence department; and harcarrahs, (Native guides or spies) who had been within the enemy's lines, were sent both to these and the left column.

Tippoo's picquets having made no attempt to interrupt the reconnoitring parties in the forenoon, he probably did not expect so early a visit. The distance of our camp seemed a circumstance favourable to his security, and he did not, perhaps, imagine, that Lord Cornwallis would attack his lines till strengthened by the junction of the armies commanded by General Abercromby and Purseram Bhow.

The Sultan had still less imagined that a fortified camp, defended by a powerful army, with a large field train, and under the guns of his capital, would be attempted by infantry alone, without cannon, and in the uncertainty of the night.

The plan of attack was indeed bold beyond the expectation of our army, but, like a discovery in science, which excites admiration when disclosed, it had only to be known to meet with general applause. The troops, delighted to find themselves unincumbered with cannon, relied with perfect confidence on their musquets and scaling ladders, under cover of the night, as the fittest instruments for opening their way into the enemy's camp.

While the columns were on their march, the camp left under the command of Colonel Duff, was struck, and the baggage packed, in consequence of the orders he had received; the corps of artillery and the quarter and rear guards of the line, standing to their guns and arms in readiness for its defence, while the reserve, consisting of the cavalry and the 7th brigade, under Colonel Floyd, was drawn up in front of the camp, to support the infantry, or to act as occasion might require at day-break.

The anxiety of the corps of the reserve, and of the troops in camp, may be more easily imagined than described in terms that could do justice to their feelings, while their fellow-soldiers were employed in an assault so arduous and important.

The allies, to whom the intended attack was not mentioned till after the columns had marched, were, it is said, in a state of the greatest consternation, on hearing that Lord Cornwallis had ventured out with part of his infantry only, and without cannon, to attack all Tippoo's army in a fortified camp under the walls of his capital. Their surprize was still greater, on knowing that his lordship in person commanded the division that was to penetrate the centre of the enemy's camp, and had gone himself, as they termed it, to fight like a private soldier. They thought it next to impossible that the enterprize should succeed, and dreaded that the ruin of the allied armies might be involved in the attempt.

Between ten and eleven o'clock, the centre column, within a mile of the bound hedge, touched upon the enemy's grand guard, or a body of cavalry, that were coming with rocket boys to disturb our camp, as they had done on the preceding night. The horsemen instantly galloped off to their lines, leaving the rocket boys to harrass the column, and endeavour to impede its march. They threw numberless rockets, that, like the flashes of distant lightning which precede a storm, were effectual only in declaring our approach.

The left column, when the rocketing commenced, was ascending the great Carighaut hill, which soon became illuminated by the discharge of musquetry; and the front division of the centre column, pushing briskly forward on being discovered, reached the hedge, and entered the lines about a quarter of an hour after the intelligence could have got to the enemy.

The right column, meeting with more impediments to retard its progress than the other columns, and led to a more distant point than intended by Lord Cornwallis, was considerably later in reaching the hedge than the centre column, notwithstanding his Lordship's precaution in halting his column for half an hour early in the evening on that account. About half past eleven o'clock this column also entered the bound hedge, and, turning to the right, advanced rapidly against the enemy's principal redoubt in that quarter, distinguished by the white ead-gah, or mosque, which, shone upon by the moon, was seen clearly on the eminence.

The battle now became general throughout the whole extent of the enemy's lines, the discharge of cannon and peals of musquetry shewing that our troops had every where closed with the enemy. The fort and capital, situated low, and seen but faintly in the moon-light, remained silent amidst the conflict.

The particulars of the operations of the several divisions will be best understood by detailing them separately, and following the arrangement in the general orders, beginning with the right attack.

Operations of the Right Division, commanded by General Medows.

General Medows, whose column was destined for the attack of the left of the enemy's position, gave the following orders, in addition to those of the commander in chief.

"The 22d coast battalion, commanded by Captain Oram, to "march on the right flank of the front division; and, on approaching the bound hedge, to make a circuit to the right, "keeping without the hedge, in order to draw the attention of "the enemy to that quarter, while the column is to enter the "hedge to the left, and penetrate the enemy's camp."

"The two rear battalions of the column, being part of "Lieutenant-Colonel Cockerell's brigade, to form in line close "to the hedge, under the command of the senior officer, Captain Richard Scott, and to remain as a reserve, ready to support, but not to advance, without special orders."

That part of the column which, under the immediate orders of the general, was to penetrate into the enemy's camp, consisted of the 36th and 76th regiments, commanded by Captains Wight, and Shawe, and the 13th battalion of Bengal Sepoys, commanded by Capt. Macleod, in the order detailed for the march of the column.

The general's station, as fixed by the orders of the commander in chief, was in the centre of the column. He was attended by Colonel Harris, Major Hart, Captains Macauley and Bordes, his aids de camp, and by Lieutenant Grant, with his body guard. Majors Dirom and Close, the officers of the general staff with this division, accompanied Lieutenant-Colonel Nesbitt at the head of the column.

Colonel Nesbitt, meeting with no opposition, nor finding any camp on penetrating the bound hedge, and seeing the ead-gah or mosque, to his right, thought it his duty to advance without hesitation against this work, as being within the enemy's lines, and one of the posts which defended the left of their position. He wheeled his division to the right, and marching first along the hedge, and afterwards to his left, along the bank of the canal, crossed it, and ascended the hill towards the redoubt.*

The enemy, forewarned of their danger, by the previous commencement of the other attacks, were here prepared for their defence.

A few cannon had been fired from the redoubt, and a few musquet shot from the advanced centinels, as our pioneers

* Lord Cornwallis did not intend that the ead-gah redoubt should be attacked, from its being considerably advanced beyond the main line of Tippoo's encampment; and it was owing to the mistake of the harcarrahs (native guides) that the column was brought upon this post.

cut down the hedge; but whether it was that the enemy reserved their fire till they should be able to give it with full effect, or that their attention was successfully drawn off by the march of the 22d battalion to their front, the leading division met with no opposition till they had crossed the canal and approached near to the redoubt, when a heavy fire of grape and musquetry was directed against the column.

The gleam of this discharge gave a momentary view of the enemy and their post. The redoubt and covert-way were full of men, and troops were seen drawn up to the right and left, but chiefly to the left of the redoubt.

Lieutenant-Colonel Nesbitt, assisted by Major Close, formed the battalion company of the 36th regiment which led the column, and some farther part of the battalion, as it advanced to oppose the enemy on the left, while the flank companies of the 36th and 76th regiments rushed forward to the redoubt.

The enemy, who had continued their fire, now received ours. The assailants drove them from the covert-way, but being severely galled by the multitude that manned the inner works, repeated ineffectual efforts were made to pass the ditch. Several of the ladders were missing, and without them, in the face of such resistance, it seemed impossible to get into the redoubt.

While the troops that had extended to the right and left of the mosque, were thus unsuccessful in the assault, a path-way was fortunately discovered, which was left across the ditch, and led from the end of the mosque into the redoubt. Officers and men crouded to it from both sides, where they had been stopped by the ditch. A slight gateway, which closed the sortie or entrance, was soon forced; and, after a severe conflict, the assailants got possession of a large traverse between the gateway and the body of the redoubt.

The enemy, now driven to the inner circle of the redoubt, faced towards the traverse, and turned one of the guns against the gorge. Their retreat was cut off, and they seemed determined to die or defend their post. Ranged along the circle of the rampart, they directed a heavy fire against the gorge and traverse, crouded by our people, who continued to press in from without, while an irregular fire was returned from a smaller front on our side.

Captain Gage, with Brigade-Major Nightingall and Ensign M'Coll, had got a party of grenadiers of the 76th regiment upon a banquette to the right of the gorge, from which they fired into the redoubt, and a few men had also got upon a similar banquette behind the magazine to the left of the gorge: these parties, in some measure, secured the traverse; but the enemy's fire being evidently superior, it became necessary to cease ours, and charge them with our bayonets. The firing was stopt with some difficulty; the men were formed and brought forward by their officers, and, headed by Major Dirom and Captain Wight, were led in at the gorge of the redoubt. The enemy, who had seen this intention, reserved their fire till the assailants advanced, when a discharge of grape from the gun they had directed against the gorge, seconded by their musquetry, brought down nearly the whole party, and repulsed the charge. Captain Gage, recommencing his fire from the banquette within, prevented the enemy from taking advantage of the confusion that followed this check, while the men below in the traverse were rallied and exhorted to renew the attack. They came forward with great spirit, and were again led in by Major Dirom and Captain Wight. Captain Gage and his party mounted the parapet to the right; Captain Burne, with part of his remaining grenadiers, at the same time, mounted the works to the left of the gorge; and Major Close, who had come into the redoubt, also zealously assisted at this critical period of the attack.

The enemy fired their musquetry, but not having been able to reload the gun which raked the gorge, and dismayed at this second more powerful effort, broke as the assailants closed with them; and such as escaped immediate death by leaping from the embrasures into the ditch, were fired upon, or taken by the main body of the column, which was formed by General Medows to support the attack and cut off the enemy's retreat.

While the attack was carried on in the redoubt, and before the rest of the column had come up, Lieutenant-Colonel Nesbitt, after routing the body in his front, saw a corps advancing with drums beating and colours flying. The officer who led, on being challenged in Moors, answered (*Agari que logue*) " We belong to the " advance,"—the title of Lally's brigade, supposing the people he saw to be their own Europeans, whose uniform also is red; but soon discovering his mistake, the commandant called out (*Feringy Banchooot !—Chelow*) " They are the rascally English! " Make off;" in which he set his corps a ready example. Lieutenant John Campbell of the 36th grenadiers, who had come out of the redoubt wounded, was the person who challenged this corps; and, on seeing it break, rushed forward and seized the standards. Colonel Nesbitt also, finding that this body of the enemy had not come to lay down their arms, nor had been beat-

U 2

ing a chamade, as at first supposed, gave orders to fire upon them, and dispersed the whole.

This event took place during the heat of the contest within the redoubt; and had this corps, which, it seems, was late in following up the rest of the brigade from Somarpett, advanced with less noise, or had it not been opposed by Colonel Nesbitt's party before it reached the redoubt, it is hard to say what turn it might have given to the assault.

This work, which defended the left of the enemy's position, was supplied with eight pieces of cannon, and flanked by three, which were taken on the glacis, said to be the field pieces of Lally's brigade. The commandant, Syed Hummeed, a Moorman of high rank, and near four hundred of his men, fell in its defence.

The loss on our side was also considerable; eleven officers and about eighty men, killed and wounded. The officers killed were Lieutenant Stuart of the Bengal engineers, Lieutenant Robertson of the 73d, doing duty with the 36th regiment; Ensign Smith of the 36th, and Lieutenant Jones of the 76th regiment. The wounded were Lieutenants Brownrigg, Robert Campbell, and John Campbell, of the 36th regiment; Captain Markham, Lieutenants Robertson, Philpot, and Shaw, of the 76th regiment.

Lieutenant Stuart, who had charge of the scaling-ladders, was killed when gallantly pressing forward to the ditch; and several Lascars, who carried them, having fallen at the same time, occasioned the inconvenience that arose at first from the want of ladders in the assault.

Captain Markham, who was severely wounded at the storming of Bangalore, had the misfortune to be disabled in the first onset at this redoubt. The other officers, who were killed or wounded, fell close to the enemy; some in forcing the gateway, others in leading on their men to charge in at the gorge: amongst the latter Lieutenant Brownrigg, adjutant of the 36th regiment, when exerting himself to bring forward the men, received a dangerous wound in the neck.

The loss in private men fell chiefly on the 36th regiment, that corps and the flank companies of the 76th regiment, being the troops which formed the front division of the column. The grenadiers of the 36th, who led, in advancing to the redoubt, had twenty men killed and wounded.

A deserter from our army, who belonged to Lally's corps, gave himself up at this post. From his account, it appeared that Monsieur Vigie with his Europeans, about three hundred and sixty, was stationed in the angle of the hedge in front of the redoubt. Captain Oram's battalion, upon which they fired, had attracted their attention, till finding themselves surrounded, they broke, and endeavoured to make their escape; some along the hedge to the left, but chiefly by passing through the intervals of our column as it continued advancing to the redoubt. The colour of their uniform contributed essentially to the effecting of their escape; and to the same circumstance Monsieur Vigie himself owed his safety; he was seen to go through the column mounted on a small white horse, but, being mistaken for one of our own officers, was suffered to pass unmolested.

General Medows, having ordered four companies of the 36th regiment, under Captain Austin, who had commanded the leading company of the column, and Captain Oram's battalion, to be left for the defence of this post, directed that the troops should be formed again in their original order, and wheeled to the left, that he might move down as quickly as possible, to co-operate with Lord Cornwallis. The column being again in motion, the general directed one of his suite to go at the head of it, and gave him two troopers of his guard, that he might take the first opportunity of pushing on to acquaint his Lordship with what had been done, and to inform him that the column was coming down to his support.

The deserter, who had given himself up at the redoubt, undertook to be the guide into the enemy's camp and to the island. On recrossing the canal, at a bridge a little higher up, he mentioned that some houses seen on fire to the right, were Monsieur Vigie's quarters at Somarpett, by which he judged that post was abandoned; at all events, it did not appear to be in the proposed line of attack. The column soon after crossed a large ravine, and then ascended an eminence, on which the deserter said there was a redoubt, commanded by Syed Guffar, and a larger one to the right not quite finished, between it and the fort. The general sent orders to halt and close up after crossing the ravine, and came himself to the front.

At this time the firing every where had ceased, except a few cannon shot from the redoubt, which was some hundred yards in front of the column; it was consequently supposed that the two other columns were victorious or repulsed. Being now in possession of the enemy's principal redoubt in this quarter, which must probably oblige them to evacuate the other posts on the left of their position; and the loss sustained having been very considerable, it became an object of deliberation, whether it might be more advisable to storm these redoubts also, and get directly to the island; or, by leaving them to the right, avoid the farther delay which might be occasioned by this attack. The latter measure was adopted. The general resolved to get into the track by which Lord Cornwallis had marched, and to advance and support his Lordship in that direction. The column recrossed the hedge and canal; but finding it necessary, from the rice swamps, to make a larger circuit than was intended, it unfortunately missed the track of the centre column; and the general reached the Carighaut or Pagoda hill without receiving any intelligence of Lord Cornwallis. Two Sepoys were met, who gave a confused account of our troops having been repulsed from the island. Still there was no firing. The column was halted, and an officer dispatched with a few troopers to endeavour to gain intelligence. But on his return, without obtaining any information of the centre column, a heavy firing commenced in that part of the camp that lay between the fort and the Carighaut hill, upon which General Medows gave orders to countermarch his column, and was advancing to support the troops that appeared to be engaged, when the day broke; and he found it was unnecessary to proceed, as will appear in the account of the operations of the centre division.

Operations of the Centre Division, under the immediate Orders of Earl Cornwallis.—Second in Command, Lieutenant-Colonel Stuart.

The operations of this column and main body of the army, directed against the centre and head quarters of the enemy's camp, were, during the night, various and extensive.

The front division, after forcing through the enemy's line, had for its immediate object to pass into the island with the fugitives. The corps in the centre, employed first in clearing the right of the camp, had, for their ultimate object, to gain possession of the island; while the corps in the rear formed a reserve, under Lord Cornwallis, who took a position whence he might support the other parts of his column, and wait the co-operation of the columns on his right and left, commanded by General Medows and Lieutenant-Colonel Maxwell.

To give a clear idea of the centre attack, it will therefore be necessary to consider this column as subdivided into three parts, and to detail its operations under the heads of front, centre, and rear divisions.

Front Division.—The front division, under the command of the Honourable Lieutenant-Colonel Knox, consisted of six European flank companies, the 52d regiment, and 14th battalion of Bengal Sepoys, as more particularly detailed in the order of march.

In conformity to the spirit of the Commander in Chief's orders, Lieutenant-Colonel Knox gave directions to the captains commanding the leading companies, after passing the bound hedge and dispersing the enemy they might find immediately in their front, not to suffer themselves to be delayed in the camp, but to push, with the utmost expedition, to the great ford near the north east angle of the fort, and pass into the island. Each captain was to be considered responsible for his own company, as success depended upon the celerity, not the solidity of the movement of the leading troops.

The 52d regiment and the 14th Bengal battalion, were directed to follow the flank companies in regular order, and general directions were given to avoid firing as much as possible.

About eleven o'clock the head of the column forced thro' the bound hedge, under a very heavy, but ill directed fire from the guns of the Sultan's redoubt, and the field pieces stationed in the intervals of Tippoo's line. The fire of the musquetry was for some time very heavy, but also ill directed, and, on the column's advancing, the enemy giving way, the leading companies pushed to the river, passing the Sultan's tent, which appeared to have been abandoned with much precipitation.*

From the badness of the ground, which between that part of the camp and the river, was a tract of rice fields, from the nature of the orders given to each captain, and from the uncertain light and the tumult of a night attack, the advanced companies separated into two bodies.

* Many pikes, ornamented with plates of silver, belonging to the Sultan's sewary or state equipage, were seen scattered round the tent, in which, among other articles, was found a case of mathematical instruments of London make; which gives probability to the accounts we had received that the Sultan had turned his attention to the science of fortification, and that he had been his own engineer.

The first body that reached the river, consisted of the battalion company of the 52d regiment, which led the column, commanded by Captain Hamilton Brown, the grenadiers of the 52d, 71st, and 74th regiment, commanded by Captain Russell, the honourable Captain Lindsay, and Captain Wallace, and the light company of the 52d regiment, commanded by the honourable Captain Monson, who was the senior officer. They were conducted to the ford by two excellent harcarrahs, accompanied by Captain Allen and Lieut. Macleod. They crossed the river under the very walls of the fort without opposition; and had it not been found that the east gate of Seringapatam was shut, and the bridge drawn up, that night might have put an end to the war, as Capt. Lindsay pushed into the sortie (the entrance which leads through the glacis into the fort) in hopes of entering the gates with the fugitives.

This party, led by the harcarrahs, proceeded along the glacis through an extensive bazar, which stretched towards the south branch of the Cavery, destroying numbers of the enemy, who did not expect to meet our troops in that quarter, and dispersing several bodies, chiefly of horse, of which there was a large encampment on the island.

The troops then took post, part at a bridge over a nullah or canal, which runs nearly across the island, part at a redoubt that defended the Mysore or southern ford. The second body that reached the river, with Lt. Col. Knox, consisted of the light companies of the 71st and 74th regiments, commanded by Captains Robertson and Wood: they were directed by the fugitives to the same ford, which had been passed about five minutes before, by the first party.

The passage of the river was difficult from the number of the enemy pressing into the island: crowds of followers, tumbrels, bullocks, &c. had nearly choked up the ford. The enemy, however, intent only on their own safety, made no show of resistance, though many of them were killed with the bayonet in the water. Three or four guns were now fired from the fort, but the shot were not directed to the ford.*

This second body, on reaching the opposite bank, was joined by Captain Russell with part of the grenadiers of the 52d regiment, who, having understood that the operations were intended to be carried along the northern branch of the Cavery, had waited for the remaining part of the front division.

Instead of continuing along the glacis, Lieut. Colonel Knox turned immediately to the left, and proceeded to the Dowlat Baug, at the gate of which a Moorman, apparently of some consequence, was seized: Captain Robinson, aid de camp to the commander in chief, who had crossed the river with this division, spoke to the prisoner in Moors, and promised him security, if he would direct the party to the pettah of Shaher Ganjam; to this proposal he gladly assented. His assistance, however, was soon rendered unnecessary by the capture of two Frenchmen, who conducted the division to the western gate of the pettah.

* It is no incurious circumstance here to observe, what was afterwards learned from some French deserters, that, at the time of the firing of these guns, the Sultan was at the Mysore or southern gate of the fort, which he refused to enter: he was much enraged that the guns had opened without his orders, and sent immediately directions to cease firing, lest it might be imagined in his camp that the fort itself was attacked, and the panic among his troops in consequence become universal. To this order, wise as perhaps it was in its principle, may be attributed the little damage sustained by the troops, who crossed into the island, within reach of grape from the bastions of the fort.

In the march from the ford to the pettah, near a mile, numbers of the enemy were seen flying in different directions, but in no regular bodies. The gate, on that side, was found shut, but was soon forced open, as the troops stationed for the defence of the place had, on the first alarm, moved out to man the lines and batteries on the northern branch of the river.

The French prisoners were directed to conduct the party through the pettah to the gate which led to the batteries. This they did, but cautioned the officers to be on their guard, as a body of the enemy was generally posted at that gate: none however appeared: the guard house was deserted, and the gate open.

As this party did not consist of more than a hundred men, Lieut. Colonel Knox took post in the street, leading to the gate, expecting to be joined by others of the troops, which composed the front division. The grenadiers march was beat as a signal; but before any reinforcement arrived, a firing commenced from the lines and batteries on the river. This shewed that our troops had penetrated the right of the enemy's camp, and were possibly attempting to force their passage into the island.

Lieutenant-Colonel Knox, who had directed his march to that quarter of the island, with an intention to clear the batteries which commanded the ford opposite to the Pagoda hill, found that no time was now to be lost, and detached three parties under Captains Russell, Robertson, and Wood, to take the batteries in reverse, from which the firing was heard, and thereby facilitate the passage of the river to the troops engaged in the attempt; he remained himself at the gateway with about thirty men, either to support any of the parties, which might meet with a check, or to resist any attempt made by the enemy to recover possession of the pettah.

The enemy, compleatly surprised by the parties which moved down to the river; unable to judge of their numbers in the night; and strongly impressed with the terror of the bayonet in the hands of Europeans, deserted the lines and batteries, which were all open to the rear, and dispersed.

Some of the enemy fled for shelter to the gate of the pettah, where they were seized; and from one prisoner, Lieutenant-Colonel Knox received information of several Europeans being confined in a house at no great distance. A party was immediately sent, who released twenty-seven half-starved wretches in heavy irons: among them was Mr. Randal Cadman, a midshipman, taken ten years before by Suffrein, and by him delivered to Hyder. The remainder were private soldiers; some of whom had been taken by the Looties; others were deserters, but who had not, on that account, met with better treatment.

During this period, no attempt was made by the enemy to dislodge the party in the pettah. They had not yet recovered from their panic, and their attention was distracted by the bodies of our troops, that had taken post in different parts of the island, and with whose strength they could not possibly be acquainted.

The two parties under Capt. Monson and Lieutenant-Colonel Knox, which have been mentioned, were followed by the seven battalion companies of the 52d regiment, commanded by Captain Hunter, and soon after by three companies of the 14th Bengal battalion, commanded by Lieutenant White. The 52d regiment had marched through the camp in regular order, and reached the river soon after the last division of the flank companies had passed into the island. The principal ford not being perceived, they crossed the Cavery opposite to the Dowlat Baug, or Rajah's garden, which they entered, after forcing open the river gate.

Ignorant of the route taken by the flank companies, and from the information of two officers and some soldiers of that corps, who had separated from these companies and joined the 52d regiment, Captain Hunter did not believe that any troops had passed before him into the island. He therefore resolved to remain in the Dowlat Baug till the remainder of the column should arrive, or till circumstances should point out where his co-operation might be necessary to any other attack.

His position was soon discovered by the enemy, who collected in great numbers round the garden, and even brought some pieces of cannon to bear upon it from the fort, and from a redoubt on the bank of the river. Captain Hunter foreseeing that his post could not be tenable after day-light, as he would then be exposed to the fire of all the guns on the eastern face of the fort; engaged two serjeants, for a considerable reward, to repass the river, and give information to Lord Cornwallis of his determination to defend the garden, till near break of day, and then to leave it unless he was reinforced, or should receive fresh instructions from his Lordship. Lieut. Dowse of the pioneers, offered himself for this dangerous service, and accordingly crossed the river, but was soon forced to return into the garden, being driven back by a party of horse.

These troops had now remained two hours in the garden, and morning was drawing near, when a party of the enemy was perceived with two field pieces on the opposite bank of the river. Whether this party was retreating into the island, with two guns which they had saved from the general wreck, or whether they had an intention to open them and fire across the river upon our troops in the Dowlat Baug, could not be known. Their appearance decided Captain Hunter, who, quitting the garden, rushed with his corps into the river, and passed it under a heavy fire of cannon and musquetry, to attack them before they could have time to unlimber their guns, in which he succeeded, though with some loss. He then returned through the camp, and most opportunely joined Lord Cornwallis, with his reinforcement, and contributed essentially to his Lordship's safety, as will appear in the sequel of the operations of this column.

The 14th Bengal battalion unfortunately lost their commandant, Captain Archdeacon, who was killed near the bound hedge; and some confusion which arose in taking ground to the right, (a movement ordered with a view to get through the hedge at the same time with the 52d regiment), occasioned a break in this corps. Lieutenant White, with the leading grenadier company, and two other companies with the colours, penetrated the hedge, and, having charged the enemy in line with the 52d, continued to act with that corps during the night; but the other companies of this battalion, having misunderstood, or not heard the order given by Lieutenant White, unluckily separated from the three companies that have been mentioned; and instead of forming part of the front division, joined the other Bengal battalions of Major Russel's brigade, on their advancing to the hedge.

Centre Division.—Upon the 14th Bengal battalion's falling into disorder, Lord Cornwallis ordered Major Dalrymple to advance with the 71st regiment, which came forward immediately, and passed the bound hedge, followed by the remainder of the 14th, and two other Bengal battalions. Lieutenant-Colonel Stuart proceeded with these corps, which, separating from the corps in the rear, are considered as the centre division of the column. He moved to the left, as directed in the general orders for the attack, with a view to break the right wing of the enemy's army.

On approaching the Sultan's redoubt, a large body of horse opposed itself to the progress of the column; Major Dalrymple formed the 71st regiment, and gave them orders to fire one round, to load and shoulder. This order was executed with great steadiness; and, on the clearing up of the smoke occasioned by the volley, the horse were seen at a distance scattered over the field.

The regiment advanced to the storm of the Sultan's redoubt; but, on mounting the walls and entering the embrasures, they found it abandoned: it was immediately taken possession of, and Colonel Stuart ordered two companies of the 71st regiment, under the command of Captain Sibbald, two lieutenants, and a detachment of artillery, and a lieutenant, with fifty Sepoys, to be left in it for its defence: the colonel proceeded, and completed the defeat of Tippoo's right wing, the flank of which had been turned by Lieutenant-Colonel Maxwell, as will be seen in the detail of the operations of the left division.

The detachment of artillery, under Major Montague, besides the party furnished for the Sultan's redoubt, were actively employed in securing the field artillery in the enemy's camp. Instead of spiking the guns, he directed that they should be thrown off their carriages, and the wheels rolled different ways, by which means the guns taken were secured without being damaged, and the parts afterwards easily collected. Captain Ross, of the royal artillery, was wounded in assisting on this important service.

Rear Division.—The front and centre divisions of Lord Cornwallis's column having each advanced in the directions mentioned, his Lordship ordered the 74th regiment, commanded by Captain Dougald Campbell, and the 2d and 21st battalions of Coast Sepoys, commanded by Major Langley, to be formed near the Sultan's redoubt, where he waited in anxious expectation of General Medows's column from the right; but as there was no firing, which might have served to direct the general in his march, he had, as before observed, crossed the track on which the centre column advanced, and must have passed within a few hundred yards of the place, where Lord Cornwallis had taken post with his reserve.

About two hours before day-light, the seven companies of the 52d regiment, and the three companies of the 14th Bengal battalion, joined his Lordship. Their arrival was most fortunate, as scarcely had they time to replace their ammunition (their cartridges having been damaged in passing the river) when a large body of troops, part of Tippoo's centre and left, who had recovered from the panic occasioned by the first operations of the night, marched down and attacked him with much resolution. Animated by the presence, and under the immediate orders of the commander in chief, these four corps received the enemy with firmness, returned their fire, and, on their approaching nearer, charged them with their bayonets. They, however, renewed the attack repeatedly, and it was near day-light before they were finally repulsed. Lord Cornwallis then ordered his reserve to retire towards the Pagoda hill, that they might not be exposed to the fire of the fort at day-light, nor be surrounded by the enemy; and, on coming near the foot of the hill, he met General Medows, whose column was in motion to have supported his Lordship.

Operations of the Left Division, commanded by Lieutenant-Colonel Maxwell.

Lieutenant-Colonel Maxwell was destined to attack the Carighaut hill, on the right of Tippoo's fortified camp. It is immediately above the river, and terminates the range of hills along which the colonel had pursued the Sultan's troops, when he broke the corps on the left of his position on the 15th of May, 1791. After dislodging the enemy from this post, he was to descend the hill, and continue the attack in that quarter till he could force his way into the island.

The front division of this column, under Lieutenant-Colonel Baird, consisted of the flank companies of the 72d regiment, commanded by Captain Drummond, and Lieutenant James Stuart, and the 1st battalion of Madras Sepoys, commanded by Captain Archibald Brown.

The main body of this column, consisting of the battalion companies of the 72d regiment, and the 6th battalion of Madras Sepoys, commanded by Captain Macpherson, was, as detailed in the orders, led by Lieutenant-Colonel Maxwell. He was accompanied by his aids de camp, Captain Agnew, and Lieutenant Wallace; and also by Lieutenant Capper, of the Madras establishment, who, with great zeal, had served as a volunteer with the army during the two last campaigns, and attended Colonel Maxwell in this attack.

The Carrighaut hill, which is steep, and of great height, was defended by a double breast-work in front of a stone redoubt lately completed on its summit. Commanding one of the fords and the eastern part of the island, and protecting the right wing of the Sultan's camp, this post was of great consequence to his safety; and a considerable body of infantry, but without artillery, was stationed on it for its defence.

Colonel Maxwell ascended the hill at the time the rocketing commenced on the centre column; and so vigorous and well conducted was the attack, that this post, strong both by nature and art, made but a slight resistance, its late additional works being instantly scaled by the flank companies of the 72d regiment, by which corps it was stormed on the 15th of May.

The loss on our side was trifling in taking this important post, owing partly to the enemy being surprised, and to their commander, a sepadar, (an officer of the rank of brigadier) being mortally wounded in the assault.

A party being left in possession of this redoubt, the column proceeded to the hill on which is built the Carrighaut pagoda, and which may be called a shoulder of the great hill, by which it is entirely commanded.

The Pagoda hill was incapable of much defence, as the wall had been lately levelled by Tippoo, who relied on the works of the great hill, and who supposed, not without some reason, that the batteries of the island would also render a lodgment on the Pagoda hill, if not an impracticable, at least a dangerous attempt.

The column then moved down towards the enemy's camp, and was much galled by a corps, who had sheltered themselves behind the bank of the water-course, which winds round the bottom of the hill.

The troops had also to sustain the fire of the right of Tippoo's line, stationed within the bound hedge, and which was also defended by the Lockany river: the column, however, forced its way through every obstacle, and entered the enemy's camp, through which it proceeded till met by the 71st regiment and the centre of Lord Cornwallis's division. In descending the Pagoda hill to the Lockany river, Major Fraser of the 72d regiment, was severely wounded, and Captain Mackenzie, of the same regiment, killed.

An attempt was now made to pass the north branch of the Cavery: the depth of the water, the rocky bottom, and a heavy fire from the lines and batteries on the island, rendered the event doubtful. The 71st and 72d regiments lost many men in the river. At last Lieut. Colonel Baird reached the opposite bank, with Lieut. Sutherland, the adjutant of the 72d regiment, and about twenty men, followed by another party commanded by Major Petrie. The ammunition, unavoidably damaged in the river, which at that place was neck deep, left the troops without a cartridge fit for service; but the desperate decision of the bayonet was rendered unnecessary, as the fire suddenly ceased; the enemy being driven from their batteries at this critical period, by the parties of the flank companies, which Lieut. Colonel Knox had detached from the pettah on the island.

Lieut. Colonel Maxwell having discovered a more practicable part of the river a little to the left of where the first troops had crossed, passed into the island with the remainder of his column, followed soon after by the rest of the troops under Lieut. Colonel Stuart, who also joined Lieut. Colonel

Knox at the pettah, and took the command of the whole as senior officer.

In order to gain some knowledge of the situation of the pettah of Shaher Ganjam, Colonel Stuart, with a party of Sepoys, was making a circuit on the outside of the walls, a little before day-light: a straggling party of horse rode up, who had probably sheltered themselves during the night in the Laul Baug, or great garden; and at the same time, a body of Europeans was discovered marching across from the southern side of the island. The horse were soon dispersed, and the Europeans proved to be the leading companies of Lord Cornwallis's column, which had first entered the island. They had, under the orders of Capt. Monson, remained during the night, at the posts they had occupied, as already mentioned; but not finding themselves supported, they had drawn off before day-light, and were then on their way to join the troops, which they expected to find on the eastern extremity of the island.

The positions taken by those companies, as well as that taken by the 52d regiment, had this most essential advantage; they kept the enemy in check, and prevented them from detaching to reinforce their posts on the river, or to make a speedy effort to dislodge our troops in that quarter, which it was now too late to effect, as a force had got footing on the island, so considerable as effectually to secure every post which it might be thought necessary to occupy for the first operations of the siege.

Major Scott, deputy-adjutant-general to the Bengal troops, who had accompanied Lieut. Colonel Stuart, and Capt. Robinson, Lord Cornwallis's aid de camp, who had accompanied Lieut. Colonel Knox, now returned to his Lordship, to report the success of the centre and left divisions.

The operations of the several columns being detailed, it remains to state the general result of the attack. On collecting the information of the events of the night, it appeared that the centre division, commanded by Earl Cornwallis, and the left division, commanded by Lieut. Colonel Maxwell, had executed fully the parts allotted to them; and that the right division, commanded by General Medows, although unfortunate in the direction of their operations, had also their share in the dangers and fatigues of the night; and in taking the ead-gah redoubt, had gained a post of such consequence that the enemy could not possibly remain in force on the north side of the river, nor retain any position opposite to that face of the fort which might enable them to retard the siege. Every material object was attained, and the loss on our side, though considerable, was small in comparison with that of the enemy, and in proportion to the importance of the victory.

Lord Cornwallis had himself run no small risk: he was on horseback during the whole of the night, in the midst of the attack; and in the last onset of the enemy, had his left hand grazed by a musket shot. His Lordship was attended by Lieut. Colonel Ross, Majors Skelly, and Haldane, Captains Madan, Kyd, and Apsley; Mr. Cherry, Doctor Laird, and Lieut. Turner, with his Lordship's body guard; and by Lieutenant Colonels Malcolm and Richardson, and Major Smart, of the general staff. Lieut. Colonel Martin, who, though at an advanced age, and independant in his fortune, had come from the service of the Vizeer in Bengal to assist in this interesting war, also attended his Lordship, as did Mr. Kingscotte, commissary of provisions, who had been a volunteer on former occasions of danger.

Lieutenant Colonel Patrick Ross, chief engineer, Lieutenant Mackenzie his aid de camp, and some other officers of his corps, had likewise been with Lord Cornwallis, but joined the division under Lieutenant Colonel Stuart, and crossed with him into the island.

Lieutenant Colonel Malcolm, shot through the leg in the last attack made by the enemy, was severely wounded, but still on horseback; and was the only one of his Lordship's suite hurt during the night. Major Skelly was missing, but there was reason to hope, as fortunately proved to be the case, that having been sent with some orders, he had remained in the Sultan's redoubt.

CHAPTER IV.

Operations of the 7th of February—Position on the Island—Defence of the Sultan's Redoubt—Advanced Position of the Camp—Final Repulse of the Enemy on the Island.

ALTHOUGH the night was over, the battle was not at an end: the fort now opened on such of our troops as were within its reach, and the scattered remains of the enemy began to collect in different parties. They had still possession of the redoubts between the Sultan's and the mosque redoubt, and of several batteries and posts on the island, between the pettah and the fort.

Lord Cornwallis, on joining General Medows at the Pagoda hill, detached the remaining six companies of the 36th regiment, and the 3d battalion of the Bengal Sepoys, towards the Sultan's redoubt, to assist the troops that had been with his Lordship in making good their retreat, and sent two more battalions from that column to strengthen the escort with the baggage, which was now ordered to move from the former ground of encampment to a new position, with the left to the Pagoda hill, the better to support and defend our new possessions. His Lordship and the general then went to the hill, from which they could see every thing, leaving the rest of the general's column at the foot of it, to be in readiness to act as might be required. Observing that the troops, to whose support the 36th regiment and 3d battalion had been detached, were clear of the enemy's lines, his Lordship sent Lieutenant-Colonel Richardson and Captain Kyd, to recal those corps, and with orders for them to reinforce the island, where the enemy had begun to attack our troops.

Lieutenant-Colonel Stuart, on going into the island, had taken the command as senior officer. It being impossible during the night, to reconnoitre the situation of the pettah, the nature of the ground around it, and to ascertain the practicability of keeping up a communication between it and the Pagoda hill; the colonel judged it expedient to retire from thence, and took up a strong position across the island in front of the Laul Baug; his right covered the ford, which leads across from the island to the Pagoda hill, and between the pettah and the river, occupied lines and batteries which had been constructed as an additional defence to that part of the island.

Colonel Stuart had scarcely effected his change of position before a body of the enemy's infantry, a little after day-light, advanced under cover of old houses and walls, firing upon our troops, who were, however, sufficiently protected to prevent their being much annoyed in their new post. The enemy seemed emboldened by finding that their fire was returned but faintly; this was a measure of necessity, as most of the cartridges had been either expended during the operations of the night, or damaged in passing the river, which having been reported to Lord Cornwallis, he sent, not only a supply of ammunition, but also the reinforcement above-mentioned, upon which the enemy drew off.

Lieutenant-Colonel Maxwell, seeing that his services were no longer necessary in the island, and might be wanted elsewhere, joined Lord Cornwallis on the Pagoda hill.

The attack on our forces in the island was scarcely repulsed, when the attention of our commanders and the army was drawn to the Sultan's redoubt, upon which the enemy were keeping up a constant fire, and assembling around it from every quarter, chiefly under cover of some rocks, which were within musquet-shot. It had been shamefully lost without resistance, and they seemed determined to recover it at any expence.

The Sultan's redoubt was nearly of the same size and construction as that which had defended the left of Tippoo's position at the ead-gah or mosque, but with this essential difference to it's new possessors, that it was within reach of the guns of the fort; and the gorge, instead of being covered by any traverse, or outwork, was left open to the fort and the island, that, if taken, the fire from thence might render it untenable. The party put into it for its defence, commanded by Capt. Sibbald, consisted of his own and another company of the 71st regiment (the two about eighty men), two lieutenants, and fourteen men of the artillery, and a subaltern, with fifty Bengal Sepoys; in all one hundred and fifty.

Towards morning, while the enemy attacked Lord Cornwallis and his reserve, Major Skeily had been sent to the Sultan's redoubt, to bring such men to reinforce his Lordship as he might find in or about it, who did not belong to the detachment ordered for its defence. Several parties of the enemy being near, and firing upon the redoubt, the Major made his way to it with considerable difficulty, and had scarcely got into it, when they advanced to the attack; but, on receiving the fire of a party posted at the gorge, or entrance, they moved off.

Major Skelly finding no men in the redoubt, besides the party that was put into it for its defence, and some of the wounded who had been brought thither, determined to remain in this post, where his services were most likely to be of use. Among the wounded were Captain Hunter, and two lieutenants of the 52d, and the Hon. Captain Maitland, of the 72d regiment.

Day-light soon shewed, that to maintain this post would require every exertion of a vigorous defence; for it was not only exposed to the cannonade of the fort, but to the musquetry and assault of the enemy; who being collected in large bodies, prepared for the attack, as if emulous to retrieve part of their disgrace, by retaking their Sultan's redoubt, and regaining a post that might still be of infinite importance in retarding the siege. Our army, being kept at a distance by the guns of the fort, the small party in the redoubt were left to their fate, and to have all the honour of disputing this point with the remains of the enemy's forces.

The first object which appeared to require attention, was to endeavour to shut up the gorge of the redoubt, which was open towards the fort. This was attempted by throwing some broken doolies (litters) across it, and the carriage of a gun; which was no sooner perceived from the fort than they opened three guns on the gorge, and sent two field pieces to the rocks, which soon destroyed this slender barrier, and did much execution in the work. The enemy, on seeing the gorge clear, advanced to the assault, but were beat back with considerable loss, and retired to their station behind the rocks.

In this attack, which was made about ten o'clock, a most valuable officer, Lieutenant Buchan, of the Bengal artillery, and several men were killed in defending the entrance of the redoubt. Captain Sibbald, who had distinguished himself with great bravery, was soon after killed by a cannon shot; and Captain

Hunter, who, though wounded, was gallantly exerting himself, received a second wound, which, however, did not deprive his friends of his able services.

Major Skelly, who had assisted hitherto by his advice and personal exertions, took upon himself the command after the fall of Captain Sibbald. The enemy still annoyed them severely from the rocks, to which there were constantly coming fresh troops. The day was extremely sultry, and many of the wounded were dying for want of water, of which there was not a single drop in the place; and, in addition to these embarrasments, a quantity of powder blew up, by which Captain Maitland, already severely wounded, and several of the men, were much scorched. But the chief object of concern was the want of musquet ammunition. Major Skelly, when using every means in his power to husband the little that remained, was informed by one of the officers that he had observed two loaded bullocks in the ditch, which, he believed, to be of those appointed to each regiment for the purpose of carrying spare ammunition. The officer had judged right, the bullocks had wandered into the ditch of the redoubt in the night, and were more precious to the major and his party at this juncture, than if they had been loaded with the richest jewels in Tippoo's treasury.

The men had scarcely filled their cartridge boxes, when a body of cavalry (at least two thousand strong) were seen advancing to the redoubt, and, with so determined a countenance, that it would seem they intended to charge at once into the gorge. They halted, however, beyond the reach of musquet shot, when three or four hundred of them dismounted, drew their sabres, and made a most daring attempt to storm the redoubt. Fortunately its brave defenders were now prepared to receive them. Their fire brought down many; and the rest, getting into confusion, retired, while their friends behind the rocks redoubled their fire of cannon, musquetry, and rockets, to cover their retreat.

This happened at one o'clock in the afternoon, and about an hour after, the Sultan's redoubt had to sustain a third attack.

The troops that now advanced, headed by Europeans, were probably the remains of Lally's brigade, commanded by Monsieur Vigie. The major expected to find them more resolute than their Musselmen friends. They did not, however, deserve the opinion he had formed of them, for they advanced but a little way from the rocks, when two or three of the foremost falling, they stopped short, got into great disorder, and went off.

This was the last effort made by the enemy to recover the Sultan's redoubt; nor did its defenders wish for the honour of another attack. It had become a horrid scene of carnage; two officers and nineteen privates lay dead among their feet, and three officers and twenty-two privates, miserably wounded, were imploring assistance which it was not in their power to give. About four in the afternoon, the enemy's fire from behind the rocks slackened, and they soon after began to quit their post and retire to the island. Water was then brought from a ditch and pond near the redoubt, which afforded a most welcome refreshment to the wounded, and to the remaining part of the troops, who were nearly exhausted with want and fatigue.

Lord Cornwallis and General Medows, having on the Pagoda hill seen the gallant defence of the Sultan's redoubt, and that the enemy seemed to have every where given up the battle, went down to the new camp which was pitched about three o'clock, where his Lordship gave directions for the troops in the Sultan's and ead-gah redoubts, to be relieved in the evening, and for provisions to be sent to the troops on the island; while the general, as usual, inspected the position of the new encampment.

The troops on the island had remained undisturbed, so long as the enemy's attention and exertions were employed in attempting to retake the Sultan's redoubt; but about five o'clock in the afternoon two cushoons, (brigades) and a body of dismounted troopers, with a party of rocket boys, entered the pettah, drove out a number of our followers, who were dispersed through it in search of plunder, and pursued them through the gate, which led to our lines. They threw many rockets, and were advancing seemingly with great confidence.

Lieut. Colonel Stuart, on this appearance, ordered the 1st coast battalion, under Captain Archibald Brown, to drive back the enemy, who, upon the advance of the battalion, returned within the gate. Captain Brown pursued, but finding them in greater force than was expected, sent back for a reinforcement. The 71st regiment, under Major Dalrymple, now moved on to join the 1st battalion. These two corps drove the enemy before them, who, retiring from street to street, were at last forced to evacuate the pettah.

In this last affair Captain Brown and Lieut. Nicoll of the 1st battalion were wounded.

A prisoner, taken at the pettah, whose appearance denoted him to be of the better class, gave Colonel Stuart information, that Tippoo had convened his principal sirdars, and had exhorted them to make a bold effort to drive the English from the island, and to recover the tomb of Hyder: that the chiefs had thrown their turbans on the ground, and had sworn to succeed, or perish in the attempt. The attack, the prisoner said, was to be made in the night, and the march of the assailants was to be directed along the bank of the northern branch of the river, to turn the right flank of our line, and to cut off the communication with the camp.

This account, so circumstantial, seemed to deserve credit, and Colonel Stuart made his arrangements to repulse the expected attack.

Major Dalrymple, with the 71st regiment, and Captain Brown's battalion, was directed to keep possession of the pettah, and two field pieces were sent to strengthen their position.

Lieut. Colonel Knox had charge of the right wing, in which was posted the 72d regiment; Lieut. Colonel Baird was stationed on the left, with the six companies of the 36th regiment; and a proportionable number of sepoys were posted according to the space to be defended by each wing. Lieut. Colonel Stuart himself, with Major Petrie, took post in the centre in the rear of Shaher Ganjam, with a small body, as a reserve.

The regimental field pieces were posted in the most convenient stations, and the guns of the batteries were turned towards the fort. Small parties were also detached, as picquets, to the front, and Major Dalrymple was directed to seize the most favourable opportunity of sallying upon the flank or rear of the enemy, as they passed Shaher Ganjam to the attack of the lines.

Lieut. Colonel Stuart having reported this intelligence to

the commander in chief, he immediately ordered four field pieces into the island, which arrived in the course of the night; and Major Gowdie with his brigade, after furnishing the detail for the relief of the Sultan's and the ead-gah redoubts, was directed to take post at the foot of the Pagoda hill, to be in readiness to pass the ford into the island on the first alarm.

Every possible precaution having been taken to insure success, the troops lay upon their arms anxiously expecting the approach of the enemy; but the night passed in silence, and day broke without an alarm.

That an attack was intended, could not be doubted; but the repulse in the pettah had either slackened the ardour of the chiefs; or the soldiery, dispirited by the fatal events of the last twenty-four hours, could not be brought to second the zeal and enthusiasm of their commanders.

On the evening of the 7th of February, Earl Cornwallis was pleased to issue the following orders.

" The conduct and valor of the officers and soldiers of this " army, have often merited Lord Cornwallis's encomiums; but " the zeal and gallantry which were so successfully displayed " last night in the attack of the enemy's whole army, in a posi- " tion that had cost him so much time and labour to fortify, " can never be sufficiently praised; and his satisfaction on an " occasion, which promises to be attended with the most sub- " stantial advantages, has been greatly heightened by learning " from the commanding officers of divisions, that this meritorious " behaviour, was universal through all ranks, to a degree that has " rarely been equalled.

" Lord Cornwallis, therefore, requests that the army in general

" will accept of his most cordial thanks for the noble and " gallant manner in which they have executed the plan of the " attack. It covers themselves with honor, and will ever com- " mand his warmest sentiments of admiration."

CHAPTER V.

Consequences of the Victory—Return of Cannon taken—Of the killed, wounded, and missing, in the British Army, and some account of the Enemy's Loss.

THE fatigue and danger of the two preceding days were amply compensated on viewing the extent and importance of the acquisitions gained by that brilliant contest.

The Sultan, repeatedly foiled in his attempts to dislodge our troops from the island, and having found his broken army unable even to recover an open redoubt, judged it necessary to order the other redoubts between his own and the ead-gah redoubt to be abandoned during the last night; consequently every thing on the north side of the river was now quitted by his troops; and his capital, exposed to view, was clearly seen in all its extent from the redoubts and commanding ground, where his fortified camp had been intended to guard it from our approach.

On the island, which we divided with the enemy, we were also well established. The pettah, or town of Shaher Ganjam, full of good houses, and laid out in regular cross streets, surrounded by a strong mud wall, not only afforded excellent shelter for the troops stationed in it, but was also very defensible as an advanced post within about fifteen hundred yards of the outworks of the fort.

Nor were these all the advantages of the victory. The enemy, driven from the rich fields of pasture to which they had but a few days before removed their camp, the forage which they had so carefully preserved for themselves, afforded a seasonable relief for our horses and cattle. In the pettah, which was inexhaustible in fire-wood, our followers also collected considerable quantities of grain; and in a public store there was found a supply of gram (a kind of pulse) for the cavalry. Tippoo's noble garden (the Laul Baug), which occupies the eastern end of the island, shaded with walks of large cypress trees, and full of fruit trees of every description, promised ample means of forming materials for the siege, while the Sultan's new palace, and the square of Faquier's buildings round his father's tomb, would afford excellent accommodation, and make comfortable hospitals for the sick and wounded officers and soldiers of the army.

The enemy having thus quitted every post on the north side of the river, our camp was advanced as near to the bound hedge as the guns of the fort would permit, and picquets were sent into the redoubts, which, with other small parties in their front, completed a chain of posts that, connecting along the north and east faces of the fort, converted the enemy's fortified camp and works on the island into lines of countervallation to our army for the attack of his capital.

The proud city of Seringapatam, which we could scarcely discern from our first ground, was now in forty-eight hours strongly and closely invested on its two principal sides: the enemy's army broken and dispirited; ours in perfect order, and highly animated by their success.

Such were the consequences of the battle of the 6th and 7th of Feburary, 1792; an event that will ever be contemplated with admiration in the annals of the British transactions in India, not less from the signal advantages gained over an able and obstinate adversary, than from the consummate wisdom displayed in the plan of attack. Formed on the result of the experience acquired in the course of the war, it was the boldest and most masterly measure that the relative position and circumstances of the contending armies could suggest; and executed with a degree of vigour, which gave way to no resistance, and with a steadiness of discipline, which no temptation of plunder could allure; the only spoils secured were the arms, the standards, and the cannon of the enemy.

Return of Cannon taken from Tippoo Sultan in the Assault of his fortified Camp, and the Island of Seringapatam, on the 6th and 7th of February, 1792.

Quality	Calibre.								Total.
	4	18	12	9	6	4	3	2 & under	
Brass Guns - -	—	—	—	2	19	5	1	9	36
Iron Guns - -	2	5	3	17	11	6	—	—	44
Total	2	5	3	19	30	11	1	9	80

N.B. Most of the brass guns were taken in the lines, and belonged to the Sultan's field train; the iron guns were found in the redoubts in his camp, and in the batteries on the island.

The loss, on our side, as collected from the returns, was as follows :

Return of killed, wounded, and missing, in the Assault of Tippoo Sultan's fortified Camp, and Island of Seringapatam, on the 6th and 7th of February, 1792.

Divisions.	European Officers.				European N. Cd. Officers and Privates.				Native Officers and Privates.				Total, including Officers.			
	Killed	Wounded	Missing	Total	Killed	Wounded	Missing	Total	Killed	Wounded	Missing	Total	Killed	Wounded	Missing	Total
Right, Gen. Medows	4	7	—	11	6	41	—	47	17	17	3	37	27	65	3	95
Centre, Earl Cornwallis	4	14	—	18	37	105	20	162	26	123	13	162	67	242	33	342
Left, Lt.-Col. Maxwell	1	6	—	7	15	43	—	58	6	21	6	33	22	70	6	98
Total	9	27	—	36	58	189	20	267	49	161	22	232	116	377	42	535

List of Officers included in the above Return.

Right Division.

Engineers.—Lieut. Stuart, Bengal Establishment, killed.

36th Reg.—Lieut. Robertson of the 73d, doing duty in the 36th, and Ensign Smith, killed; Lieutenants Brownrigg, Robert Campbell, and John Campbell, wounded.

76th Reg.—Lieut. Jones, killed; Capt. Markham, Lieuts. Robertson, Philpot, and Shaw, wounded.

Centre Division.

Gen. Staff.—Earl Cornwallis, commander in chief, wounded; Lieut.-Col. Malcolm, adjutant-general, wounded.

Artillery.—Lieut. Buchan, Bengal establishment, killed; Capt. Ross, royal artillery, wounded.

Engineers.—Lieut. Hemming, Coast establishment, wounded.

52d Reg.—Lieut. Hutchinson, killed; Captains Hunter and Zouch; Lieuts. Irvine, Madden, and Rowan, wounded.

71st Reg.—Capt. Sibbald, and Lieut. Bayne, killed; Surgeon's-Mate Paley, wounded.

74th Reg.—Lieut. Farquhar, and Ensign Hamilton, wounded.

14th Bengal Batt.—Captain Archdeacon, killed.

2d Coast Batt.—Lieut. Martin, wounded.

Left Division.

72d Reg.—Captain Mackenzie, killed; Major Fraser, Hon. Capt. Maitland, Lieuts. Macpherson, and Ward, wounded.

1st. Coast Batt.—Capt. Brown, and Lieut. Nicoll, wounded.

The enemy's loss was more considerable at the ead-gah redoubt than at any other post or part of their lines. From the numbers of dead that lay wherever our troops had been on the ground of encampment, and on the island, and from the number of bodies floating in the river, it is supposed their killed did not amount to less than four thousand. But Tippoo's principal loss was in the vast desertion that took place in consequence of this overthrow. His Sepoys threw down their arms in great numbers, and, taking the advantage of the night, went off in every direction to the countries where they had been impressed, or enlisted: many came into our camp; and that continued to be the case during the siege. From their reports, it appeared, that, on a muster taken of the Sultan's army, some days after the battle, his killed, wounded, and missing, were found to amount to twenty thousand!

Fifty-seven of the foreigners in Tippoo's service, took advantage of the battle of the 6th and 7th of February, to quit his service and come over to our army. Among them were Monsieur Blevette, an old man, who was his chief artificer, or rather chief engineer, and Monsieur Lafolie, his French interpreter, both of whom had been long in his, and his father's service. Monsieur Heron, who was taken at Bangalore, and released on his parole, to enable him to bring away his family, also took this opportunity to fulfil his promises; several other people of some note were likewise of the number; some of them of the artificers sent to Tippoo from France, when his ambassadors returned in 1789.

Thirty of these foreigners, headed by Joseph Pedro, a Portuguese, who held the rank of captain in Tippoo's service, engaged immediately with the Mahrattas. Some requested to go to the French settlements in India, others to return to Europe; a few might, perhaps, be taken into our service, and the remainder have probably engaged in the Mahratta or Nizam's armies.

The remains of the Sultan's army, which had withdrawn in the course of the day and night of the 7th, were collected on the morning of the 8th; his infantry on the glacis, and within the outworks of the fort; his baggage and cavalry on the south side of the river towards Mysore. The croud in and about the fort was very great; but his army never again encamped in order, or made any formidable appearance.

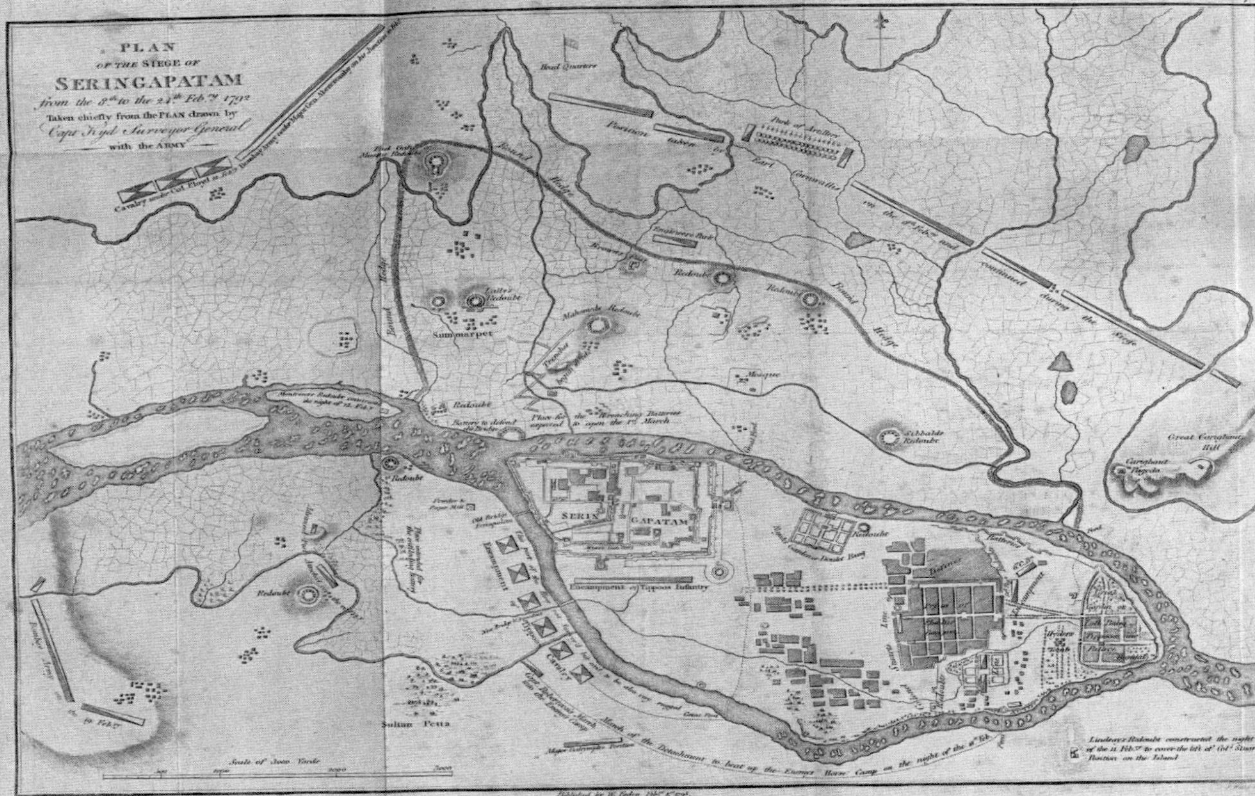

N.° 7
PLAN
OF THE SIEGE OF
SERINGAPATAM
from the 8th to the 24th Feb.y 1792
Taken chiefly from the PLAN drawn by
Capt. Kyd Surveyor General
with the ARMY
Head Quarters
Park of Artillery
Earl Cornwallis on the 6th Feb.y and continued during the Siege
Bound Hedge
Summarpet
Mahomeds Redoubt
Redoubt
Mosque
Sibbalds Redoubt
Great Carighaut Hill
Carighaut Pagoda
SERIN GAPATAM
Encampment of Tippoos Infantry
Sultan Petta
Scale of 3000 Yards
Published by W. Faden Feb.ry 1st 1793.

CHAPTER VI.

Arrangements and Preparations for the Siege—Description of the Island—Tippoo's Overtures towards a Negotiation for Peace.

EXTRACT OF GENERAL ORDERS.

9th February, 1792.

" LIEUTENANT-COLONEL STUART posted on the island, in com-" mand of the troops on duty there."

" Major Petrie to remain on the island, under the orders of " Lieutenant-Colonel Stuart."

" Major Dirom, (deputy-adjutant-general to the King's troops) " appointed to conduct the detail of the troops on the island."

The force stationed on the island, consisted of three European regiments, and seven battalions of Sepoys, and a captain's command of artillery: they were relieved by turns every second day; a field officer on duty also came down every morning from camp.

Major Petrie commanded the troops in the pettah, consisting of one regiment, and two battalions, as the advanced post on the island. The lines that reached from the pettah to the river, were commanded by the senior officer of the troops stationed on each side for their defence. Other posts were also established round the eastern part of the island; the whole, excepting the pettah, under the direction of the field officer of the day, who also received his instructions from Colonel Stuart.

Lieutenant-Colonel Ross, the chief engineer, with the officers of his corps, took up his station on the island, where a park was formed for the intrenching tools and implements of that department. A corps of one hundred European pioneers was formed under Lieutenant Macpherson, of the 76th regiment; Lieutenant Lennon, with half his corps of native pioneers, about two hundred, and Lieutenant Hind, of the Bengal artillery, with three hundred gun Lascars, were also employed under the engineer, in preparing materials for the siege. The pioneers and Lascars made gabions, as requiring most skill, while working parties were daily furnished from the corps on the island, to the amount of from one to three hundred Europeans, and from five hundred to a thousand Sepoys, to make facines and pickets.

The noble garden was devoted to destruction; and the trees, which had shaded their proud master, and contributed to his pleasures, were now to be formed into the means of protecting his enemies in subverting his empire.

The sick and wounded were also sent to the island. The upper part of the palace, and the bungulo, or summer-house, were allotted to the officers, while the lower part of the palace, and the square of Faquier's Chaultries round Hyder's tomb, were divided into hospitals for the different European corps. The sick and wounded of the native corps remained in camp.

The island of Seringapatam has, upon survey, appeared to be about four miles in length, by one mile and a half in breadth, across the middle part of it, where it is also highest, and from thence falls and narrows gradually towards the extremities. The west end of the island, on which the fort is built, slopes more, especially towards the north; the ground rising on the opposite side of the river, commands a distinct view of every part of the fort.

The fort and outworks occupy about a mile of the west end of the island, and the Laul Baug, or great garden, about the same portion of the east end.

The whole space between the fort and the Laul Baug, except a small inclosure, called the Dowlat Baug, or Rajah's garden, on the north bank near the fort, was filled, before the war, with houses, and formed an extensive suburb, of which the pettah of Shaher Ganjam is the only remaining part, the rest having been destroyed by Tippoo to make room for batteries to defend the island, and to form an esplanade to the fort.

This pettah, or town, of modern structure, built on the middle and highest part of the island, is about half a mile square, divided into regular cross streets, all wide, and shaded on each side by trees, and full of good houses. It is surrounded by a strong mud wall, and seemed to have been preserved for the accommodation of the Bazar people and merchants, and for the convenience of the troops stationed on that part of the island for its defence.

A little way to the eastward of the pettah, is the entrance into the great garden, or Laul Baug. It was laid out in regular shady walks of large cypress trees, and full of fruit trees, flowers, and vegetables of every description.

The island of Seringapatam is watered not only by a river,

but also by a canal cut from it, at a considerable distance, where its bed is higher than the island, and brought from thence in an aqueduct across the south branch opposite to that face of the fort. This stream, conducted in various canals to all the lower parts of the island on the south side, afforded great convenience to the inhabitants in that quarter, and was the means of keeping the gardens in constant beauty and abundance.

The fort, thus situated on the west end of the island, is distinguished by its white walls, regular outworks, magnificent buildings, and ancient Hindoo pagodas, contrasted with the more lofty and splendid monuments lately raised in honor of the Mahomedan faith. The Laul Baug, which occupies the east end of the island, possessing all the beauty and convenience of a country retirement, is dignified by the mausoleum of Hyder, and a superb new palace built by Tippoo. To these add the idea of an extensive suburb or town, which filled the middle space between the fort and the garden, full of wealthy, industrious inhabitants, and it will readily be allowed that this insulated metropolis must have been the richest, most convenient, and beautiful spot possessed in the present age by any native Prince in India.

The Sultan's proud mind could not be tranquil, in seeing his beautiful garden, and all his improvements, in the possession of his enemies, who were also preparing to deprive him of his last citadel, and all that remained of his power. His anger was expressed in a continual discharge of cannon from the fort, directed to the island, to the redoubts, and to every post, or party of ours within his reach. Some of his shot even ranged to the camp, and seemed aimed at head quarters; but the distance on every side was considerable, and his ineffectual cannonade rather served to proclaim the wrath of the sovereign, than to disturb or materially annoy his enemies.

Sensible that he could not extricate himself by such vain resistance, the Sultan began to meditate seriously on making overtures for peace, and as the first step to an accommodation, and the only means of having his proposals received, he determined to release Lieutenants Chalmers and Nash, the officers taken in Coimbettore, whom he had detained contrary to the terms of capitulation.

On the evening of the 8th of February, Tippoo sent for these officers. They found him sitting under the fly of a small tent, (the roof without the walls) pitched on the south glacis of the fort, apparently much dejected, very plainly dressed, and with only a few attendants. After giving them the welcome tidings of their intended release, he asked Lieut. Chalmers, who had commanded in Coimbettore, whether he was not related to Lord Cornwallis, and an officer of considerable rank in our army. On being answered in the negative, he then asked whether he should see his Lordship on going to camp; and being told he probably should have that honour, requested him to take charge of two letters on the subject of peace, which he said he had been very anxious to obtain ever since the commencement of the war, as it was not his intention to break with the English; and requested his assistance in effecting that important object. He further expressed his wish that Mr. Chalmers would return with the answer; told him their baggage should be sent after them; gave him a present of two shauls and five hundred rupees, and ordered horses and attendants to go with them to camp. Lieut. Chalmers told the Sultan, it might not be in his power to serve him, but (happy to get away upon any terms,) said he should not fail to execute his commands, and this morning waited on Lord Cornwallis with the letters.

Lieutenants Chalmers and Nash, although detained contrary to the rules of war, had not been ill-treated in their confinement. Their baggage and servants were allowed them; they had a good house in the fort, and were not put in irons in the cruel manner in which Tippoo used to treat his prisoners. It would seem he expected their detention would be of use to him in negotiating for peace, and with that view had refused to ratify the capitulation they had made with Cummer-ud-Deen Cawn, and had ordered him to bring them and the garrison prisoners to Seringapatam. The company of topasses, commanded by Lieut. Chalmers, and part of the sepoys, commanded by Lieut. Nash, had been released in the pettah by our troops in the night of the 6th of February, but the officers, confined in the fort, remained to be now sent as a peace-offering to Lord Cornwallis.

CHAPTER VII.

Attempt to cut off Lord Cornwallis—Junction of the Bombay Army—Plan of Attack, and Arrangements for opening the Trenches.

TIPPOO, while thus suing for peace, had determined to try another expedient of force, and by aiming a blow at our commander in chief, endeavour to extricate himself from all his difficulties.

On the 8th of February, in the forenoon, his cavalry were seen marching from their encampment down the south side of the Cavery. Some deserters said they were going to bring a convoy from Caveriporam, or to forage in that quarter; their march was reported from the island, but they went off without attracting much notice, or raising any suspicion of their destination being to our side of the river; they crossed at a ford, six miles below the island, near Arakery, probably on the evening of the 9th, and by day-break in the morning of the 10th, got round to the rear of our left wing undiscovered, and entered between our camp and that of the Nizam.

Our allies seldom had any picquets or out-posts of their own; and a party of horse, seen between our camp and theirs, was thought by our picquets and rear guards to belong to their army. The head quarters were in the rear of the right wing, and so near to the right flank of the line, that the party of the enemy on passing the park of artillery, which was posted between the wings, asked some of the camp followers, for the Burra Saib, or commander. Not suspecting them to be enemies, and supposing these horsemen wanted Colonel Duff, the commanding officer of artillery, they pointed to his tent. The horsemen then drew their swords, and galloped towards the tent, cutting some lascars and people as they advanced, till being fired upon by a party of Bombay sepoy drafts and recruits, encamped in the rear of the park, who had turned out with great alacrity, they were dispersed before they could do any further mischief. Some shot were afterwards fired at them from the park as they went off, but they got away across the hills again with very little loss.

This scheme was one of those daring projects that have been so frequently practised by the native powers against each other in effecting revolutions in the East: and had those assassins been conducted by a guide, or their judgment been equal to their spirit in the attempt, it is possible they might have effected their murderous purpose. But the Mahometan horsemen, in the service of the native powers in India, are generally intoxicated with bang, a plant mixed with their tobacco in smoking, or with opium, of which they take a large dose before they enter upon any dangerous enterprize; this inebriation renders their exertions so wild and disunited, that it is almost impossible for them ever to prove successful against a vigilant enemy.

This incursion, though soon over, created a general alarm in the army; the safety of Lord Cornwallis was not less the universal object of public than of private concern, and it was highly satisfactory to find that he had escaped from this second attempt made against his life during the war. His Lordship had always declined having any guard over his own tent, except a couple of native troopers from his body guard, but was now prevailed upon to have a captain's guard at night from one of the European regiments.

The operations of the Bombay army having been detailed in the first part of this Narrative until they ascended the Ghauts, and advanced to the enemy's frontier, it remains to give an account of their march from thence to join the main army, and assist in the siege of the capital.

General Abercromby, having sent back his sick to his hospitals at Poodicherrim, and leaving a detachment strongly posted at the foot of the Seidaseer Ghaut, proceeded on the 8th of February according to the orders he had received from Lord Cornwallis. On the 10th he passed Periapatam (then in ruins, and not repossessed as a post), and leaving the great road on his right, directed his march northward, and on the 11th crossed the Cavery, at Eratore, a good ford, about thirty miles above Seringapatam.

On the 13th, in crossing a small river which falls into the Cavery, a party of the enemy's horse, that had been sent to harass the march of this army, broke in among the baggage, and took some part of it, and infested them the whole of that day.

On the 14th, the enemy's horse were again hovering round the army, and the appearance of a much larger body soon occasioned a greater alarm in front; the line was halted, and formed for action, when Captain Dallas, who had been sent forward by Colonel Floyd, announced the glad tidings of his approach with our cavalry, a detachment of 4000 of the allied horse, and a battalion of sepoys. The whole encamped at Caniambaddy, and on the 16th General Abercromby joined Lord Cornwallis without further loss or interruption on the march.

Tippoo had meant a more serious opposition to this junction, and for that purpose had detached the whole of his cavalry on the evening of the 13th; they had crossed a few miles above the fort, and lay in wait till Colonel Floyd moved in the morning of the 14th. The detachment of allies, in despite of the colonel's orders, and the remonstrance of Major Scott, who was sent with them, remained loitering on the ground for some time after the Colonel had marched: the Sultan's horse seized the opportunity, and attacked them with great vigour. They stood their ground for some time, and then retreating towards Colonel Floyd, he returned to support them, and soon put the enemy to the rout.

The Bombay army, consisting of four European regiments, and seven battalions of sepoys, formed in three brigades, could still furnish about 2000 Europeans and 4000 native troops fit for duty, a very important reinforcement for the service of the siege.

This force having joined, and a considerable stock of materials (2,000 gabions, 10,000 fascines, and 20,000 pickets)* having been prepared, every thing was now in readiness to commence the attack of the place.

* Pickets are round pointed stakes, which are driven through the fascines, and fix them together. This word is also used for the out-posts or guards for the security of a camp.

The fort of Seringapatam, of a triangular figure, constructed on the west end of the island, is embraced by the branches of the river on its two longest sides; the third side, or base of the triangle towards the island, being the face most liable to attack, is covered by strong out-works, and is defended by two very broad and massy ramparts, the second at a considerable distance within the first, both having good flank defences, a deep ditch, with draw bridges, and every advantage of modern fortification.

The two other sides of the fort being protected by the river, it was intended that the main attack should have been carried on from the island, by making a lodgment in the Dowlet Baug, or Rajah's garden, and from thence to run regular approaches against the north east angle of the fort, which would also be subject to a powerful enfilade attack from batteries on the north bank of the river. Much time and many lives must probably have been lost in this attack; the undertaking was arduous; but there being no impediment, besides those of art to encounter, the superior power of our troops and artillery could not fail of success.

Lieut. Colonel Ross, the chief engineer, had in the mean time been able to reconnoitre the north face of the fort very closely, and from what he saw, and the information he received from Monsieur Blevette, the head artificer, and others of Tippoo's Europeans, who had come over to us, it was judged more adviseable to make the principal attack across the river against the north face of the fort. The curtain there was evidently very weak, and extending close along the bank of the river, left no room for outworks, and the flank defences were few and of little consequence.

The ditch, excavated from the rock, was dry, and said to be inconsiderable; and it appeared to be so from what could be observed in looking into it from the Pagoda hill. The stone glacis, which, built into the river, covers that face, was broken, or had been left incomplete, in two places, including several hundred yards of the curtain; the walls might therefore be breached to the bottom, and would probably fill up great part of the ditch. The fort built on the declivity of the island on the north was there exposed in its whole extent, and every shot fired from that quarter must take effect, while the slope the island has also to the west end, exposed that part of the fort to a very powerful enfilade attack from the ground by which it is commanded on the south side of the river, opposite to the south west face of the fort.

The north branch of the river, which would intervene between the main attack, and the fort, was the only objection. It seemed possible, by repairing an old dam or embankment, to throw the water entirely into the other branch; at all events the channel, though rugged, was not deep or impassible, and the embarassment of such an obstacle was in some measure compensated by the security it gave against sallies, and the cover it would afford in breaking ground at once within breaching distance of the fort. The fire, too, from that side, could not be very considerable, and there was a certainty of carrying on the approaches rapidly, and breaching the place with little loss. It might not be necessary to storm, and if it should, an extraordinary exertion must be made at the general assault.

Such were understood to be the principal reasons which determined Lord Cornwallis to relinquish the attack from the island against the east face, and adopt, in preference, that across the river against the north face of the fort.

Lieut. Colonel Stuart was informed by Lord Cornwallis of this determination; and that he must strengthen his position in the island by some additional works, as it would be necessary to withdraw part of the troops from thence to reinforce the camp and enable them to furnish a detail for the trenches.

Two European regiments, four battalions of Sepoys, and the captain's command of artillery already stationed in the island, composed the force that was to remain for its defence, and for keeping up the stock of materials for the siege. The Sultan's, now called Sibbald's redoubt, was also to be relieved from thence, which, and a new redoubt constructed on the south side of the river, were considered as out-posts from the island, and were also under the command of Colonel Stuart.

On the 18th of February, in the course of the day, a part of the materials prepared in the island, was carried over to the north side of the river, also the intrenching tools, as directed in the following orders, which were issued for opening the trenches that night.

GENERAL ORDERS.

Head Quarters, Camp before Seringapatam, 18*th February,* 1792.

"The following arrangement, ordered for conducting the
" duties of the line and the operations of the troops during the
" siege.

"An engineer's party to be established immediately near the "bound hedge, in the rear of Captain Brown's redoubt, as the "rendezvous of the corps of engineers, for the stores, &c. of that "department, and for the corps of European and native pioneers, "who, being placed under the orders of the chief engineer for "the period of the siege, are to be considered as a distinct detail "for working service, and regulated accordingly.

"The intrenching tools, lodged with the commissary, to be "removed to the engineer's park in charge of a conductor of "stores, who is to remain there, and, under the direction of the "chief engineer, regulate the delivery of the tools to working "parties, and see that, when no longer wanted, they are care- "fully returned into store.

"Lists of artificers in European corps, but particularly carpen- "ters, to be sent forthwith to the deputy-adjutant-general.

"The field officer for the island discontinued. The picquets (out-posts) from the line to report to Lieutenant-Colonel Maxwell, as usual.

"The following corps posted on the island under the command "of Lieutenant-Colonel Stuart, until farther orders.

"The 52d and 72d regiments, and the 13th and 14th Bengal, "and the 6th and 21st coast battalions.

"These corps to be accommodated with a few tents from "camp; but his Lordship recommends that the number only "indispensably necessary to cover the troops, may be taken from "the lines.

"The remainder of the troops on the island to return to camp "in the course of to-morrow morning.

"A detail, including a field officer, to be relieved daily, will "be ordered as a guard for the trenches, to be furnished from "camp, or the troops under Major-General Abercromby.

"The field officer for this duty to have authority over the "advanced redoubts, which, Sibbald's excepted, are to be oc-"cupied, until farther orders, by the 1st native battalion.

"The working parties for the trenches will be ordered in like "manner, and, so long as numerous details are required for "working service, a field officer will be appointed to command "them: he is to regulate, in communication with the engineers "on duty, the details required to work, and frequently visit "the different parties employed, but is not to interfere in the "command of the guard for the trenches; which is to be under "the orders of the field officer included in that detail.

"Lieutenant-Colonel Knox, to meet the chief engineer at four "o'clock, at the engineer's park, and make himself acquainted "with the situation of the out-posts, and receive from him the "commander in chief's directions regarding the manner in "which the troops are to be employed, and disposed of for the "protection of the working parties during the night.

"Working party to march at three this afternoon, to carry "fascines, ropes, and pickets, from the depot of materials near the "ford, to the engineer's park, the 7th Bengal and 2d coast batta-"lions. After one trip, this party to return to camp.

"Working party for the trenches, this evening, to be furnished "by the troops under Major-General Abercromby, and march "so as to arrive at the engineer's park by sun-set.

"Lord Cornwallis is convinced that the same military ardour, "which has been so often manifested by the officers and soldiers "of this army during the course of the present war, will call forth

" the most animated exertions of all ranks, upon an occasion which " may eventually bring the contest to a speedy and honourable " conclusion; and, he therefore, only thinks it necessary to de- " sire, that both officers and soldiers will recollect, that gallantry " under arms, forms but one part of the duty of a soldier during " a siege; and that the ultimate success cannot be secured, with- " out the most vigorous and unremitting exertions of industry " and labour.

" His Lordship will enter into all the details of the arrange- " ments for carrying on the siege; and he feels a peculiar satis- " faction, in possessing the advantage of General Medows's zeal " and activity, for assisting to superintend the execution of " them. He requests that the general will be pleased to visit the " works as often as he may judge it expedient; and that he will " give such orders upon the spot, as may from time to time, ap- " pear to him to be calculated for preserving our own troops, " and for rendering our fire more effectual against the enemy, " communicating the nature of such orders to his Lordship, as " soon as may be convenient for him: and in every other respect, " his Lordship relies with the utmost confidence upon the Ge- " neral, both for suggesting what may be useful for improving " any of the arrangements, and for executing with energy, what- " ever may be directed for promoting the success of the present " enterprize."

CHAPTER VIII.

Diversion made to draw the Attention of the Enemy to the South Side of the Fort, while the Trenches were opened on the North Side—Description of the Ground, and Work done during the Night—The Bombay Army crosses the River and invests the South-West Face of the Fort.

YESTERDAY, the 19th of February, in the afternoon, when the orders were issued for opening the trenches, Lord Cornwallis gave directions, at the same time, for a diversion to be made from the island, and to beat up the enemy's horse encampment on the south side of the river, in order to draw off their attention from the north side.

Major Dalrymple, with the 71st regiment, and the 13th battalion of Bengal Sepoys, commanded by Captain Macleod, without their field pieces, was ordered for this service, accompanied by Lieutenant Macleod, of the Intelligence Department, with some of Tippoo's deserters as guides. Lord Cornwallis had directed that these corps in particular, should be employed upon this service; and that Captain Robertson, of whose gallantry and good conduct he had repeated proofs, should be sent forward with a party consisting of four companies of the 71st regiment (of which his own light infantry company was to be one), and four companies of the 13th battalion, to beat up the enemy's camp. The detachment marched from the island, and crossed the south branch of the river about eight o'clock; and, making a detour of several miles, over rice swamps and broken ground, approached the enemy's camp before midnight.

The flank companies of the other corps in the island were ordered to the ford soon after, to be in readiness to cross and support this detachment, in case they should be pressed in their retreat.

Major Dalrymple, according to his instructions, halted when within about a mile of the enemy's camp, and sent forward the party which has been mentioned, under Captain Robertson, who gave strict orders to his men not to fire, nor to break their ranks, nor plunder. He entered the camp undiscovered, and, with the bayonet, killed above an hundred troopers, and double that number of horses, till, the alarm having become general, he then retired; first firing a few vollies to keep up the consternation he had raised with so much success.

The fort was now a blaze of fire on all sides, illuminated every where with blue lights, as if they expected a general assault. One shot was fired in the direction of the musquetry, and went through the ranks of the party; but the firing was not continued from the fort, the garrison fearing, no doubt, that they should do more hurt to their friends than to the enemy, and waiting, perhaps, to be in readiness for a closer attack.

Captain Robertson rejoined Major Dalrymple, without having lost a man on this important service; and, much to his own credit, and that of the discipline of his detachment, not a man had broken his rank to plunder, nor did they bring in even one horse, although many had broken loose or might have been easily cut from their pickets; nor was any article of value whatever, brought from the camp. Major Dalrymple returned with his detachment to the island, at four o'clock in the morning, and proceeded from thence to the head-quarters of the army, with the 71st regiment, which was one of the corps ordered up from the island, in consequence of the plan of attack being changed from thence to the north side of the fort.

Lieutenant-Colonel Ross, the chief engineer, and the Honourable Lieutenant-Colonel Knox, who was to command the guard for the trenches had, in the afternoon, visited the outposts, and looked at the general situation of the ground opposite to the north face of the fort, as directed in the general orders.

The large redoubt, called Mahomed's, which was constructed for the defence of the centre of the Sultan's camp, is nearly opposite to the middle of the fort on the north side, and at the distance of about 1500 yards from that face. The approaches were to connect with that redoubt; but in order to take full advantage of an attack so unexpected on that side, it was determined to break ground within breaching distance of the fort, and, having formed a sufficient parallel, to work back from thence to the redoubt.

A deep ravine, in which there is a stream of water on the right of the redoubt, turns along its front, and is branched into several nullas, or canals, for the cultivation of the rice fields between the redoubt and the river. One of these nullas, running nearly parallel to the north face of the fort, and being also at the distance wished, about 800 yards, was to be formed into a first parallel for the attack, to which the ravine or water-course itself formed an imperfect approach.

About 1000 yards to the right of the ground fixed upon for

the parallel, there was a square redoubt of the enemy's near the river, and a mosque with very strong walls, at nearly the same distance on the left, both convenient posts to be occupied by the guard for the trenches.

The troops for working, and for guarding the trenches, having assembled at the engineer's park as directed, marched down as soon as it was dark, to commence the interesting operations of the night.

The disposition of the guard for the trenches, or covering party, consisting of the 36th regiment, and two battalions of Sepoys, being the first arrangement, was made by Lieutenant-Colonel Knox, according to the plan fixed with the chief engineer, and was as follows:

Captain Wight, with the grenadiers, and a battalion company of the 36th regiment, accompanied by Lieutenant Mackenzie, aid de camp to the chief engineer, with a party of pioneers with gabions for closing the gorge of the work towards the fort, was sent to dislodge the enemy, and take possession of the redoubt on the right of the parallel: the light infantry company of the 36th regiment, under Captain Hart, and two companies of Sepoys, were to occupy the mosque to the left. Serjeants' parties were distributed along the front and flanks of the parallel, to prevent the possibility of surprize. A battalion of Sepoys was sent into the nulla intended for the parallel, and the remainder of the covering party lay upon their arms, on each side of the water-course in the rear of the parallel, under shelter of some banks near the burying-ground of Tippoo's Europeans, whose quarters had been at Somarpett.

The chief engineer having detailed the working parties under the different officers of his corps, proceeded to execute the parallel which he had marked out the preceding night. They worked undiscovered, and so ineffectual were the blue lights of the fort, that, when illuminated on all sides, in consequence of the diversion which was made from the island, they did not enable the garrison to see the people who were at work within 800 yards of the walls; nor can those lights be of any service to discover an enemy, unless in a very close attack, where they are generally of still more use to the assailants.

General Medows, accompanied by the officers of his suite, came down in the evening to the advanced redoubt, where he remained during the night, in readiness to give his orders in case any thing particular had occurred. In the morning he inspected the work that had been executed, and afterwards continued his daily visits to the trenches during the siege.

By day-light, the nulla was formed into a wide and extensive parallel, and a redoubt was constructed to cover its left flank, the right being protected by the ravine.

The party that had been sent to possess the redoubt near the river, having found it evacuated, and too open to be rendered tenable, in the course of the night rejoined Colonel Knox. In the morning the parties were withdrawn that had been posted in front, and on the flanks of the parallel during the night; but the party was continued in the mosque on the left, as it was thought strong enough to resist the cannon of the fort.

Day-light shewed the Sultan that the exertions of his enemy had been directed to a more material object than beating up his horse camp during the night; and that his attention had been successfully drawn off to a different quarter, during the most interesting operation of the siege. He opened every gun he could bring to bear upon the parallel, and upon the mosque, and sent parties of infantry across the river to harass our troops in flank, and to interrupt the work.

Tippoo, finding all his exertions from the fort would be ineffectual, in repelling the attack on that side, thought of employing another expedient in his defence, by turning off the water from the large canal, which, being cut from Caniambaddy for the cultivation of the grounds on the north side of the river, supplied the greatest part of our camp.

This measure, he knew, would distress our troops, and, by depriving the camp of a large stream of running water, soon render it unhealthy; and moreover, by increasing the quantity of water in the bed of the river, would add to the difficulty of our approach.

It is probable that the Bombay army, previously to their junction, prevented the Sultan from an earlier attempt to deprive us of this source of health and comfort, to which he was now urged by the opening of our trenches, and the commencement of the attack on that side of the fort.

The sudden deficiency of the water, soon indicated that the enemy had diverted the stream from the canal. The 14th battalion of coast sepoys, commanded by Captain Wahab, was immediately detached with a party of pioneers to dispossess the enemy, and endeavour to repair the damage. Tippoo's troops did not attempt to defend the position they had taken on the bank of the canal, which they had broke down in order to turn the stream into the bed of the river; and the embankment being very massy, the little they had been able to destroy was soon repaired, and the stream again confined to its former channel. But to prevent a repetition of such inconvenience, it was necessary to leave Captain Wahab stationed there with his battalion during the remainder of the siege.

The main attack having been commenced, the Bombay army was directed to cross the river this morning, to invest the south-west side of the capital, and prepare for the enfilade attack to be carried on against that face of the fort.

Lieut. Colonel Hartley's brigade was to have crossed on the afternoon of the 18th, and to have made the diversion afterwards ordered from the island, but the ford was so little known, and found to be so extremely difficult and rugged, that he could not have returned, or been supported so speedily as might be necessary. Orders were therefore sent to the Colonel to desist from the attempt, but to be in readiness to cross early the next morning,

Major Dow, with an advanced guard, consisting of two companies of Europeans, commanded by the Honourable Captain St. John, and the grenadier battalion of Sepoys, commanded by Captain Gore, having crossed at four in the morning, to possess the opposite bank, was followed at day-break by Lieutenant-Colonel Hartley, with the remainder of his brigade. It was necessary to unload the tumbrels; and it proved a work of time and labor to get them, and the guns, over this wide and rugged river.

General Abercromby crossed, himself, with this brigade, and on ascending the heights on the opposite side, saw a body of several thousand horse formed in his front, and to his left a line of infantry with guns drawing out from the fort, apparently to give him battle.

Major Stirling, who had been directed to follow down to the ford, with his brigade, saw also from his side of the river, that the enemy were advancing in force. He anticipated the general's wishes, by crossing instantly to his support, and by possessing the ground between him and the river, prevented the enemy from getting between the advanced brigade and the main body of the general's force.

It would seem that Tippoo did not suppose that our troops would find it possible to pass the river with guns at the place they had crossed, until he heard of their being actually on the south side; and from the alarm of the preceding night, it had probably required some time to collect and marshal his horse. Jealous of our getting a footing on that side of the river, and apparently more than ordinarily anxious to prevent our possessing a redoubt, and a tope, or grove, between the heights and the fort, he had come out in person at the head of his infantry.

On gaining the heights, and possessing a village upon them, Lieut. Colonel Hartley went down with the grenadier battalion to reconnoitre the redoubt. The enemy, thinking he was advancing to attack, withheld their fire till they saw him face about to return, upon which they gave him a discharge of musquetry, and opened their guns from the tope, which galled his party as they returned to the village.

The Sultan, secure in the tope under the guns of the fort, continued to cannonade and rocket our line on the heights, and sent a part of his infantry to attempt to recover the village, while his cavalry hovered round to support them, and be in readiness to take advantage of any confusion, in case our troops should be obliged to retreat. The infantry were soon beat off, and the Sultan finding his efforts ineffectual, slackened his fire towards night, and drew off to the fort, upon which Lieut. Colonel Hartley advanced again, and after a slight resistance of musquetry, took possession of the redoubt. The loss on our side, at the close of the day, was found to be inconsiderable, only a few men killed, but a good many wounded, though in general but slightly, chiefly by the rockets.

Colonel Balfour, with the 1st brigade of the Bombay army, having been directed to move down to cover the crossing of the other two brigades, on seeing them at length established, returned to his ground on the north side of the river, where he was posted with one regiment, and one battalion of his brigade, to keep up the communication, and assist in furnishing the details for the trenches.

General Abercromby's force, on the south side of the river, consisted of three regiments of Europeans, and six battalions of Sepoys. His camp, strongly situated on heights, was pitched just beyond gun-shot of the fort.

CHAPTER IX.

Progress of the Attack—Operations on the Island—Admission of Tippoo's Vakeels—His Action with the Bombay Army on the 22d of February.

ON the night of the 19th, some improvements were made to the parallel, and traverses begun which were to connect it with the large redoubt in the rear. On the 20th, and 21st, these traverses were finished, and an approach carried on to the line fixed for a second parallel, which was marked out the night of the 21st, 200 yards farther advanced than the first parallel, and within less than 600 yards of the fort. The bank of the river in front of this parallel being high and favourable for the batteries opposite to the breaks in the glacis, there seemed no doubt that a practicable breach might be made in both walls, without the necessity of a nearer approach.

So ineffectual was the enemy's fire from this side of the fort, that our loss in the trenches, from first breaking ground on the night of the 18th, till the morning of the 22d, did not exceed thirty men, killed and wounded.

Colonel Stuart had by this time strengthened his line of defence across the island, by reversing some of the enemy's redoubts, constructing others, and adding to the solidity of the breast-work by which they were connected. This line, including the pettah, was defended by 23 pieces of cannon, chiefly the iron guns taken on the island. The two largest, a 26 and a 24 pounder, were placed in a battery masked by the front wall of the pettah, to check any attack the enemy might make in that quarter, and to be ready to enfilade the fort, which might be done from thence with good effect, whenever the batteries were ready to open at the main attack.

The colonel, having completed those works, could employ a greater number of men for providing materials for the siege. The working parties from the several corps, vying with each other who should make the greatest quantity, and of the best quality, were become so expert in this military manufacture, that 1200 men produced daily 100 gabions, 2,000 fascines, and 3,000 pickets.

The Sultan's garden, which had flourished under the mild influence of a climate, where the seasons of spring, summer, and autumn, reign with uninterrupted and united power, became a melancholy spectacle, devoted to the necessities of military service; and appeared for the first time as if it had suffered the ravages of the severest winter. The fruit trees were stripped of their branches, while the lofty cypress trees, broken to the ground by the troops, to be formed into fascines, were rooted up by the followers to be consumed as fire-wood. The mausoleum, palace, and bungalo, at first scarcely discerned in the high surrounding shade, were now laid open to view. These the Sultan might regain, but, to speak in the eastern style, the remaining years of his ill-fated life, would be unequal to renew the beauties of his terrestrial paradise.

This devastation, unavoidable on the part of Tippoo's enemies, must have been a subject of the more poignant regret to himself, from seeing that the same precaution which led him to sacrifice his suburb to the improvement of his defence, and to cut down every tree and bush in the adjoining country that might afford materials for the siege, ought also to have dictated the necessity of destroying this extensive garden. Sensible of his error, and misjudged obstinacy, his people were now cutting down the Rajah's, or Dowlat Baug, with as much diligence as we were employed in felling his own garden; so that the island, which, shaded by large groves, was green and beautiful on our arrival, now presented a most wretched and barren appearance. The Sultan's fort and city, only remained in repair, amidst all the wrecks of his former grandeur.

Tippoo's affairs were now drawing to a crisis. He was seen frequently every day on the ramparts, particularly at the north face, viewing our approaches, and giving directions to his own troops. He was constantly bringing guns to the works and cavaliers on that side, and had a multitude of people at work thickening the inner rampart, filling up the embrasures to strengthen the parapet where he could not have guns, and repairing such as had been blown and damaged by the firing of his cannon. He had first employed his people in completing the glacis and strengthening the works on the east face of the fort towards the island; but, since the opening of our trenches on the north side, all his attention and exertions were turned to that quarter. He was at work day and night, making every preparation possible for a vigorous defence.

The horse camp, that was beat up on the south side of the river, on the night of the 18th, was since removed to Mysore.

Hundreds of the followers that belonged to it, deserted to us every night, and came in with their cattle and effects, which the post established from the island on the south side of the river, greatly facilitated. The desertion from the Sultan's Sepoys, continued also to be considerable, from the parties that were posted on the outworks of the fort at night, and even some of his horsemen were now treating with the Mahrattas and the Nizam's chiefs, and coming over to them with their dependants. The deserters reported that some baggage which we had seen removing to Mysore, was merely what belonged to his camp; that his family, the families of his chiefs, and all his own, and their riches, were in the fort; that the troops, as well as the other people in the place, were in a state of the greatest consternation; that the head men were even holding cabals among themselves; and that nothing kept them quiet but the assurances of peace.

Tippoo, having sent in the prisoners taken at Coimbettore, Lord Cornwallis again listened to his solicitations for peace, and agreed to receive vakeels with his proposals. Tents were pitched near the mosque redoubt, for the conference, where they were met by Sir John Kennaway and Mr. Cherry, on the part of his Lordship, and by vakeels from the Nizam's son, and from Hurry Punt, on their part. The first meeting was on the 15th, a second on the 16th, a third on the 19th, and a fourth on the 21st, after which the general talk was of peace. Still the operations of the siege went on with unabated ardour. The negotiations of the vakeels excited the exertions of the troops; and Tippoo's well known pride and obstinacy, gave hopes that he would yet hold out, till the loss of his fort was inevitable.

On the 22d of February, the Sultan unawed, either by the

formidable appearance without, or the uneasiness within the fort, had not yet brought his haughty mind to grant the concessions which he found he must make to the allies to obtain peace. Extremely straitened in the fort, and having reason to apprehend that he should also be soon blockaded on the south side, the only quarter open to him from the country; he was obliged to send off all the working people and persons he was not desirous to protect, to the fort of Mysore. Still, he probably imagined, that such immense armies could not much longer subsist in a desolated country before his capital, and he himself hourly expected Cummer-ud-Deen Cawn's detachment, with a convoy from the Biddenore country, which would both reinforce and supply his garrison.

The position of General Abercromby, opposite to the weakest part of the fort, seemed to give the Sultan particular uneasiness, and, finding the picquets of that army farther advanced this morning, he determined to endeavour to dislodge them, and protract the siege on that side.

The circular redoubt, or battery, in front of the general's camp, being within reach of the guns of the fort, was quitted on the morning of the 20th, and remained unoccupied either by him, or the enemy, till the night of the 21st, when Lord Cornwallis having directed that preparations should be made for commencing the enfilading attack against that face of the fort, the redoubt was again possessed, as well as a tope, or grove, in front between it and the fort.

Captain George Mackenzie, of the 75th regiment, was sent with a party consisting of two subalterns, Lieutenants Doherty and Filmer, and 80 men, to take post in the redoubt on the evening of the 21st, and with orders to take possession of the tope, or grove, next morning. He remained quiet in the redoubt during the night, and at day-break sent on Lieutenant Doherty, with 30 men, to the tope.

On seeing that the tope was possessed by the enemy, Captain Mackenzie followed immediately with the rest of his party; and finding Lieutenant Doherty engaged, charged the enemy, drove them out, and took post in front of it, opposite to the batteries of the fort.

The enemy kept up a distant scattered fire at the sentinels, and threw rockets into the tope till eight o'clock, when the guns of the fort opened upon it; and the enemy advanced both horse and foot, in considerable force, directing their march so as to leave the tope open to the fire of the fort, while the infantry took it in flank with their musquetry.

Two companies of the Bombay European regiment, under Captains Cameron and Macdonald, and two companies of the 10th battalion of Sepoys, were sent to reinforce Captain Mackenzie. The possession of the tope was long very hotly disputed on both sides, till our troops, having expended all their ammunition, it became necessary to retire. The enemy gained confidence with their apparent success, and, headed by a body of dismounted troopers, advanced shouting, and rushed in on all quarters, to the number of between two and three thousand. Captains Mackenzie and Cameron could not brook being pressed in this manner; they faced about, charged the enemy with their bayonets, and, driving them through the tope, pursued them till checked by the fire of the fort.

The enemy, reinforced by still greater numbers, advanced again, and commenced a heavy fire on this small party, who, being without ammunition, were again obliged to fall back. They retired slowly, and before the enemy could attempt another charge, were met by the 12th battalion of Sepoys, with a supply of musquet cartridges. Captain Oaks, who commanded this battalion, possessed the tope till Captains Mackenzie and Cameron, having replenished the cartouch-boxes of their party, returned and took post again in front of the tope, when the contest was renewed, and maintained with determined perseverance on both sides.

General Abercromby had also sent down Major Stirling, with the remainder of the European regiment, commanded by Major Lampard, and the 2d battalion commanded by Captain Burchall, to support this advanced post. These corps, forming to the right and left of the tope, opposed the enemy with a heavy and more equal fire, while Captain Hawkes, of the artillery, from his post in front of the village, directed his guns, and checked a body of horse, that threatened the right flank of the troops in action. The engagement continued in this manner for near an hour, when about four o'clock, the enemy slackened their fire, and, by sun-set, withdrew to the fort.

This action, which lasted the whole day, occasioned considerable uneasiness in the great camp, and on the island. The fire of cannon and musquetry, was, at times, extremely heavy, as if the whole of General Abercromby's force had been engaged; and, seeing troops occasionally retreating on both sides, it was impossible to judge of the event.

Lieut. Colonel Stuart, supposing the general might be attacked not only by Tippoo from the fort, but also on the other side, by Cummer-ud-Deen Cawn, who had been daily expected, ordered the flank companies of the corps on the island, to be assembled at the ford, and directed the officer who was sent in command of them, to be in readiness to cross over to reinforce the general, in case of his changing his position and moving to that quarter.

General Abercromby imagined, himself, that the attack on his advanced post might be probably a feint, and had formed the rest of his troops on the heights, expecting Cummer-ud-Deen in the rear. This precaution, which the general system of Tippoo's conduct rendered so necessary, prevented the general from detaching so freely to reinforce the tope, as he otherwise would have done; and the European regiment and 10th battalion, which he had first sent down to the support of the troops engaged, meeting bodies of horse advancing on their right, Major Stirling found it necessary to form, to oppose them, instead of proceeding directly to the tope, which was also the means of prolonging the engagement.

The loss on our side, was fifty-one Europeans, and fifty-three Sepoys; in all, 104 killed and wounded in this affair.

Lieutenants Douglas and Lloyd, of the Bombay regiment, Lieutenant Mears, of the 2d, Lieutenant Hunt, of the 10th, and Ensign Kennedy, of the 6th battalion, were among the wounded, but none of them mortally. The enemy's loss, from having greater numbers engaged, must have been much more considerable.

CHAPTER X.

Farther Progress of the Siege—Prospects of Success—Tippoo's Situation—His Submission to the Terms demanded, and Cessation of Hostilities.

DURING the nights of the 22d and 23d of February, the second parallel was completed, and the ground fixed upon for the breaching batteries, in a very advantageous situation on the bank of the river opposite to the two breaks in the glacis, and within about 500 yards of the fort.

On the night of the 23d, a detachment of three companies of Europeans, and seven companies of Sepoys, commanded by Captain Montresor, was sent to possess a small island in the river, and to construct a redoubt on it for its defence. That island, within 1500 yards of the north-west angle of the fort, became a necessary post, as commanding a good ford, and shortening the communication with the attack on the south-west face of the fort.

Major Sartorius, the chief engineer with the Bombay army, had already begun to prepare materials on the south side of the river; a work had been thrown up in front of the tope, to secure that post; and next evening a lodgment was to be made in a ravine farther advanced, beyond which the battery was to be erected, in a commanding situation, from which shot and shells might be thrown into every part of the fort.

At the main attack the enemy had possession of a battery

which had been constructed for the defence of the bridge on this branch of the river, which was thrown down on our approaching the capital the former year. They had no guns in that work, but merely a party of infantry that fired upon the trenches; but it was intended to drive them from it on the night of the 24th, which must have obliged them to quit entirely the north side of the river.

The two breaching batteries, one of twenty, the other of twelve guns, and the enfilading battery on the south-west side of at least ten pieces, would have been ready to open by the 1st of March. These, with the cross fire, which would also have been directed from the island and Sibbald's redoubt, together with the mortars and howitzers belonging to the train, would have brought a fire of fifty pieces of heavy ordnance against the place, and which might be joined by any number of smaller guns, that might be thought necessary to distract the attention of the enemy.

Colonel Duff had his park fully provided, and arranged for this expected interesting service. He had even prepared furnaces for heating shot, and would have opened his batteries with such a display of fire against this extensive fortress, crouded with houses built of combustible materials, as must, in all probability, have set it in flames in a few hours, and obliged the enemy to surrender without farther resistance. At all events, the superior fire of the breaching batteries could not fail of success.

The chief engineer, Lieutenant-Colonel Ross, was prepared, should it be necessary, to carry the approaches across the river; and if the siege should come to the last extremity, the storm was to be led by General Medows.

But supposing, in the eventful uncertainty of war, that every effort of skill and force should fail in the attack of the capital, thus covered by the rugged channel of a rapid river for its ditch, and defended by a brave and able prince, who had declared his determination to fall in the breach; supported too, by many resolute adherents and relations, who had also every thing dear to them in life at stake in its defence: admitting that the desperate valour of the defenders might prevail over the disciplined courage of the assailants, still the able arrangements of our commander in chief, seem to have gone beyond the power of fortune in ultimately securing his success.

The Mahratta army, commanded by Purseram Bhow, consisting of 20,000 horse, a body of several thousand infantry, and thirty pieces of cannon, and the brigade of Sepoys, commanded by Captain Little, was now daily expected; a force fully equal to invest the south side of the fort, and complete the blockade of the place.

Major Cuppage, from the Coimbettore country, with a brigade of 400 Europeans, and three battalions of Sepoys, with field artillery, having taken Damicotta and Sattimungulum, had ascended the Gudzelhatty Pass. Upon advancing he would also get possession of Ardinelly, and in the mean time, it would not be difficult to reduce Mysore, a new but unfinished fort, defended by only a few guns, which would give us a post of sufficient strength for a depot or magazine within six miles on the south side of the capital, when the country would be completely in our possession, and open to us on all sides.

Large supplies had been collected in the southern countries, both from Tritchinopoly and Palgautcherry, and were ready to be brought up the Gudzelhatty Pass. General Abercromby's communication was perfectly established, and supplies were coming forward constantly from the Malabar coast. Arrangements had been made for sending supplies to the Mahratta and Nizam's armies from their own countries, and in the grand army there had not been such abundance known since the beginning of the war. Lord Cornwallis had the grain merchants, or brinjarries, engaged in his service from all quarters, who had passports from him for 70,000 grain bullocks. Two large convoys had arrived from Bangalore, since the battle of the 6th and 7th of February; and others were coming forward with supplies of every sort in such quantities, that the Bombay army was furnished with arrack and other articles they wanted from the grand army; and the Mahratta and Nizam's armies were frequently supplied with grain.

The Sultan, having no army that could keep the field, and closely blockaded, and confined to one end of his small island, must soon be reduced to distress, while the allied armies, had all the resources of his and their own countries open to them from every part of the peninsula, no hope could remain to him that even the monsoon, of which the effects are partial, and only material from its swelling the river, would oblige his enemies to raise the siege.

Such was the state of the attack on Tippoo Sultan's capital, and such the prospect which the army had of acquiring riches and farther honour from its capture, when, on the morning of the 24th of February, orders were sent to the trenches to cease working, and forbear from farther hostilities.

The soldiers, dejected to a degree not to be described, could, with difficulty, be restrained from continuing their work. Still it was supposed there must be some mistake; and the men became irritated on finding that, after receiving those orders, the fire of cannon from the fort, and musquetry from the enemy's advanced parties was kept up more incessant than ever, and from every side of the fort where they could reach our troops. Brigade-Major Turing, and several men, were wounded.

This extraordinary conduct in the enemy, was supposed in camp, to arise from a mistake in the vakeels not having acquainted their master that hostilities must cease: but the Sultan could not be ignorant of the articles he had signed and sealed the preceding night; nor was this any great testimony of the sincerity of his wishes to terminate the war. Indeed, his conduct could bear no other construction, than an insolent and revengeful bravado, to fire upon us when he could with impunity, and to impose upon the ignorant part of his own subjects, and our allies, and leave their minds impressed with an idea, that his superior fire (for we had opened no guns upon the fort), and his resolute defence, had been the means of his obtaining peace.

At length, after repeated messages, the firing ceased from the fort at noon, and the cessation of arms then took place on both sides.

GENERAL ORDERS.

Camp before Seringapatam, 24th February, 1792.

" Lord Cornwallis has great pleasure in announcing to the
" army, that preliminaries of peace have been settled between
" the confederate powers and Tippoo Sultan, containing condi-

" tions highly honourable and advantageous to the Company and " the British nation; and, in consideration of the uncommon " valour and firmness that has been manifested by the officers " and soldiers of the King's and Company's troops, during the " whole course of the war, it is his Lordship's intention to take " upon himself to order a handsome gratuity to be distributed to " them, in the same proportions as prize-money, from the sum " that Tippoo has bound himself by one of the articles to pay to " the Company. It has been agreed, that from this day hostilities " shall cease on both sides; but the army is not only to retain its " present posts till further orders, but his Lordship likewise enjoins " in the strongest manner, that no troops, nor persons belonging " to Tippoo, shall be allowed to pass the picquets and approach " the encampment, without passports or permission regularly " notified; and in general, that the same vigilance and strict- " ness that has been customary during the war, shall be observed " by all officers and soldiers in the execution of every military " duty, until the troops shall arrive at the posts that shall be " allotted to them in the Company's territories. His Lordship " thinks it almost unnecessary to desire the army to advert, that " moderation in success, is no less expected from brave men than " gallantry in action; and he trusts that the officers and soldiers " in his army will not only be incapable of committing violence, " in any intercourse that may happen between them and Tippoo's " troops, but that they will even abstain from making use of any " kind of insulting expression towards an enemy now subdued " and humbled."

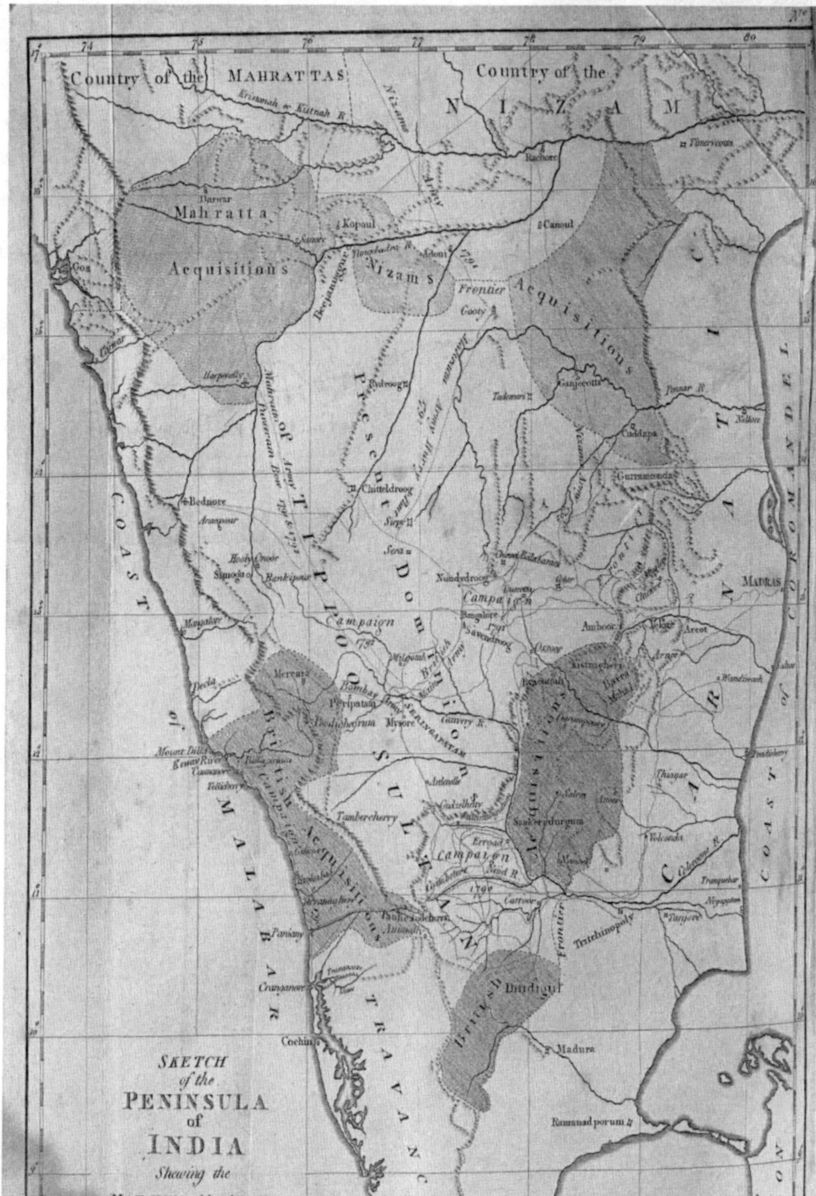

Published by W. Faden Feb. 1st 1798.

PART THIRD.

TREATIES OF PEACE, AND REVIEW OF THE CONSEQUENCES OF THE WAR.

CHAPTER I.

Preliminary Articles of Peace—Arrival of the Hostages—Their Reception, and some Account of Tippoo's Sons.

" PRELIMINARY articles of a treaty of peace concluded between " the allied armies and Tippoo Sultan."

ARTICLE I.

" One half of the dominions of which Tippoo Sultan was in " possession before the war, to be ceded to the allies from the " countries adjacent, according to their situation."

ARTICLE II.

" Three crores and thirty lacs of rupees, to be paid by Tippoo Sultan, either in gold mohurs, pagodas, or bullion."

" 1st. One crore and sixty-five lacs, to be paid immediately."

" 2d. One crore and sixty-five lacs, to be paid in three payments, not exceeding four months each."

ARTICLE III.

" All prisoners of the four powers, from the time of Hyder Ally, to be unequivocally restored."

ARTICLE IV.

" Two of Tippoo Sultan's three eldest sons to be given as hostages for a due performance of the treaty."

ARTICLE V.

" When they shall arrive in camp, with the articles of this treaty, under the seal of the Sultan, a counterpart shall be sent from the three powers. Hostilities shall cease, and terms of a treaty of alliance and perpetual friendship shall be agreed upon."

These were the terms, which, after different conferences with the vakeels, were dictated by Earl Cornwallis to Tippoo Sultan, and to which he found it necessary to submit. They were sent to him on the 22d, and returned by him, signed and sealed, the night of the 23d of February.

The allies, Hurry Punt on the part of the Mahrattas, and the Nizam's son, Secunder Jaw, and his minister Azeem-ul-Omrah, on the part of the Nizam, are said to have conducted themselves with the greatest moderation and propriety in the negotiation, and on every occasion on which they had been consulted during the war. And such was the ascendancy gained by a plain and upright conduct in all public transactions, by condescension in all points of form and religious prejudice, and by firmness in all the material operations in the field, that they professed the most perfect confidence in Lord Cornwallis, and declared their willingness to proceed with the siege, or readiness to agree to any terms of peace his Lordship should think fit to conclude with the Sultan.

Tippoo is said to have been prevailed upon with infinite difficulty to subscribe to the terms of peace; and now that all was settled, the uneasiness in the seraglio became extreme in parting with the boys, who were to be sent out as hostages. The Sultan was again entreated to request they might be allowed to remain another day, in order to make suitable preparations for their departure, and Lord Cornwallis, who had dispensed with their coming at the time the treaty was sent, had again the goodness to grant his request.

The vakeels had been instructed to acquaint Tippoo that his Lordship would wait upon the Princes as soon as they came to their tents; and besides the guards and attendants, about 200, allowed to be sent with them, that his Lordship would appoint a careful officer, with a battalion of Sepoys, for their protection. The Sultan sent in answer, "that he was fully sensible of his "Lordship's goodness; that he could not agree to his being at the "trouble to go first to wait on his sons; and having the most "perfect reliance on his honour, it was his own particular desire "and request, that he would be pleased to allow them to be "brought at once to his tent, and delivered into his own "hands."

On the 26th about noon, the Princes left the fort, which appeared to be manned as they went out, and every where crouded with people, who, from curiosity or affection, had come to see them depart. The Sultan himself, was on the rampart above the gateway. They were saluted by the fort on leaving it, and with twenty-one guns from the park as they approached our camp, where the part of the line they passed, was turned out to receive them. The vakeels conducted them to the tents which had been sent from the fort for their accommodation, and pitched near the mosque redoubt, where they were met by Sir John Kennaway, the Mahratta and Nizam's vakeels, and from thence accompanied by them to head quarters.

The Princes were each mounted on an elephant richly caparisoned, and seated in a silver howder, and were attended by their father's vakeels, and the persons already mentioned, also on elephants. The procession was led by several camel harcarras, and seven standard-bearers, carrying small green flags suspended from rockets, followed by one hundred pikemen, with spears inlaid with silver. Their guard of two hundred Sepoys, and a party of horse, brought up the rear. In this order they approached head quarters, where the battalion of Bengal Sepoys, commanded by Captain Welch, appointed for their guard, formed a street to receive them.

Lord Cornwallis, attended by his staff, and some of the principal officers of the army, met the Princes at the door of his large tent as they dismounted from the elephants; and, after embracing them, led them in, one in each hand, to the tent; the eldest, Abdul Kalick, was about ten, the youngest, Mooza-ud-Deen, about eight years of age. When they were seated on each side of Lord Cornwallis, Gullam Ally, the head vakeel, addressed his Lordship as follows. "These children were this "morning the sons of the Sultan my master; their situation is "now changed, and they must look up to your Lordship as "their father."

Lord Cornwallis, who had received the boys as if they had been his own sons, anxiously assured the vakeel and the young Princes themselves, that every attention possible would be shewn to them, and the greatest care taken of their persons. Their little faces brightened up; the scene became highly interesting; and not only their attendants, but all the spectators were delighted to see that any fears they might have harboured were removed, and that they would soon be reconciled to their change of situation, and to their new friends.

The Princes were dressed in long white muslin gowns, and red turbans. They had several rows of large pearls round their necks, from which was suspended an ornament consisting of a ruby and an emerald of considerable size, surrounded by large brilliants; and in their turbans, each had a sprig of rich pearls. Bred up from their infancy with infinite care, and instructed in their manners to imitate the reserve and politeness of age, it astonished all present to see the correctness and propriety of their conduct. The eldest boy, rather dark in his colour, with thick lips, a small flattish nose, and a long thoughtful countenance, was less admired than the youngest, who is remarkably fair, with regular features, a small round face, large full eyes, and a more animated appearance. Placed too, on the right hand of Lord Cornwallis, he was said to be the favourite son, and the Sultan's intended heir. His mother (a sister of Burham-ud-Deen's, who was killed at Sattimungulum), a beautiful delicate, woman, had died of fright and apprehension, a few days after the attack of the lines. This melancholy event made the situation of the youngest boy doubly interesting, and, with the other circumstances, occasioned his attracting by much the most notice. After some conversation, his Lordship presented a handsome gold watch to each of the Princes, with which they seemed much pleased. Beetle-nut and otter of roses, according to the eastern custom, being then distributed, he led them back to their elephants, embraced them again, and they returned, escorted by their suite and the battalion, to their tents.

Next day, the 27th, Lord Cornwallis, attended as yesterday, went to pay the Princes a visit at their tents, pitched near the mosque redoubt, within the green canaut or wall, used by the Sultan in the field, of which we had so often traced the marks during the war.

The canaut of canvas, scollopped at top, was painted of a beautiful sea-green colour, with rich ornamented borders, and formed an elegant inclosure for the tents. It was thrown open to the front, and within it the pikemen, Sepoys, &c. of the Princes' guard formed a street to a tent, whence they came out and met Lord Cornwallis. After embracing them, he led them, one in each hand, into the tent, where chairs were placed for his Lordship, themselves, and his suite. Sir John Kennaway, the Mahratta and the Nizam's vakeels, also attended the conference.

The eldest boy, now seated on his Lordship's right hand, appeared less serious than yesterday; and when he spoke, was not only graceful in his manner, but had a most affable, animated appearance. The youngest, however, appeared to be the favourite with the vakeels; and, at the desire of Gullam Ally, repeated, or rather recited some verses in Arabic, which he had learned by heart from the Koran, and afterwards some verses in Persian, which he did with great ease and confidence, and shewed he had made great progress in his education.

Each of the Princes presented his Lordship with a fine Persian sword, and in return he gave the eldest a fuzee, and the youngest a pair of pistols, of very fine and curious workmanship. Some jewels, shawls, and rich presents were then offered to his Lordship as matter of form; after which, beetle-nut and otter of roses being distributed, the Princes conducted his Lordship without the tent, when he embraced them and took his leave.

The tent in which the Princes received Lord Cornwallis, was lined with fine chintz, and the floor covered with white cloth. The attendants sprinkled rose water during the audience; and there was a degree of state, order, and magnificence in every thing, much superior to what had been seen amongst our allies. The guard of Sepoys drawn up without, was clothed in uniform, and not only regularly and well armed, but, compared to the rabble of infantry in the service of the other native powers, appeared well disciplined and in high order.

From what passed this day, and the lead taken by the eldest son, it seemed uncertain which of them might be intended for Tippoo's heir. Perhaps, and most probably neither; for Hyder Saib, about twenty years of age, has always been said to be Tippoo's eldest son; had been educated accordingly, and had accompanied his father constantly during the war, till lately, when he was sent on a separate command, and distinguished himself very eminently in the relief of Gurramconda. The vakeels, however, asserted that he was not a legitimate son, nor in favour with Tippoo, from being of an unpromising disposition; but there is reason to suspect that they were directed to make this sacrifice of truth to policy, in order to prevent the demand of Hyder Saib as one of the hostages, which, to a prince at his time of life, must have been extremely disagreeable; though the others, from their early age, would feel less in that situation, and would not suffer essentially by removal from their father's care.

Hyder Saib is, from all accounts, a most promising youth, and should he be destined to succeed to the kingdom of Mysore, it may be hoped that the misfortunes which the inordinate ambition of his father has brought upon their family, will lead him to recur to the prudence of his grandfather; and that his reign, as well as the remainder of Tippoo's life, will be employed rather to preserve and improve what remains, than to attempt to recover the half which they have lost of the extensive dominions so lately acquired by the wisdom and valour of old Hyder.

CHAPTER II.

Adjustment of the Definitive Treaty—Difficulties with respect to the Country of the Coorga Rajah, and the Exchange of the Money to be paid by Tippoo—Preparations for the Recommencement of Hostilities—The Sultan's final Submission, and the Delivery of the Definitive Treaty by the Princes.

On the morning of the 28th of February, a royal salute was fired from the fort, said to announce the Sultan's satisfaction on hearing of the reception and treatment his two sons had met with from Lord Cornwallis, and seemed an additional testimony of his sincerity in wishing to ratify the terms of peace.

Sir John Kennaway, Tippoo's vakeels, and the vakeels of the allies, now met every day for the purpose of adjusting the definitive treaty. Mr. Hoare, paymaster of the army, and the shroffs of the allies, also attended to receive the money. The captured guns were brought up from the island, and from the redoubts, and every preparation was making to be in readiness to withdraw from the capital.

There being now full leisure and opportunity to view this celebrated metropolis on the sides invested by our army, every thing farther that could be discovered, corroborated the eligibility of the quarter fixed upon for the attack. The Sultan found himself hemmed in so closely, that he was under the necessity of requesting that the Bombay army might withdraw a few miles to prevent interference between their followers and his on that side of the river. That army was in consequence directed to fall back about six miles to the heights opposite to Caniambaddy, a measure that became desirable also for their own convenience.

On the north side of the river, it was necessary to keep possession of the trenches, in front of which there was a line of centinels on our side, within less than six hundred yards of the fort. The enemy, in possession of the work which had been constructed for the defence of the bridge on that side, were entitled to have centinels between ours and the river; and they were planted opposite to ours, at the distance of ten or twenty yards. The Sepoys on both sides were ordered not to speak; but using the same language, being frequently of the same cast, and differing only in masters, they would sometimes transgress their orders, which generally began from our side; perhaps, as an intended civility, from the victor to his vanquished enemy. One of our Sepoys, after repeatedly inviting his sullen adversary to converse, was answered, "It is my orders not to speak to you; "and I am, besides, not inclined to talk to people who come like "thieves in the night, and attack their enemy when unprepared "for their defence!"

Many inquiries were made at this time, respecting the fate of the few officers who had fallen into the hands of the enemy during the war, particularly respecting Mr. Home, surgeon of the 36th regiment, a man universally respected, who had been taken by a party of horse in returning from visiting his hospital in Bangalore, in September last. Accounts had been received, both in the main army, and in the Bombay army, of his being in Seringapatam, and we had great hopes of his immediate release; but from circumstances mentioned by Tippoo's deserters, of such a person having been sent down to the bank of the river and put to death, and the vakeels asserting that they knew nothing of Mr. Home, there was but too much reason to fear that such might have been his unhappy fate. They said, the only prisoners that were in Seringapatam, had already been sent, and the others, if there were any, must be in the hill forts, and would be ordered without delay. The prisoners they alluded to, were Mr. Peacocke, and a boat's crew of the Dublin Indiaman, that had been taken at Mangalore. The assertion of the vakeels, that there were no other prisoners, must have been false, as several soldiers were seen by Lieutenant Chalmers in Seringapatam, that were taken in the night of the 6th of February, and ought to have been sent back, unless, what may be too probable, Tippoo had given orders to put them also to death. The people belonging to the Dublin being in a different line, might fortunately not have been such immediate objects of vengeance.

This system of cruelty, which continued to brand the conduct of Tippoo's government, was exemplified in another instance: ten of the followers of the Bombay troops were taken the day that army fell back to Caniambaddy, and now came into camp, each mutilated of a hand. They said a chubdar, with a silver stick, one of the Sultan's messengers of justice, had taken them from the place where they were confined, to the public Bazar, where their hands were cut off, after which they were dismissed. They were shewn to the vakeels, who, after inquiring, said they were caught plundering, but had been punished without the Sultan's knowledge. The vakeels gave the same answer, on being asked with respect to the treatment of our prisoners, and said that the Sultan had never authorised any such severity, and could not inquire into all the details of his government.

While the arrangements for quitting the capital were proceeding with perfect reliance on the sincerity of the Sultan, it was observed that his people still continued at work in the fort, contrary to the rules of an armistice and the custom of war.

On receiving a remonstrance against this unwarrantable conduct, Tippoo is said to have replied to Lord Cornwallis with a degree of insolent effrontery and ostentatious submission, that affords a strong additional trait of his character, "That his Lord-"ship must have been misinformed; but for his satisfaction, if "he desired it, he would throw down one of the bastions that he "might see into the fort."

The Sultan's vakeels seemed as studious to procrastinate the arrangement of the treaty, as their master was active in carrying on his preparations for a further defence.

The business had proceeded slowly the first week, and there was now a stop in sending out the remainder of the money from the fort. The vakeels pretended that the revenue accounts of many of the provinces were lost, and attempted to give in statements over-rating the provinces that would be claimed, and under-rating those that would remain in the possession of the Sultan. They also valued the Sultan's specie or coins, at an exorbitant rate, and declining to abide even by the standard fixed in his own public regulations, asserted, that the rates there stated, were only those at which money was received into the treasury, but when issued, that it was always paid at a higher exchange.

Although such might be the practice under the Sultan's arbitrary government, where his pagodas and gold coins are declared worth a certain number of rupees and annas (silver coins) at his pleasure, and the month, generally reckoned at forty-five days in the payments to his troops and public servants; yet this system of economy, so well calculated to lessen the disbursements of his treasury, was not so readily admitted in a payment to be made to his enemies, who, now masters, insisted on having his gold at the rate he exacted it from his own subjects. The value of the countries, and the value of the money, were both in dispute; the confederates had above a crore of rupees (a million sterling) of his money, and his two sons in their possession; he had gained a fortnight, and, notwithstanding his violent protestations, had continued constantly at work day and night, strengthening the north face of the fort, and bringing every gun he could to the works on that side. Cummer-ud-Deen Cawn had joined him with his detachment and a convoy from Bidenore, and the Sultan seemed determined to settle the definitive treaty in his own way, or risk the consequences.

During this time, the Mahratta and Nizam's vakeels having produced papers, which, they contended, were accurate accounts of the revenues of Tippoo's countries, in which, perhaps, they did not fail to depreciate the value of the provinces they demanded; the Sultan's vakeels were under the necessity of producing more authentic documents. A schedule was at length brought forward, and admitted as a just statement, by which it appeared that the whole amounted annually to two crores and thirty-seven lacs of rupees; and from that list, countries were selected to half the amount, in which were included the strong and extensive district of the Coorga Rajah, stated at a low tribute, which had been lately fixed with that prince.

By this arrangement, the three confederate powers would each acquire an accession of territory equal to thirty-nine and a half lacs of rupees, about four hundred and thirty thousand pounds sterling a year,* defended by strong posts, that would also strengthen their respective frontiers; and the English, in particular, would have the satisfaction of securing the Coorga Rajah's possessions to him, and supporting him as an independent prince, in a strong frontier post, against Tippoo; while the commerce to be derived from his country, was an object of infinitely greater importance than the amount of the tribute which he had agreed to pay to the Sultan.

Upon farther inquiry into the relative value of Tippoo's coins, it was found, that they might be received at a medium between the rate at which he had desired to pay them, and that at which the confederates had insisted to have them, upon the authority of the regulations of his government. On this point it was therefore agreed to divide the difference with the Sultan; but the list of the countries to be ceded was to admit of no alteration.

The demand of the country of the Coorga Rajah seems to have been equally unexpected by Tippoo and his vakeels; and the Sultan having reason to consider this Rajah as one of the main instruments of the war, and doubtless harbouring the severest vengeance against him in his breast, is said to have received this proposal with astonishment and disdain. He asserted,

* The rupees are reckoned throughout this work, at the rate of 365 to 100 star pagodas, or £40, the exchange at which they were issued from the Company's treasury, about 2 s. 2½d. the rupee. On this principle Tippoo's revenues amounted to £2,597,259; and the cession to the three confederate powers, being one-sixth part to each, would amount to £432,876.

and not without some reason, that as the territories of the Coorga Rajah approached close to his capital, and were by no means contiguous to any of the countries of the allies, they could not be demanded according to the preliminary articles of peace. Lord Cornwallis was, on the other hand, as determined not to sacrifice the Rajah, whose cause could not be relinquished with justice or honour. The vakeels represented the Sultan to have been irritated to a state of phrenzy by this demand; and, on returning to camp on the morning of the 15th, said, he refused to see them, or enter again upon this subject.

Lord Cornwallis, in consequence of what was passing, had ordered the guns to be sent back to the island and to the redoubts; and working parties to bind up the old fascines, and prepare a farther stock of materials for carrying on the siege.

The hopes of the army were again revived; and, there was no doubt, that our Commander in Chief, should hostilities recommence, would be as determined in his perseverance to reduce the capital, as his conduct had been signal for moderation, in sparing its master in the hour of victory.

The suspension of hostilities, although amply paid for by Tippoo, was not, however, unattended with serious inconvenience to a renewal of the attack. The greater part of the materials, formed of the cypress trees, was become so dry and brittle as to be unfit for use; the garden was exhausted, and the new stock of materials must be brought from a considerable distance; the trenches, particularly the parallels, from the bursting of the gabions, had fallen into disrepair; but, above all, the troops, particularly the Europeans, in this tedious respite of three weeks after hard labour; confined to a fixed camp, which had become extremely filthy and nauseous; without vegetables and suitable refreshment in sultry weather, were of late very unhealthy. The army, sensible that the war had been concluded with great honour and public advantage, had made up their minds to peace; and although ready to recommence the attack, some time would be required to re-animate their exertions, and bring every department again into action. To a cause supported by forces less numerous, or more precariously supplied, the Sultan's artful delay might have proved fatal, or given him the ascendancy he aimed at, in the final adjustment of the definitive treaty of peace.

The confederate army had now been six weeks before Seringapatam; and so successful were the arrangements of Earl Cornwallis for the subsistence of his troops, that he had not only occasionally supplied the allies with rice, but such was the ample store in camp, that the last convoys of brinjarries were directed to come no further than Outredroog.

The magnitude of the supplies required, and of the combinations in action to insure the success of the last campaign, may be judged of from the annexed statement of the forces above the Ghauts at this period; which, with the followers of the armies, and the people employed in bringing forward supplies, would be little short of four hundred thousand strangers in Tippoo's country, of which number it may be reckoned that above one half were now collected in the neighbourhood of his capital.

STATEMENT *of the* ALLIED ARMIES *above the Ghauts, 16th March,* 1792.

	Cavalry.		Artillery.		Infantry.		Total.		Total Europeans and Natives.	Cannon.
	Europ.	Natives.	Europ.	Natives.	Europ.	Natives.	Europ.	Natives.		
British Main Army - - -	444	723	1,245	3,117	5,745	16,818	7,434	20,658	28,092	158
Ditto Bombay Army - - -	—	—	203	269	2,942	4,390	3,145	4,659	7,804	36
Ditto Detachment at the Gudzelhatty Pass	—	—	50	200	350	2,100	400	2,300	2,700	6
Purseram Bhow's Army, including the Bombay Detachment - - -	—	15,000	56	120	62	2,173	118	17,293	17,411	30
Hurry Punt's Army - - -	—	8,000	—	—	—	—	—	8,000	8,000	20
The Nizam's Army, including the Madras Detachment - - -	—	12,000	58	185	38	1,825	96	14,010	14,106	4
Rajah of Travancore's Troops - -	—	500	—	—	—	1,200	—	1,700	1,700	—
Coorga Rajah's Troops - - -	—	—	—	—	—	4,000	—	4,000	4,000	—
Total	444	36,223	1,612	3,891	9,137	32,506	11,193	72,620	83,813	254

N. B. The Mahratta and the Nizam's horse are stated at one-third less than they called their force. Their infantry not being considerable, nor their numbers ascertained, are not included.

The 80 guns captured at Seringapatam being in use for the defence of the lines and of our posts on the island, are included with the main army.

I i

The followers of an army in India, on being reckoned at four times the number of fighting men, will appear to be a moderate estimate on considering the particular circumstances and customs of the country.

The number of black people employed in the public departments, is immense, particularly in charge of the cattle that carry the supplies for the army, for which is required, at the rate of one man for every two or three bullocks. This article, including the public and private cattle of the confederate armies, and of their brinjarries, the whole probably amounting to near half a million of cattle, may be reckoned to bring into the field one hundred thousand followers. The elephants, of which there were several hundred, and the camels several thousand, had also many attendants; and every horse in the cavalry and in the army, besides the trooper or rider, has two attendants, one who cleans and takes care of him, called the horsekeeper, and the other the grass-cutter, who provides his forage; and a number of bullocks with drivers, is, besides, required to carry grain for the horses. The palanquin and dooly-bearers, for the conveyance of the sick, are also a numerous class of followers.

Field officers, including the people who carry or have charge of their baggage, cannot have less than forty, captains twenty, and subalterns ten servants. The soldiers have also their attendants, particularly a cook to every mess; and the Sepoys, most of whom are married, have many of them, as well as of the followers, their families with them in camp.

The bazar people, or merchants, and their servants, are also very numerous; nor are the adventurers few who accompany an army, with no other view than to plunder in the enemy's country; and even they, far from being a nuisance, search for and dig up the pits of grain in the fields and villages, which would otherwise remain undiscovered, and bring in numbers of cattle that could by no other means be collected in the country.

Early in the war, many of the Sepoys were prevailed upon to send back their families, and other arrangements were made for reducing the number of followers; but those measures tended to create desertion and increase distress. In short, no man will carry his family to camp who does not find his convenience and advantage in doing so; no person will pay for servants he does not want, nor will followers attend an army without pay, who do not earn a living, which they can do only by contributing to its support. There are no towns to be depended upon for supplies; and an army in India, not only carries with it most of the means of its subsistance for several months, but also a variety of necessaries, which are exposed daily in the bazars like merchandize in a fair: a scene altogether resembling more the emigration of a nation guarded by its troops, than the march of an army, fitted out merely with the intention to subdue an enemy!

But to resume the account of the negotiations with the Sultan, which had now come to a crisis: the Princes, on the return of the vakeels from the fort, were informed that they must prepare to move off the next morning to the Carnatic, and the guard they had of their father's troops, were disarmed and treated as prisoners.

On the 16th of March, in the morning, they accordingly

moved off, guarded by Captain Welch's battalion, and were to be met by Colonel Floyd with the cavalry, by whom they were to be conducted to Bangalore.

The Princes were said to have been much affected by this change in affairs, and prepared for their departure with great regret. On having palanquins brought to them (with which, from some accident, they had not been provided from the fort), the eldest, in particular, asked whose they were, and hesitated in going into them, till they were told they belonged to Lord Cornwallis.

The vakeels had entreated the night before, that his Lordship's orders might be suspended for one day, and again renewed their solicitations in the morning, with many assurances that the Sultan would hear reason. The Princes were allowed to halt, and encamped on the road to Bangalore, in the rear of the army, but were not permitted to return to their former ground. The vakeels were at the same time informed, that if the Sultan did not instantly agree to execute the definitive treaty, as drawn out, he must expect no farther delay, and orders would be given to recommence hostilities.

Purseram Bhow, who had joined some days ago with his division of the Mahratta army, and Captain Little's brigade, crossed the river this morning to join General Abercromby, and be in readiness to invest the south side of the fort.*

* It may appear extraordinary that the other Mahratta army, or the Nizam's army, had not been employed to act with General Abercromby, in the absence of Purseram Bhow. Lord Cornwallis mentions in one of his dispatches, that it suited neither the health nor inclination of Hurry Punt to go upon any detached service; and that the Nizam's minister, although he, with great zeal, offered to supply the place of the Bhow,

The Bhow, eager for Tippoo's destruction, was also anxious to make amends for his late unwarrantable conduct, in going first to Bidenore instead of advancing immediately to the capital, by now exerting himself with redoubled vigour; and he, or part of his horse, exceeded their orders, by ravaging the country as soon as they crossed the river, and captured a number of camels and cattle belonging to Tippoo's army, which they brought in from the neighbourhood of Mysore.

The Sultan, whether awed by the reluctance of his troops to defend the place, or prevailed upon by the entreaties of his mother, family and relations; or seeing that the moderation he met with from Lord Cornwallis, proceeded from wisdom, and not from any apprehension of failing in the enterprize, now consented to see the vakeels, and submitted to the dictates of the conqueror.

Full of that policy which marks the character of an able Mahomedan, and teaches him, after failing in every subtlety of art, to appear dignified even in his submission, the Sultan is said to have written to Lord Cornwallis on this occasion, expressing "his concern for the misunderstanding that had taken place; "that he meant only to remonstrate, not to refuse; that he was "greatly indebted to his Lordship's indulgence, and was the "more desirous that his sons should not be sent off to the Car- "natic, as he wished that the treaty should be delivered by them "to his Lordship, with every mark of solemnity, both as a testi-

was so completely ignorant of military affairs, and so total a want of arrangement prevailed in every department of his army, that he was equally unable to put his troops in motion, or to provide for their subsistence, even for a few days, if removed from our army!

"mony of his own sincerity; and that they might also thereby "consider themselves as parties for its due performance."

On the 17th, the vakeels did not come out with the treaty as expected, which still kept up the anxiety in camp. The Sultan, like all Indian princes, who think that dignity consists in deliberation and delay, did not probably relish the appearance of its being forced upon him so abruptly; but the vakeels sent assurances of every thing being agreed to, and that they would bring out the treaty without fail, the next morning.

The 18th was another day of anxiety, till late in the afternoon, when the vakeels came out; the Princes guard was then restored to them, and the next morning fixed for the delivery of the treaty to the confederate powers.

The vakeels, while they returned from the Sultan with all the necessary documents for concluding this first calamitous war experienced by his family, were charged with a letter or message from the Sultan, that shewed how little his proud mind was inclined to peace with our allies, and how lightly he treated their force. After remonstrating against the conduct of Purseram Bhow, in the ravages he had committed, and requesting that he (with his 20,000 horse) might be recalled across the river, and brought to an account for this outrage, the Sultan added, or directed his vakeel to add, "he should consider it as a still greater "favour, if his Lordship would be pleased to permit him to go "out and punish the Bhow himself!"

In the course of the negotiation, Tippoo is said to have expressed his wishes through his vakeels, to have a meeting and conference with Lord Cornwallis, which his Lordship declined, probably from an apprehension of giving cause of jealousy to our allies, from having no great respect for the Sultan's character, and from seeing it would answer no essential public purpose.

On the 19th of March, the young Princes, attended and escorted in the same manner as when they first arrived in camp, came to perform the ceremony of delivering the definitive treaty to Lord Cornwallis and the allies. They arrived at head-quarters, at ten o'clock, which was the hour appointed, and were received by his Lordship, as formerly, with the greatest kindness and attention. The boys had now gained more confidence; the eldest in particular, conducted himself with great ease and propriety; and, after some general conversation, having a parcel handed to him, which contained the definitive treaty in triplicate, he got up and delivered the whole to Lord Cornwallis.

The Nizam's son, or Mogul Prince as they call him, and the Mahratta plenipotentiary, Hurry Punt, did not think it consistent with their dignity to attend on this interesting occasion, any more than on the first day that the Princes arrived in camp. Even their vakeels were late in making their appearance. At length, on their coming, the eldest Prince receiving two of the copies of the treaty, returned to him by Lord Cornwallis, delivered a copy to each of the vakeels of the other powers, which he did with great manliness; but evidently with more constraint and dissatisfaction than he had performed the first part of the ceremony. One of the vakeels (the Mahratta) afterwards muttering something on the subject, the boy asked at what he grumbled; and, without giving him time to answer, said, "they "might well be silent, as certainly their masters had no reason

" to be displeased." These may not be the precise words, but something passed to that effect, which did great honour to the boy's manliness and spirit.

The Princes having completed the ceremony, and delivered this final testimony of their father's submission, took their leave and returned to their tents; and thus ended the last scene of this important war.

CHAPTER III.

Retrospect of the Military Transactions in India since the former Peace; and a short Statement of the general Consequences of the late War.

THE dominions of Tippoo Sultan, previous to the war, rendered his power formidable, not only from their extent and value, but also from their advantageous position; which, strengthened by numerous fortresses, commanded the frontiers of the adjoining countries; and the restless enterprizing spirit of the sovereign, obliged all around him to be in a state of constant preparation for their defence.

The Sultan's revenues, it appears, amounted annually to about two and a half millions sterling. He was, besides, possessed of very great treasures, and had an army consisting of 18,000 cavalry, 50,000 regular infantry, formed in brigades, completely appointed with field artillery; and twice that number of irregular infantry, employed to garrison his forts, and for the collection of his revenues.

Whether from the operation of the system established by Hyder; from the principles which Tippoo had adopted for his own conduct; or from his dominions having suffered little by invasion for many years; or from the effect of these several causes united; his country was found every where full of inhabitants, and apparently cultivated to the utmost extent of which the soil was capable; while the discipline and fidelity of his troops in the field, until their last overthrow, were testimonies equally strong, of the excellent regulations which existed in his army. His government, though strict and arbitrary, was the despotism of a politic and able sovereign, who nourishes, not oppresses, the subjects who are to be the means of his future aggrandizement: and his cruelties were, in general, inflicted only on those whom he considered as his enemies. He had been diligently employed ever since the former war, in improving his army, and in strengthening his principal forts; and had laid in such ample supplies of military stores in his frontier posts to the north, as shewed that he meditated extensive conquests.

Confiding in his superior power and talents, and aiming at universal conquest, this active Prince not only disclaimed the paramount authority of the Emperor of Delhi,* and declared himself to be the greatest king on earth, but also pretending to derive his descent from the founder of his religion, announced himself to be the restorer of the Mahommedan faith. He sent forth proclamations† inviting all true Mussulmen to join his standard; and thus, to the advantages of military discipline, adding the enthusiasm of religion, declared his intention to drive the European infidels out of India, and to extend the empire of Mahommed over the world.

The great seal which Tippoo adopted soon after his father's

* Tippoo is the first Mahommedan prince who, since the establishment of the Mogul empire, has openly disclaimed the authority of the king of Delhi, or great Mogul; and who has presumed to impress coin with only his own titles. Even the government of Bengal, still preserve that external mark of respect to the fallen representative of the house of Timur. On this subject, see the Introduction to Major Rennell's Memoir, page lxxi.

† See Appendix, No. II.

death, and which goes affixed to all his public dispatches, is sufficiently expressive of his ambition to appear both as a prophet and a conqueror.

In the middle of the seal, which is a large oval, there is the following sentence in Arabic, from the Koran—

"I am the messenger of the true faith."

Round the edge of the seal, beyond the compartment which contains the Arabic sentence, there is a couplet in Persian to the following purport:

"From conquest, and the protection of the Royal Hyder,
"comes my title of Sultan: and the world, as under the sun and
"moon, is subject to my signet.*"

Ambition thus avowed, to an extent so inordinate, created immediate alarm in the powers on the Peninsula of India, and rendered an union necessary between the Mahrattas and the Nizam; people and powers differing in religion, in government, and in every point of interest, except the fear which united them against this powerful adversary, who commanded their southern frontiers. So formidable was he also to the British government in India, that the revenues of two of their three presidencies, Madras and Bombay, were inadequate to support forces equal to their defence.

The experience of the former war; the insolent conduct of the Sultan since the peace; and the fluctuating state of politics all over India; indicated the necessity of establishing a vigorous government, and a powerful army, for the protection of the British possessions in that distant quarter of the globe.

* For a further explanation of this seal, see Appendix, No. III.

Early in 1786, the powers of Governor-general and Commander in Chief being vested in Earl Cornwallis, he went out to take the command in India; and a commission was sent at the same time to Sir Archibald Campbell, then Governor of Madras, vesting him with similar powers in the Carnatic.

In 1787, on the appearance of a rupture with France, in which Tippoo Sultan was ready to have espoused their cause, four regiments were raised in Great Britain as a necessary addition to our force in India; and, although embarrassing to the finances of the Company, were sent out after the immediate necessity had apparently ceased; a precaution which events soon arose to justify, as a most wise and prudent measure on the part of the administration in England. General Medows was, at the same time, appointed Governor and Commander in Chief at Bombay; Colonel Abercromby, at the head of one of the new regiments, to be his second in command; and Colonel Musgrave, at the head of another of those regiments, was destined to be second in command in Bengal.

There were in India, in 1788, a regiment of British dragoons, nine regiments of British, and two of Hanoverian infantry, in all about eight thousand European troops, in addition to the Company's establishments. Several of the first officers in the British service, were in command in that country; and a system was established, which, by joining the powers of governor to those of commander in chief, united every advantage which could give efficacy to the operations of war.

The discipline, which had lately been ordered by the King for establishing uniformity in his army, was now equally practised by his Majesty's and the Company's forces in India. The field equipment was refitted and enlarged at the several presidencies; and every preparation made to act with the promptitude and effect which unforeseen exigencies might require. Public credit, increasing with the security afforded to the country, and also in consequence of like able arrangements in the conduct of the civil line of the government, the Company's funds rose daily in their value; and their affairs, as stated to parliament, by the minister at the head of the India department, were not only retrieved from supposed ruin, but soon appeared to be in a state of decided and increasing prosperity.

The Carnatic, which had been the seat of the former, and would probably soon be the seat of a future war; at least the scene where our army must assemble, and the source whence it must be supplied; required extraordinary exertion of military science and arrangement, to prepare it for the operations of defensive or offensive war.

To protect a weak and extensive frontier; to discipline a detached army; and to provide resources in a lately desolated country, fell to the lot of Sir Archibald Campbell. Skilled in every branch of military science; with knowledge matured by experience in various countries and climates; indefatigable in all public duties; and endued with a degree of worth and benevolence, which attached to him all ranks in the army, and excited voluntary exertion in every officer to second the zeal of his general; he had a task to perform, which, though great and complicated, was not beyond the reach of such distinguished talents.

Granaries were established in the frontier and other stations in the Carnatic, containing supplies for near 30,000 men for twelve months; and furnished in such a manner as to provide against the exigencies of famine or of war, without incurring additional expence to the public; a complete train of battering and of field artillery was prepared, far surpassing what had ever been known upon the coast; a store of camp equipage for an army of 20,000 men, was provided; the principal forts were repaired, and more amply supplied with guns and stores; the cavalry were, with infinite difficulty, completed to their full establishment; and a general uniformity of discipline and movement was established in the cavalry, in the infantry, and in the artillery.

During the government of Sir Archibald Campbell, the revenues of the Presidency of Fort St. George (including the acquisition of the Guntoor circar and the additional subsidy from the Nabob of Arcot); were increased from nine hundred and sixty thousand to fourteen hundred thousand pounds sterling a year;* and not only did his able conduct improve the re-

	Lacs		Lacs
* Company's revenue in 1785 Pags.	16	Company's revenue in 1789 Pags.	19½
Nabob's subsidy - - - -	4	Guntoor circar - - - -	2½
Rajah of Tanjore, ditto - -	4	Nabob's subsidy - - - -	9
		Rajah of Tanjore, ditto - -	4
	24		35

The Guntoor circar was, by the treaties of 1766 and 1768, to be ceded to the Company by the Nizam, after the death of his brother, Bazalet Jung. He died in 1782, but a fit opportunity did not offer for making good this claim, till 1788, when Lord Cornwallis sent Captain Kennaway to Hyderabad to make this demand of the Nizam; and, at the same time, gave orders to Sir Archibald Campbell, to detach a force from Fort St. George, to take possession of it; measures which were accomplished with a degree of promptitude that prevented hesitation on the part of the Nizam, or the interference apprehended from Tippoo Sultan. The arrears of tribute, due to the Nizam, for the other northern circars, which was paid on this occasion; and the tribute of seven lacs of rupees a-year, stipulated by those treaties, since regularly paid, may be considered as the purchase-

sources of that coast, and preserve it in peace during his administration, but such were the extent and importance of his arrangements, that every person who is acquainted with the subject, will readily acknowledge, that the preparations made by Sir Archibald Campbell in the Carnatic, were of infinite consequence, and in a great measure laid the foundation for the success of the late glorious war.

Tippoo Sultan, though awed by the vigorous and decisive measures of Sir Archibald Campbell, had evidently his views turned towards Travancore; and his enmity to the Rajah, as well as the importance of the acquisition of his country, which would not only complete the conquest of the Malabar coast, but greatly facilitate a future invasion of the Carnatic, seem to have marked the kingdom of Travancore as the first object of the Sultan's ambition. He encouraged the Rajah of Cochin to claim some possessions, formerly the property of his family, upon which part of the lines are built that defend the Travancore frontier; and employed him to work upon the fears of the Rajah, and to endeavour to persuade him by threats or promises, to withdraw from the friendship of the English, and to put himself under his protection; "for who," says the Sultan, "ever found truth or good faith in Europeans?"

In 1788, apparently in prosecution of this plan, Tippoo had carried down his army to the Malabar coast, and having excited the Chereka Rajah, one of his tributaries, to seize the island of

money, or deductions from the value of the Guntoor circar: but still the acquisition was of great importance, not so much from the addition of revenue it brings to the Company, regarding it as a purchase, as from the advantage of possessing the whole of the coast, and the strength which Guntoor gives to our frontier by connecting the Carnatic with the other circars.

Darmapatam, dependent on our settlement of Tellicherry, he blockaded that place with his army, in order that by cutting off all communication with his countries, he might render it untenable for want of provisions, without committing any direct act of hostility against our government. He at the same time threatened the Dutch at Cochin, which lies within the territory of Travancore, and was using every means short of actual warfare, to gain possession of the remaining part of the Malabar coast.*

The Rajah of Travancore, aware of the Sultan's character, and alarmed at his conduct, reported the conversation that passed with the Rajah of Cochin, and every thing that had occurred, to Sir Archibald Campbell,† by whom he was prevailed upon to pay the expence of two battalions of Sepoys, which, with a detachment of artillery and four field pieces, were sent to reinforce his army; a measure no less desirable for our ally, than important to the safety of the Carnatic, thereby adding essentially to the security of a frontier country, and to the number of our forces, without any increase of expence.

The Sultan, finding that the Rajah adhered to his alliance, and that Lord Cornwallis had confirmed the declaration of Sir Archibald Campbell to avenge his cause, if attacked, withdrew his army. His proud mind, however, was not at rest; and no sooner had Sir Archibald left India, where he had sacrificed his

* The settlement of Tellicherry, in consequence of the Sultan's policy, was supported at so great an expence, and partook so little in the commerce of the country, that the Bombay government had in contemplation to recommend its being relinquished as an unnecessary and unprofitable post and factory.

† See Appendix, No. IV.

health to the fatigues and duties of his station, than the Sultan again descended the Ghauts to the Malabar coast.

The Rajah of Travancore had lately made a purchase of the small territory of Cranganore and Ayacotta from the Dutch at Cochin, a measure which, though not sanctioned by the government of Madras, the Rajah thought necessary, in order to complete and strengthen his frontier to the sea. Tippoo took advantage of this transaction. He asserted that the Rajah had no right to make the purchase, nor the Dutch to dispose of the territory, without his permission, as sovereign of that part of the Malabar coast;* and upon the Rajah's refusal to relinquish the purchase, advanced with his army, and approached his frontier. For several days, from the 23d to the 28th of December, 1789, the Sultan's horsemen rode up to the Rajah's lines, and made use of every insulting expedient to draw the first act of hostility from the Travancore troops; but finding them aware of his artifice, and that the detachment of English troops was stationed at some distance, he at last gave way to his rage, and on the 29th of December, attacked the lines by storm. His troops being repulsed with disgrace, and himself thrown into the ditch in the retreat, he is said to have made an oath, that he never would wear his turban again, till he took the Rajah's lines, and accordingly prepared to attack them by regular approach.

An enterprise, directed to so distant a quarter, while it alarmed and united the powers on the Peninsula, against the common

* The Dutch conquered Cochin and those districts from the Portuguese in 1662. They never paid tribute to any prince for their possessions on the Malabar coast; nor did they ever acknowledge allegiance either to the Rajah of Cochin, or to Hyder's or Tippoo's government. See the papers laid before the House of Commons in 1791.

enemy, also enabled them to collect their resources, and commence their operations against him with every advantage.

The wise and provident measures of the administration in England, in the vigorous government which they had established in India, became fully evinced in the prosecution of this war; and but for the energy of the system, which placed the power and resources of the country in the hands of those who took the field in its defence; and but for the wisdom and talents of the person to whom the supreme power and military command were entrusted; this, like the former wars with the Mysore government, must have probably ended in the accumulation of debt without adequate advantage; in the desolation of the Company's possessions; and in the aggrandizement of the power and pretensions of their most formidable adversary.

It is impossible to recollect the busy scene, which has passed in India, without wishing to give some farther idea of the conduct of the personage who directed that great confederacy: not in the operations of the field alone, part of which have been detailed, but in the more laborious duties of office which required the most assiduous and indefatigable attention. Lord Cornwallis, on marching days, was in his tent from the time the army came to the ground of encampment; and on halting days, after visiting the out-posts in the morning, was there constantly employed till the evening, attending to the affairs depending on his station. The business which pressed upon him from the several armies, and from every part of India, may easily be imagined to have been so complicated and various as to have required every exertion of diligence and arrangement for its dispatch. He gave his instructions, in person, to all officers who went on detachments of importance, and saw them on their return. Officers at the heads of departments applied to himself on all material business; and there was no branch of the service with which he was not intimately acquainted. In the detail of business, he was ably assisted by his secretary, Lieutenant-Colonel Ross, and other gentlemen of his suite; and his Lordship's tents, and the line of head quarters, appeared more like the various departments of a great office of state, than the splendid equipage that might be supposed to attend the leader of the greatest armies that, under a British general, were ever assembled in the east.

To this unremitting attention to business, is not only to be ascribed the general success of the administration of Lord Cornwallis in India, and in particular that of the operations of the late war, but also the unexampled economy with which it was conducted, and the readiness with which all accounts will be closed, and the expence ascertained for the information of the public. Before his Lordship quitted Madras to return to Bengal, in July last 1792, all arrears to the troops and to the public departments, were paid up; and there is great reason to believe that, after deducting the Company's share of the fine paid by Tippoo Sultan, the extraordinary expence of this glorious war (that is beyond the usual allowances to the troops on the peace establishment), will not amount to even two millions sterling!

The army having assembled in the Carnatic, and the greatest part of the corps belonging to the presidency of Fort St. George, the general detail of the army, and duties of the line, were conducted by the adjutant and quarter-master-general of that establishment; as in like manner was the charge of the hospitals, placed under their surgeon-general; and of the pay and provision departments, under gentlemen of the civil line from Madras. The talents of the persons who filled those important stations, were sufficiently evinced in the satisfactory manner in which their departments were conducted; while the duties of the officers on the general staff of the King's troops, and of the Bengal troops, having been limited to the details that respected those establishments exclusively, every duty was punctually executed without jealousy or unnecessary interference.

To return to the general view of the military transactions in India; it was under the operation of a system so well calculated for the maintenance of distant provinces, in times of danger, that the forces of our establishments in India were, for the first time, called forth and led on by the Governor-general; ably seconded by the exertions of the Governors of the two other presidencies, and supported by distinguished zeal and merit in the officers and troops which composed those armies. Thus a hope was realized, which, though sometimes indulged, was considered rather as chimerical at the commencement of the war; namely, that the three Governors would meet with the forces of their respective presidencies at Seringapatam: and not only did this event take place, but the native powers on the Peninsula were brought forward to witness and assist, in the subjugation of the common enemy!

The map prefixed to this part of the work,* which shews the

* The map referred to, see page 225, and the description of the ceded countries at the end of this chapter, are intended merely to give a general idea of the importance of those acquisitions to the allies; and of the relative state of the powers on the Peninsula at the conclusion of the war. The particulars, so far as they are known, are fully detailed by Major Rennell, in the Map and the Supplement which he has lately published to his Memoir.

ceded countries, will also give an idea of the desolated state of the Sultan's remaining provinces, from the various directions in which they will appear to have been traversed by the confederate armies during the war; and the following tables, containing an estimate of his loss in forts, cannon and troops, will assist in completing the view of the broken state of his power.

STATEMENT *of the Loss in Forts, Cannon, and Troops, sustained by* **TIPPOO SULTAN** *during the late War.*

BRITISH MAIN ARMY.

Date.	Place.	By what Army or Detachment.	Cannon.	Men killed, wounded, missing or taken prisoners.
1790. 15th June	Caroor	General Medows	2	Evacuated
5th July	Arrivacourchy	Ditto	2	150
10th Ditto	Daraporam	Ditto	3	Evacuated
22d Ditto	Coimbetore	Ditto	22	20
6th August	Perendore	Lieut. Col. Oldham	2	Evacuated
8th Ditto	Eroad	Ditto	3	200
9th Ditto	Cumulum	Ditto	2	Evacuated
22d Ditto	Dindigul	Lieut. Col. Stuart	14	700
26th Ditto	Chucklagurry	Capt. Wahab	4	100
— Ditto	Sittimungulum	Col. Floyd	2	230
14th and 15th Sept.	Do. Battle and Retreat	Ditto	—	1,000
22d Sept.	Paulgautcherry	Lieut. Col. Stuart	59	400
13th Nov.	Wimbinellore	General Medows	1	100
16th Ditto	Darampoury	Ditto	2	50
26th Ditto	Parametty	Ditto	1	50
Sept. Oct. and Nov.	Tripatore Vaniambaddy Caveripatam	Lieut. Col. Maxwell Ditto Ditto	the particulars not known. 10	300
1791. 28th Feb.	Colar	Earl Cornwallis	2	50
2d March	Ouscotta	Ditto	4	50
21st Ditto	Bangalore	Ditto	102	3,000
— Ditto	Vencatighery	Capt. A. Read	3	100
28th March	Pursuit of Tippoo	Earl Cornwallis	1	20
30th Ditto	Divanelly	Ditto	3	100
1st April	China Balaporam	Ditto	3	100
6th May	Cankinelly	Ditto	3	Evacuated.
10th Ditto	Malavilly	Ditto	2	
14th Ditto	Arrakery	Ditto	1	
15th Ditto	Battle of Seringapatam	Earl Cornwallis	5	800
20th June	Hooliadroog	Ditto	4	100
15th July	Oussoor	Ditto	6	Evacuated
22d Ditto	Rayacotta	Major Gowdie	13	300
		Carried over	281	7,920

Date.	Place.	By what Army or Detachment.	Cannon.	Men killed, wounded, missing or taken prisoners.
		Brought over	281	7,920
1791. 17th Sept.	Raymangur -	Major Gowdie -	5	300
18th Ditto	Ambajee Durgum	Capt. Alex. Read -	2	100
	Chillum Cotta -	Ditto -	2	100
18th Oct.	Nundydroog -	Major Gowdie -	17	600
19th Ditto	Cumeldroog -	Ditto -	—	100
11th July	Detachment of Tippoo's repulsed at Coimbetore	Lieut. Chalmers -	2	100
31st Oct.	Pinagra - -	Lieut. Col. Maxwell	4	200
7th Nov.	Attack of Kistnaghery	Ditto -	—	100
21st Dec.	Savendroog -	Lieut. Col. Stuart	24	1,500
24th Ditto	Outredroog -	Ditto -	2	400
22d Ditto	Ramgurry and Sheria Gurry -	Captain Welch -	13	300
1792. 6th and 7th Feb.	Storm of Tippoo's lines and the Island of Seringapatam	Earl Cornwallis -	80	20,000
		Total by the Main Army	432	31,720

BOMBAY ARMY.

Date.	Place.	By what Army or Detachment.	Cannon.	Men killed, wounded, missing or taken prisoners.
1790. 25th April	Cudroor -	Major Dow -	2	50
— Ditto	Cartinade -	Ditto -	—	Evacuated
26th Sept.	Chagaut -	Lieut. Col. Hartley	15	50
28th Sept.	Travancore guns dug out of the Paniany at Turtolla -	Ditto -	37	
26th Nov.	Paniany -	Ditto -	4	
7th Dec.	Vincaticottah -	Ditto -	3	20
10th Ditto	Battle and capture of Tricalore -	Ditto -	3	2,000
12th Ditto	Ferokabad -	Ditto -	50	1,300
— Ditto	Baypoor -	Ditto -	20	Evacuated
16th Ditto	Avery -	General Abercromby		
— Ditto	Carlee -	Ditto	68	5,000
17th Ditto	Cananore -	Ditto		
— Ditto	Biliapatam -	Major Dow -	5	
— Ditto	Narracarow -	Ditto -	—	
27th Ditto	Barragurry -	Captain Oakes -	6	200
— Ditto	Cootapore -		6	200
1791. — May	Periapatam -	General Abercromby	5	Evacuated
1792. 22d Feb.	Action with Tippoo in the defence of an advanced post at Seringapatam -		—	200
		Total by the Bombay Army	224	9,020

MAHRATTA ARMY.

Date.		Place.	By what Army or Detachment.	Cannon.	Men killed, wounded, missing or taken prisoners.
1791.	3d April	Darwar - -	Purseram Bhow's Army and Colonel Frederick's Detachment -	30	4,000
	— Ditto	Kosugul - -		4	200
	21st Dec.	Nagimungulum -	Ditto - and Captain Little's Detachment -	2	100
	— Ditto	Hooly Onore -		2	350
	24th Ditto	Bankapoor -		6	200
	29th Ditto	Battle of Simoga -	Ditto -	10	1,500
1792.	4th Jan.	Fort of Simoga -	Ditto -	12	500
			Total	66	6,850

NIZAM'S ARMY.

Date.		Place.	By what Army or Detachment.	Cannon.	Men killed, wounded, missing or taken prisoners.
1791.		Sedhout -	Nizam's Army and Major Montgomery's Detachment -	6	200
	17th April	Kopaul - -		20	1,000
	19th Ditto	Bahauder Bunder		6	200
	7th Nov.	Lower Fort of Gurramconda -	Ditto, and Capt. Andrew Read's Detachment	4	150
			Total	36	1,550

Abstract of Tippoo Sultan's Loss during the War.

	Forts.	Guns.	Troops.
By the British main army - -	40	432	31,720
Ditto —— Bombay ditto - -	16	224	9,020
Ditto Mahratta army and Bombay brigade -	6	66	6,850
Ditto Nizam's ditto, and Madras brigade -	4	36	1,550
Ditto his Majesty's squadron at Fortified Island	1	43	200
Total	67	801	49,340

N. B. The guns taken by Tippoo Sultan during the war, were the thirty-seven at the Travancore lines, belonging to the Rajah (found afterwards in the Paniany river); six field-pieces, which the detachment at Sittemungulum were, from the cattle being killed, under the necessity of quitting in their retreat; two or three guns at Permacoil, in the Carnatic; and the few guns which the detachment commanded by Cummer-ud-Deen Cawn retook in Coimbetore.

The only forts of consequence that remained in Tippoo's possession, at the conclusion of the war, were, Seringapatam, Chittledroog, Bidenore, Mangalore, or a new fort near it, called Jemaulghur, Kistnaghery, and Sankeridurgum. The two last forts being in the ceded countries, there are only four places which have not either been in the possession of his enemies during the war, or made over to them in consequence of the peace.

It may be asked, what advantage has arisen to the troops that have been employed in the reduction of so many forts and countries? This, therefore, shall be stated as briefly as possible.

At the commencement of the war it was agreed, with the approbation of the Commander in Chief, that the plunder taken should form one general fund, and prize agents were appointed by the army to take charge of all captured property. The King's officers nominated two agents, and the officers of the Company's troops, on the coast, two more, to whom one was afterwards added on the part of the Bengal troops.

The officers who were thus appointed agents for the army, desirous to approve themselves worthy of the trust, proposed to lodge all money received for the captured property with the paymaster of the army; both as a temporary aid to the public service, and to obviate any idea that might arise of their having a separate interest in delaying the payment of the prize money, from employing the funds, in the mean time, for their own advantage. They, besides, requested that a committee of seven officers, of different ranks and departments of the army, might be appointed to examine their accounts from time to time; and from the reports of that committee, upon the examination of their accounts, after the close of each campaign, there can be no doubt that the department of the prize money was conducted with strict integrity, and with great attention to the interests of the army. The war, however, having been carried on gradually from the extremities to the centre of the enemy's country, every thing of value was withdrawn to the capital. The military stores, and the grain found in the forts, were estimated at a low rate, as they were to be charged to the Company; and these articles, together with the horses taken from the enemy, which, if fit for service, were sent to the cavalry; and the cattle and sheep collected on the march, which were delivered to the commissaries, also at a low rate, on account of the Company, formed the principal articles of capture, which in all amounted to the following sums.*

Abstract of the Prize Money of the British Main Army in India during the War.

Prize money for the first campaign, or year 1790 -	£19,804
Ditto ditto — second campaign, to the 31st July, 1791 - - - - - -	52,618
Ditto ditto — third campaign, from 1st August, 1791, to 24th February, 1792 - -	21,162
Total	£93,584

N. B. This sum includes 921*l.* arising from the tax on spiritous liquors, during the two last campaigns. This was the only tax levied in the bazars or markets of the army, which, during that period, were under the superinten-

* The military stores, although more valuable in the interior country, were charged only at the estimated rate of such stores at Madras; and the grain not at the high rates at which it would have sold in the bazars, but according to the usual stoppage paid by the troops. The horses fit for service were few, and never valued higher than the cavalry price in time of peace. The cattle and sheep, which are of a much smaller size than in Europe, were paid for at the rate of twenty shillings a head for draft and carriage bullocks; eight shillings a head for cattle for slaughter; and one shilling a head for sheep.

dance of Mr. Bushby of the Bengal establishment; and the balance, after paying his salary, and the other expences, was ordered by Lord Cornwallis to be added to the prize-money.

Lord Cornwallis and General Medows were pleased to give up their shares of prize money to the army, and recommended to the Court of Directors to relinquish the moiety claimed by the Company of all public stores, which amounts to near one-third part of the captures. There can be little doubt that the Directors will be disposed to comply with this request in favour of the army, as soon as the necessary authority can be obtained from the Crown for that purpose, which will make the dividend of prize money equal to four months and three days batta to the troops that served with the main army during the whole of the war, and less in proportion to those who served only part of that period.

The prize money of the Bombay army, amounting to about two lacs of rupees, would not exceed the dividend in the main army; and the detachments serving with the Mahrattas and the Nizam have profited still less by their campaigns.

The Court of Directors having not only approved of the gratuity of six months batta given to the army by Earl Cornwallis, but having, with great liberality, directed as much more to be distributed, in testimony of their approbation of the services of the army; both sums, amounting to forty-five lacs of rupees, make an addition to the prize money of £493,150, and afford the shares to the several ranks contained in the following statement.

Distribution of Prize Money, and Gratuity to the several Ranks of the Main Army in India.

	Prize Money.			Gratuity by Earl Cornwallis.			Gratuity by the Court of Directors.			Total.		
	£.	s.	d.	£.	s.	d.	£.	s.	d.	£.	s.	d.
Colonel -	297	12	0	432	0	0	432	0	0	1,161	12	0
Lieut. Colonel	248	0	0	360	0	0	360	0	0	968	0	0
Major - -	198	8	0	268	0	0	268	0	0	734	8	0
Captain -	78	2	0	115	4	0	115	4	0	308	10	0
Lieutenant -	52	1	6	76	16	0	76	16	0	205	13	6
Ensign - -	39	10	6	57	12	0	57	12	0	154	14	6
Serjeant - -	7	11	6	10	16	0	10	16	0	29	3	6
Corporals, drummers, and privates	3	15	9	5	8	0	5	8	0	14	11	9
NATIVE TROOPS.												
Subidar - -	7	0	6	10	5	9	10	5	9	27	12	0
Jemidar - -	3	10	3	5	2	10½	5	2	10½	13	16	0
Havildar - -	3	0	2	4	8	0	4	8	0	11	16	2
Naics, drummers, and privates -	1	10	1	2	4	0	2	4	0	5	18	1

N. B. The shares of the prize money in the Bombay army, and in the detachments with the Mahratta and the Nizam's armies, are not known, and will vary according to the amount of their captures; but the gratuity, equal to twelve months batta, is general to the whole of the troops that were employed above the Ghauts at the conclusion of the war.

Officers on the general staff, or on the staff of corps, shared according to the rate of batta, or field allowance, attached to their appointments.

The Commander in Chief being entitled to one-eighth part of all prize money, of which eighth one-third is divided among the other general officers; the sums relinquished by Earl Cornwallis and General Medows are as follow:*

	Prize Money.	Gratuity.	Total.
Earl Cornwallis - -	£6,148	41,096	47,244
General Medows - -	4,724	10,273	14,997
Total	£10,872	51,369	62,241

N. B. His Lordship's and the General's shares of the prize money consequently increased the dividend for the army; but their proportions of gratuity were not drawn, and remained a saving to the Company.

Although the army has not profited considerably by this successful war, its consequences have not been the less important to the public; and considering the debt or expence of the two millions incurred, as a burden on the acquired revenue of four hundred and thirty thousand pounds a year; or as a general

* General Medows was commander in chief the first campaign; Lord Cornwallis the second and third campaigns; to which it is necessary to advert, else these calculations may appear erroneous.

burden on the possessions in India; the inconvenience will remain unfelt in the prosperity arising from the following advantages.

I. The enemy, whose power rendered the possessions on either coast an unprofitable tenure, and whose policy and ambition might have finally overthrown the British empire in India; is so reduced in dominion and resources, that our governments, with common precaution, can have no further apprehension of being disturbed by the restless enterprizing spirit of the family of Hyder.

II. The presidency of Madras, which lay exposed to sudden invasion from Mysore, is now in possession of every pass into the high country on that side; and being covered by an acquisition of extensive valuable territory, has a strong, contracted frontier from Amboor to the Cavery, defended by the forts of Kistnaghery, Rayacotta, Salem, Sankeridurgum, and Namcul; while the possession of the fort of Dindigul and its district, adds essentially to the revenues and protection of the southern countries. Peace and security thus established, the Carnatic may be expected to recover from every former calamity; to be defended at less expence; and to become a source of increasing wealth and commerce.

III. Bombay, which in India, like Gibraltar in Europe, has hitherto been supported at a great expence, as being necessary to the general interests of commerce, will in future take its rank in value and importance with the other presidencies. In possession of the provinces which yield the richest produce in India, extending from Travancore to the Keway river, on the north; protected by Palgautcherry, towards Coimbetore below the Ghauts, and by the Coorga frontier, above the Ghauts; the Malabar coast is in a state of still greater security than the Carnatic; and being a country, perhaps the most varied and fertile in the world, but hitherto a scene of constant warfare and bloodshed, its improvement may be carried to any extent, by a series of mild and equitable government.

Tippoo, thus circumscribed on the coasts of Coromandel and Malabar, has only the Coimbetore country, below the Ghauts, from which he can attempt to invade the English settlements; and that being a confined province, under a very steep and difficult pass, without any place of strength for a magazine; limited on one side by the Cavery, and flanked by Palgautcherry and Dindigul; there can be little reason to apprehend danger from that quarter, while the Mysore country is open to a more immediate invasion from our armies on either coast.

Such appears to be our improved relative situation with the Sultan; while, on the side of the native powers, the acquisition of strength and territory gained by the Mahrattas, whose frontier is advanced beyond Darwar to the Tumbudra; and by the Nizam, whose frontier, strengthened on the one side by Kopaul and the Tumbudra; and on the other by Gunjecotta, and the river Pennar, will better enable those powers to defend their territories against the encroachment of Tippoo and his family; and will give them a position nearer to the aid of the British power, to which they are indebted for their prosperity, and to whose alliance both inclination and interest must prompt them to look forward.

Finally; this war has vindicated the honour of the nation; has given the additional possessions and security to the settlements in India which they required; has effected the wished-for balance amongst the native powers on the Peninsula; has, beyond all former example, raised the character of the British arms in India; and has afforded an instance of good faith in alliance, and moderation in conquest, so eminent, as ought to constitute the English the arbiters of power, worthy of holding the sword and scales of justice in the East.

APPENDIX.

No. I.

DEFINITIVE TREATY of perpetual friendship for the adjustment of affairs between the Honourable English East India Company, the Nawaub Assoph Jah Behauder, and Row Pundit Purdhaun Behauder, and Tippoo Sultaun; in virtue of the authority of the Right Honourable Charles Earl Cornwallis, Knight of the most noble Order of the Garter, Governor General, &c. &c. invested with full powers to direct and controul all the affairs of the said Company in the East Indies, dependant on the several Presidencies of Bengal, Madras, and Bombay, and of the Nawaub Azien-ul-omrah Behauder, possessing full powers on the part of the Nawaub Assoph Jah Behauder, and Hurry Ram Pundit Tantea Behauder, possessing equal powers on the part of Row Pundit Purdhaun Behauder, settled the seventeenth day of March, one thousand seven hundred and ninety-two, of the Christian æra, answering to the twenty-third day of the month Rejeb, one thousand two hundred and six of the Hejeree, by Sir John Kennaway, Baronet, on the part of the Right Honourable Charles Earl Cornwallis, Knight of the most noble Order of the Garter, &c. and Meer Aalum Behauder, on the part of the Nawaub Aziem-ul-omrah Behauder, and Buchajee Pundit on the part of Hurry Ram Pundit Tantea Behauder, on one part, and by Golam Ally Khan Behauder, and Ally Reza Khan on the behalf of Tippoo Sultaun, according to the undermentioned articles, which, by the blessing of God, shall be binding on their heirs and successors, as long as the sun and moon endure, and the conditions of them be invariably observed by the contracting parties.

ARTICLE I.

The friendship subsisting between the Honourable Company and the sircar of Tippoo Sultaun, agreeably to former treaties, the first with the late Nawaub Hyder Ally Khan, bearing date the 8th of August, 1770, and the other, with Tippoo Sultaun, of the 11th of March, 1784, is hereby confirmed and increased; and the articles of the two former treaties are to remain in full force, excepting such of them, as by the present engagement are otherwise adjusted; and the 8th article of the second above-mentioned treaty, dated the 11th of March, 1784, corresponding with the 18th of the month Rubbi-ul-saany, 1198 Hejeree, confirming all the privileges and immunities of trade, which the Nawaub Hyder Ally Khan granted to the said Company, by the treaty entered into in the year 1770, is also by virtue of the present treaty, renewed and confirmed.

ARTICLE II.

In the fourth article of the preliminary treaty entered into between the allied powers and the said Tippoo Sultaun, dated the 22d of February, 1792, corresponding with the 28th of the month Jemadie-ul-saani, 1206 Hejeree, it is written " until the due " performance of the three foregoing articles" (the first article stipulating the cession of half the country, the second the immediate payment of half of the sum of money agreed to be paid; and the remainder in specie, only at three instalments, not exceeding four months each instalment, and the third engaging for the release of prisoners) "two of the sons of the said Tippoo "Sultaun shall be detained as hostages," which articles are confirmed by the present instrument; accordingly the said Tippoo Sultaun, shall divide the sum agreed to be paid at three instalments above mentioned, into three equal parts; and shall pay to the said three powers, their respective shares, at the exchange affixed for the amount; to be paid immediately at such places on the boundaries of the allies, as shall be determined on by them, and after the performance of the remaining two articles above mentioned, that is to say, the cession of one half of the country, and the release of the prisoners, in case the amount of the three instalments be paid by Tippoo Sultaun to the three powers, prior to the expiration of the period stipulated for it, the said sons of Tippoo Sultaun shall be immediately dismissed, and all pecuniary demands between the contracting parties shall cease and be at an end.

ARTICLE III.

By the first article of the preliminary treaty, it is agreed, that one half of the dominions which were in the possession of the said Tippoo Sultaun at the commencement of the war, shall be ceded to the allies, adjacent to their respective boundaries, and subject to their selection. Accordingly, the general abstract of the countries, composing half the dominions of Tippoo Sultaun, to be ceded to the allies, agreeably to their respective shares, is hereunto subjoined, and the detail of them is inserted in a separate schedule, bearing the seal and signature of Tippoo Sultaun.

DISTRICTS *ceded to the Honourable English Company.*

Calicut, 63 talooks			8,48,765 5 4¾	
Palgautcherry			88,000 0 0	
Dindigul and Pulnaveerpachry, 2 talooks			90,000 0 0	
Salim			24,000 0 0	
Koosh			8,000 0 0	
Namkool			16,000 0 0	
Sunkagherry			40,000 0 0	
Barrah Mohul, 9 talooks, viz.				
Barah Mohul		64,000 0 0		
Coveripultun		10,000 0 0		
Verbudderdroog		8,000 0 0		
Raycottah		8,000 0 0		
Kangoondie		6,000 0 0		
Darampoury		8,000 0 0		
Pennagur		10,000 0 0		
Tengrycottah		12,000 0 0		
Coverypoor		8,000 0 0		
			134,000 0 0	
Ahtoor Anuntgurry			18,000 0 0	
Permuttee			14,000 0 0	
Shadmungul			20,000 0 0	
Vamloor		Pagodas	16,000 0 0	
				13,16,765 5 4¾
Districts ceded to the Nawaub Asoph Jah Behauder.				
Jalook Herpah, 61 talooks			8,33,649 3 3¾	
The Doah, 15 talooks		16,48,099 0 0		
Deduct as follows:				
In the Peshwa's share	13,06,666 6 10			
Remains with Tippoo Sultaun				
Anagoondy	61,101 0 0			
		13,66,767 6 10		
Remains to the Nawaub Asoph Jah			2,81,331 6 8	
Bangaupilly and Chinchunmulla, 2 talooks			41,804 9 8	
Singputtun and Chilwara			20,000 0 0	
Oak			20,000 0 0	
Hanwantgooud			15,000 0 0	
Winipilly vemla			12,565 0 0	
Moaka			12,162 6 14	
In Gooty, 4 talooks, viz.				
Tarpatry		19,055 0 4		
Tamurry		13,072 8 0		

Velanoor			8,800 0 0		
Singunmully			10,855 0 0		
				51,782 8 4	
Biswapour			—	5,000 0 0	
Buthary Koorkoor, &c. 2 talooks			35,000 0 0		
Deduct					
Remains with Tippoo, 2 talooks					
Koorkoor and Dummoor			12,000 0 0		
				23,000 0 0	
In Koorkoor			—	370 2 5½	
Districts ceded to Row Pundit Purdhaun Behauder.					13,16,666 6 11
The Doab, 15 talooks			16,48,099 3		
Deduct remains with Tippoo Sultaun					
Anagooudy, 1 talook		60,101 0 0			
In the share of the Nawaub Asoph Jah.					
Kopul, 8 talooks	1,06,137 3 9				
Kaneckgurry, ditto	79,100 0 0				
In Gujenderghur	96,094 2 55				
		2,81,331 6 8			
			3,41,432 6 8		
Remains to Row Pundit Purdhaun, viz.					
Dawar, 8 talooks		1,38,536 8 5½			
Hawanoor, 2 ditto		30,604 2 5			
Dummoor		15,394 6 6¼			
Bankapoor, 16 talooks		2,50,426 6 7¼			
Sirkully, 4 ditto		64,843 7 10			
Keloor, 11 ditto		1,43,397 4 3			
Gudduck, 4 ditto		45,297 1 9¾			
Jaliekal, 5 ditto		73,185 0 14			
Dummul, 4 ditto		49,196 5 12			
Shanore, 26 ditto		3,40,946 7 13			
Laulgurry Souduntry		1,48,953 8 0			
In Gujenderghu, 8 talooks	1,01,977 9 6¼				
Deduct					
In the share of the Nawab Asoph Jah	96,094 2 5				
		5,883 6 7½		13,06,666 6 10	
From Gooty, Sundoor			—	10,000 0 0	
					13,16,666 6 0
			Grand Total*	Pagodas	39,50,698 9 8½

* The Canteray pagodas, in which this account is stated, are worth three rupees each, amounting to thirty-nine and a half lacs of rupees additional revenue to each of the three confederate powers, or one hundred and eighteen and a half lacs of rupees for the whole; being one half of the annual revenue of Tippoo's country.

ARTICLE IV.

Whatever part of Namkul Sunkaghurry, Salem, Ourupoor, Attoor, and Permuitty, which is above stated, are comprised within the division ceded to the aforesaid Company, shall be situated to the northward and eastward of the river Caveri, or if there should be any other talook, or villages of talooks, situated as above described, they shall belong to the said Company, and others of equal value shall be relinquished by the said Company to Tippoo Sultaun, in exchange for them; and if of the above districts there shall be any talooks, or villages of talooks, situated to the westward and southward of the said river, they shall be relinquished to Tippoo Sultaun, in exchange for others of equal value to the said Company.

ARTICLE V.

On the ratification and mutual exchange of this Definitive Treaty, such districts and forts as are to be ceded by Tippoo Sultaun, shall be delivered up without any cavil or demand for outstanding balances; and such talooks and forts as are to be relinquished by the three powers to Tippoo Sultaun, shall in the same manner be delivered up; and orders to this effect, addressed to the aumils and commanders of forts, shall be immediately prepared and delivered to each respectively of the contracting parties; on the receipt of which orders, the discharge of the money stipulated to be paid immediately, and the release of prisoners on all sides; of which the contracting parties, considering God as present, and a witness, shall release without cavil, all that are in existence, and shall not detain a single person. The armies of the allied powers shall march from Seringapatam; such forts and places, nevertheless, as shall be in the possession of the said Company, and on the road by which said armies are to march, shall not be given up until the said armies shall have moved the stores, grain, &c. and sick, which are in them, and shall have passed them on their return; as far as possible, no delay shall be allowed to occur in the said stores, &c. being removed.

ARTICLE VI.

Whatever guns and shot shall be left by Tippoo Sultaun, in the forts which the said Tippoo Sultaun has agreed to cede to the allied powers, an equal number of guns and shot shall be left in the forts which the allied powers have agreed to restore to Tippoo Sultaun.

ARTICLE VII.

The contracting parties agree that zemindars and aumildars being in balance to either party, and repairing to the country of either party, protection shall not be given them, and they shall be restored. If hereafter it should happen, that any disputes arise on the boundaries of the allies and the said Tippoo Sultaun, such disputes shall be adjusted with the knowledge and approbation of all parties.

ARTICLE VIII.

The polygars and zemindars of this country, who, in the course of the present war, have attached themselves, and been serviceable to the allies, shall not, on that account in any shape or manner, be injured or molested by Tippoo Sultaun.

Whenever three copies of this treaty, consisting of eight articles, shall be delivered by Tippoo Sultaun, bearing his seal and signature, accompanied by three schedules, also under the seal and signature of the said Tippoo Sultaun, specifying the detail of the countries ceded to the three powers, one to the said Company with the schedule, one to the said Nawaub Asoph Jah Behauder, with the schedule, and one to the said Row Pundit Purdhaun Behader with the schedule, three counterparts thereof, and of the schedule, shall be delivered to the said Tippoo Sultaun by the allies, that is to say, one counterpart with the schedule on the part of the Company, bearing the seal and signature of the said Nawaub Asoph Jah Behaudre, bearing the seal and signature of the said Nawaub, and of Azeem-ul-Omra Behaudre, and one with the schedule on the part of the said Row Pundit Purdhaun Behauder, bearing the seal of the said Row Pundit Purdhaun Behàuder, and the signature of the said Hurry Ram Pundit Tantea Behauder.

Signed and sealed in camp, near Seringapatam, this eighteenth day of March, one thousand seven hundred and ninety-two.

(Signed) CORNWALLIS.

No. II.

Translation of an Address to Mussulmen in General, from Fittah Ally Cawn Tippoo, sent into the Soubah's Camp, shortly after his having surprised Gazy Miaun's Detachment, in December, 1786.

WHEREAS the righteous in obedience to the commandment of God and his Prophet, in the following passage of the Koran,*

> " Extirpate those who believe not in the Lord and his
> " resurrection, who despise not such things as are an
> " abomination to the Lord and his Prophet, and who
> " conform not to the worship of the true God, likewise
> " those † who have the Book *of the Prophets* ‡ given unto
> " them, until they pay the tribute, for they hold the
> " faithful in derision,"

are continually bent upon humbling those rebellious Pagans who have shaken off the yoke of the true believers, and raised the standard of infidelity, that according to the ordinances of God they may be forced to pay the || tribute, or become pro-

* The quotations from the Koran are marked with inverted commas, to distinguish them from the contents of the paper, and to render the reading easy, by passing them over, as without that, it is difficult to carry on the sense through such a jumble of matter and length of periods.

† Jews and Christians.

‡ The words in italics are not a part of the translation, but inserted for the sake of perspicuity.

|| The tribute called Jazziah, formerly imposed by the Saracens on all Jews, Christians and Pagans, who would not become proselytes to Mahommedism.

selytes to Islamism; and whereas, by reason of the supineness of the Princes of Hind, these despicable nations, notwithstanding the grossness of their idolatries, hold the faithful in contempt; and not satisfied with that, have prepared themselves for war, laid waste our cities, demolished our strong-holds, and carried their desolation far and near, to the great destruction of Mussulmen and their property (for which they will suffer in this, and the world to come); I, who have the fear and the power of God *before me*, stand forth in support of *our* religion and in observance of the *Prophet's* admonition,

> "O ye people, who believe, behold I will instruct you
> "in an art that will save you from dreadful torments.
> "Believe in God and in his Prophet, and labour in *thy*
> "road to heaven. Sacrifice thy property and thy life if
> "thou be'st wise, it will be well for thee: thy sins shall be
> "forgiven thee, and thou shall be received into paradise,
> "in which rivers flow. In Eden there are delightful habi-
> "tations, and thou wilt be happy *there* beyond measure.
> "Besides *other benefits* thou wilt be blessed with the
> "Divine assistance. Victory is at hand, therefore rejoice,
> "O Mussulmen!!!"

am determined to make war upon them with incessant ardour.

It is indispensible according to the text,

> "The faithful admonish each other to follow the com-
> "mandments, hold what is forbidden in detestation, and
> "pay strict regard to the will of God,"

that ye depart the course of life ye have led, and repent; that ye attend to the word of God, and joining together, drive the unbelievers to the infernal regions. If ye be victorious, ye will possess the blessings of the two worlds, and if ye fall martyrs *in the cause*, ye will have paradise for your inheritance.

My chief design is to inform those who are ignorant of this sentence,

> "Obey not infidels or hypocrites, for God knoweth
> "all things,

and are now serving idolaters, that whatever is in the land of the Heathen.

> "Who ridicule the true God and those who believe in
> "him, but deceive themselves only, and are not sensible
> "thereof. There is an infirmity in their hearts, which
> "God has increased, and they shall suffer a most pain-
> "ful punishment because they have denied the truth,

may have comfort and relief, by coming to these parts, and leaving the country of the unbelievers, which is incumbent *upon Mussulmen.*

By the blessing of the Almighty, whatever be your support where ye are, shall be increased to double upon your arrival here, and your life, your fortune, and * whatever is dear to you, shall be in the hands of the Lord and his Prophet.

Moreover, such as are without the means of subsistence, shall have allowances made you according to your condition, for which purpose instructions are published thoughout my dominions, to give protection to all strangers, and to transmit to the presence, intelligence of their necessities: Please God your wishes shall be accomplished.

Whoever doth not receive these presents, knoweth not the

* Your character, literally.

ways of Mahommed, nor the advantages of a righteous life, and draweth upon himself the curse of the Almighty.* He is not of the elect, but shall be numbered with the Heathen, and damned for ever! †

* Out of the circle of Islamism.

† This proclamation was translated by Captain Alexander Read, who was stationed at the frontier post of Amboor, before the war broke out, and employed to procure intelligence from Tippoo's country. The two following Numbers in the Appendix were translated by a person not so well qualified; but will assist in giving an idea of Tippoo's ambition and designs previous to the war.

TRANSLATION OF TIPPOO SULTAN'S GREAT SEAL of STATE.

The Arabic Sentence in the middle of the Seal is taken from the Coran Chap: 44. wherein Mahomed relates that Moses when sent to reclaim the people of Egypt said to them.

"I am the Meſſenger of the true Faith"

(or)

"I bring unto you the Edicts of Truth".

This Motto has probably been adopted by Tippoo, partly from its reference to his Zeal for Religion, and from its containing the word Sultan *the Title he has aſsumed, altho' its meaning here seems to be a Meſsenger or a Mandate of the supreme Power.*

The Couplet in Persian round the edge of the Seal appears to be literally as follows.

"From CONQUEST, and the protection of the Royal HYDER comes my title of"
"SULTAN; and the World, as under the Sun and Moon, is ſubject to my Signet."

The first verse of the Couplet contains the Name of his Grandfather, his Fathers, and his own, and conveys a double meaning in the Original.

Fittah *or Conquest, was the Name or Title of his Grandfather; Fittah Naic;* Hyder, *his Father's Name, is also one of the Titles of the Prophets Son in Law, Aly, their Protector in War, to whom he has dedicated his Country, which he calls* سرکار اسد الله *the Government of the Lion of God;* Sultan *or King is the Title aſsumed by himself.*

Tippoo adopted this Seal on his succeeding to his Father, who died in December 1782, the beginning of the Year 1197 of the Hijeira. The Date is not marked in the usual manner on the Seal, but may be found by taking the letters of the Arabic Sentence in their numerical Capacity, and the middle letter, as implied by the word Der, from the first three words of more than one Syllable of the Couplet, viz. T *from Fittah,* A *from Ta Yeawerum, and* Y *from Hyder, which completes the Date.*

Published by W. Faden Charing Cross Feb: 21. 1793.

No. IV.

Translation of a Letter from the Rajah of Travancore, to Sir Archibald Campbell, K. B. Governor and Commander in Chief at Fort St. George, dated 8th June, 1788.

[After Compliments.]

THE Rajah of Cochin came here lately after a meeting he had with Tippoo Sultan at Palgautcherry, and has communicated to me as follows:

The Sultan asked "what has been the cause of your not coming sooner? have you been prevented by the Rajah of Travancore? Had you come immediately you would have done better; at present the rainy season is approaching; we must remain upon the borders till that is past, when I shall commence hostilities."

"I have heard that the Rajah of Travancore has taken possession of some of your districts, I have therefore to propose to you that you shall take such force from me as you may judge necessary, and go to recover those possessions."

I gave him for answer that, "at the time when the Rajah of Calicut declared war against my predecessors, and drove them from their country, riches and comfort, the Rajah of Travancore, by his protection and assistance, and with an army and resources, prepared on purpose, after a long opposition and war, recovered the whole of our country, replaced my predecessors, "put them in full possession of their former rights, and out of "his great goodness and friendship, left his troops for our protection, that we might not, in future, be exposed to the designs "of that enemy. Having experienced such instances of friendship and support in those difficulties, at the expence of lacs of "his treasure, my predecessors were desirous to give the Rajah of "Travancore in return the possessions called Perawar and Alingear, which produce only a small rent; but the Rajah would "by no means accept of that offer."

"My elder brother, when he became proprietor, prevailed "upon the Rajah to accept of those districts, and made a lasting "assignment of them, so that I have no claim to retake those "possessions, nor will the Rajah relinquish them, as it was all "fixed by a permanent agreement."

Tippoo having heard what I have related, said, "it appears "very improper that you should have your residence in a place "belonging to the Rajah of Travancore; you should remove to "the country under your own management, and, with the assistance of my army, drive the Dutch from Cochin." I replied, "that myself and family had long fixed our residence there; "and that the Rajah of Travancore would not approve of our "removing into my possessions, nor can I agree to expel the "Dutch, who are my old and intimate friends." To this the Sultan replied. "There are some districts belonging to me "in the neighbourhood of Calicut, which I shall make over "to you for a time, in order that you may, by degrees, in the "course of six months, remove from thence with your family. "Please God I will take the Rajah of Travancore's fort in the "space of eight days, and in four days more, will have possession "of the Dutch settlement of Cochin." I was at last obliged to agree to remove from hence with my people. The Sultan said farther "*the Rajah of Travancore is at present in strict alliance "and friendship with the English, but that will not prove long for "his advantage; for who has ever found truth or good faith in "Europeans? It is with me he should cultivate an intercourse and "friendship.*" At length, on my taking leave, he ordered his vakeel along with me, with a dress and a horse for you; and he is now upon the road.

Having heard this account from the Rajah of Cochin, I gave him the following answer. "What you said to the Sultan of "the impossibility of my relinquishing those possessions, or of "your demanding them, was properly stated, and is certainly "the fact. Neither can the other proposal ever take place. My "intercourse and friendship with the English is of long standing, "and firmly established; such connection and alliance with "them is sufficient for me, and I rest my peace and safety on the "protection of the English Company; if the Sultan sends his "vakeel with the dress, &c. he may do so."

May it please your Excellency, it appears to me, by the above relation, that the Sultan has seduced the Rajah of Cochin, by making a temporary offer of those possessions near Calicut, which are not within my limits; and it appears that the Rajah has not given me a just account, but a very contrary one, of the conversation which passed between him and the Sultan. From this, I am led to conclude, by the Sultan's thus gaining over the Rajah of Cochin, that hostilities will take place. If the Sultan should attack the Dutch settlement, or come against me on account of its being within my possessions; in either case it must end in war.

I have acquainted Major Bannerman* particularly of all that passed with the Rajah of Cochin, and have consulted with the Major, whether the dress sent by Tippoo should be received or returned; we agreed that the letter and dress should be received, and, according to custom, that an answer and like dress should be sent; it is therefore proper you should be acquainted, that while the Sultan writes and sends a dress in this manner, it is of no consequence; I shall continue to return an answer in the same style, and a like dress; but in case his letters should contain such matters as mentioned by the Rajah of Cochin, or respect business, or make proposals of alliance, I shall then act as becomes so old a friend of the Company, and give him a decided answer. On every occasion I shall be firm in my attachment to the Company, and in my wishes for their welfare; therefore, in case a decisive answer on my part should make the Sultan determine to attack me, I must then place my sole reliance in the Company for protection and assistance; and from the proceedings of Tippoo, as well as the conversation that took place with the Rajah of Cochin, it is evident that I may certainly look for an attack.

I take God to witness, that while I enjoy life, I never shall depart from my friendship and attachment to the Company; and I hope, from your great goodness, that you will always be desirous to hear of my welfare. Whatever business may happen

* Brigade-Major Bannerman of the Madras establishment, was employed as resident in Travancore, a situation of much difficulty during those transactions.

or occur here, shall be settled by the Major and myself agreeable to your directions.

On the arrival of the vakeel, a copy of the Sultan's letter and my intended answer shall be dispatched to your Excellency, and I beg to be favoured with your opinion as soon as possible, whether I ought to send back a dress in return by his vakeel, or send a person myself on purpose, that I may act accordingly.

I have likewise to mention, that when the Rajah of Cochin went from hence, he told the Governor of Cochin, that he ought to send one of his council along with him to wait on Tippoo Sultan. The Governor answered, I will first write, and when I receive an answer, some person shall then be sent. The Rajah afterwards, on his arrival at Calicut, wrote to the Governor, who then dispatched a harcarra with the letter. Tippoo, on receiving the Governor's letter by the harcarra, flew in a passion, and said, if he remains here, I will order him to be put to death; so that the harcarra was obliged to make his escape, and returned to the Governor without an answer to his letter. Hence it certainly appears that Tippoo intends likewise to attack the Dutch.

Your Excellency will be informed of more particulars in the Major's letter; and I have only farther to request, that I may be honoured as soon as possible with your answer, which I shall anxiously expect.

May your favour and friendship increase.

GLOSSARY.

BAHAUDER. A military title, similar to that of knight.

Bazar. A market.

Bound Hedge. A broad strong belt of planting, chiefly the bamboo tree, the prickly pear, and such other trees and shrubs as form the closest fence. Most of the forts and villages are surrounded with such a hedge; and the large forts have a bound hedge that inclose a circuit of several miles, as a place of refuge to the inhabitants of the adjoining country against the incursions of horse.

Brinjarries. Grain dealers, who supply the army with rice or other grain, which they bring in bags loaded on bullocks.

Buckshee. Paymaster-general, commonly also the commandant of a district, or of a body of troops in the field.

Cawn. A title similar to that of lord.

Cast. A tribe or class of people.

Chubdar. Literally, one who commands silence.—An attendant on a prince, or person in power, distinguished by a silver staff. They run before their master, who has several of them according to his rank; and they carry a whip to punish delinquents.

Circar. The government; also a district or province.

Coolies. Men or women, people of low cast, who are employed to carry loads or baggage; and with an army are commonly hired by the month.

Divan. A council of the prince and his ministers.

Duan. The prime minister.

Durbar. The court or place of audience.

Droog. A fortified hill or rock.

Ead-gah. A Mahommedan place of worship, like the gavel of a mosque, very conspicuous, with small minarets on it, but without any cover.

Ghaut. A pass; commonly that over mountains.

Ginjall. A wall-piece, or large musket of great length, used with a rest; is employed in the defence of forts.

Gram. A kind of pulse with which the horses are fed in India; and is also given to the bullocks, particularly to those used for the guns with an army.

Harcarras. Messengers employed to carry letters, and on business of trust. They are commonly Bramins; are well acquainted with the neighbouring countries, are sent to gain intelligence, and are used as guides in the field.

Half Cast. The mixed race of people between Europeans and natives, chiefly applied to the Christians of Portugueze extraction.

Havildar. A serjeant of Sepoys.

Howder. The chair or seat, which is fixed on the elephant; will hold two people, and has a canopy over it.

Jemmidar. The junior black officer in a troop or company of Sepoys.

Kiledar. The commandant or governor of a fort.

Lac. One hundred thousand.

Limber. A two wheel carriage, upon which the trail of the gun is fixed in travelling, and taken off when preparing for action, which is called unlimbering the guns.

Looty or *Looties.* Irregular horse employed to harass an enemy, and to lay waste the country.

Mosque. A Mahommedan temple.

Malabar Guns. They are made of bars of iron joined together, and are very heavy, long, and unwieldy.

Nabob. The governor or prince of a country.

Paddy. The general name for rice whilst green, or in its dry state before the husks are beaten off.

Pagodas. A gold coin of eight shillings value.

Pagoda. A Gentoo temple.

Peons. Irregular infantry, who arm themselves after their own manner, commonly with swords and matchlocks. They are employed chiefly in the defence of forts, and in the collection of the revenues.

Pettah. A suburb, generally adjoining to a fort, and surrounded with a bound hedge, wall, and ditch.

Poligars. The people who inhabit the mountains and woods, generally armed with pikes and matchlocks.

Raggy. A small but coarse grain, which abounds in the Mysore and other high countries in India.

Rajah. The Hindoo title for a prince.

Rocket. A missile weapon, consisting of an iron tube of about a foot long, and an inch in diameter, fixed to a bamboo rod of ten or twelve feet long. The tube being filled with combustible composition, is set fire to, and, directed by the hand, flies like an arrow, to the distance of upwards of a thousand yards. Some of the rockets have a chamber, and burst like a shell; others, called the ground rockets, have a serpentine motion, and on striking the ground, rise again, and bound along till their force be spent. The rockets make a great noise, and exceedingly annoy the native cavalry in India, who move in great bodies; but are easily avoided, or seldom take effect against our troops, who are formed in lines of great extent, and no great depth.

Rupee. A silver coin about two shillings and three-pence value.

Sandal. A valuable wood, used as a perfume by the natives in India.

Sepadar. An officer of the rank of brigadier general.

Seer. A measure containing somewhat more than a pint.

Sepoys. Black soldiers, or native troops.

Shroffs. Native bankers, or money changers.

Subab. Governor general, or prince over other Nabobs.

Sultan. King, the title assumed by Tippoo.

Tank. A large reservoir of water for the supply of a fort or town, or formed in advantageous situations to water the rice grounds in the country.

Topasses. Native black Christians, the remains of the ancient Portugueze.

Tope. A grove.

Tumbrels. Covered carts which carry the ammunition for the cannon.

THE END.